TOUCHING BEAUTY

Va Quang and Anh Photography, courtesy of Kim Thúy

Touching Beauty

The Poetics of Kim Thúy

EDITED BY
MILÉNA SANTORO AND
JACK A. YEAGER

McGill-Queen's University Press
Montreal & Kingston • London • Chicago

ISBN 978-0-2280-1737-0 (cloth)
ISBN 978-0-2280-1767-7 (paper)
ISBN 978-0-2280-1825-4 (ePDF)
ISBN 978-0-2280-1826-1 (ePUB)

Legal deposit second quarter 2023
Bibliothèque nationale du Québec

Printed in Canada on acid-free paper that is 100% ancient forest free (100% post-consumer recycled), processed chlorine free

Financé par le gouvernement du Canada | Funded by the Government of Canada | Canada | Conseil des arts du Canada | Canada Council for the Arts

We acknowledge the support of the Canada Council for the Arts.
Nous remercions le Conseil des arts du Canada de son soutien.

Library and Archives Canada Cataloguing in Publication

Title: Touching beauty: the poetics of Kim Thúy / edited by Miléna Santoro and Jack A. Yeager.

Names: Santoro, Miléna, 1965- editor. | Yeager, Jack Andrew. editor.

Description: Includes bibliographical references and index.

Identifiers: Canadiana (print) 20230147739 | Canadiana (ebook) 20230147763 | ISBN 9780228017677 (paper) | ISBN 9780228017370 (cloth) | ISBN 9780228018261 (ePUB) | ISBN 9780228018254 (ePDF)

Subjects: LCSH: Thúy, Kim—Criticism and interpretation.

Classification: LCC PS8639.H89 Z854 2023 | DDC C843/.6—dc23

This book was typeset by Marquis Interscript in 10.5/13 Sabon.

Miléna would like to dedicate her work on this volume to her twins, Lauren and Christopher. Their birth and becoming have changed everything in my life, giving me new purpose, abundant joy, and love beyond measure.

In the lengthening days of lockdown and isolation, Jack is grateful to have had this project to provide structure and goals. In my living alone, my thoughts would often turn to Timothy Cook, the person who made the biggest difference in my life, and I would like to recognize him again now with a dedication in his memory.

Contents

Acknowledgments

The idea for this volume was hatched after hearing several excellent papers delivered at the biennial conference of the American Council for Quebec Studies in New Orleans in the fall of 2018. It was, from the start, a meeting of minds and interests that seemed as timely as it was energizing. The research presented here includes scholars at various stages in their careers, inside and outside the university setting, from France, England, and the United States. The co-editors are grateful for their hard work and expertise.

Preparing this volume during a pandemic was no easy feat, and we are grateful to one another for the mutual support and encouragement that sustained us in our collaboration. It helped enormously to have a co-editor like Jack Yeager, whose knowledge, kindness, and generosity of spirit are so inspiring. Throughout, Miléna Santoro was a model of commitment, energy, and enthusiasm, and our conversations online and in person were always stimulating and uplifting. Our work was facilitated by contributors who made revisions in a timely fashion, some of them despite heavy workloads or health issues.

We are also grateful to McGill-Queen's University Press and its editorial staff, in particular editor-in-chief Jonathan Crago, who stepped in at a crucial moment to move this project along. Our biggest debt of thanks must of course go to Kim Thúy Ly Thanh, whose writings and personal qualities made our project a pleasure and fuelled our motivation when circumstances seemed most discouraging. She generously granted several interviews and spontaneously offered to participate virtually in a literature class at Georgetown University, providing yet another series of moving stories and reflections on her life and craft. These conversations and remarks have been condensed and edited into an interview in this volume, with her permission. The co-editors and contributors are honored by her participation in and support for this volume.

TOUCHING BEAUTY

Introduction

Miléna Santoro and Jack A. Yeager

The success story of Vietnamese-born author Kim Thúy Ly Thanh is as remarkable as it is inspiring. After leaving her native Viet Nam at age ten, spending four months in a refugee camp in Kuantan, Malaysia, and then being granted refugee status by Canadian authorities and moving to Quebec with her family in 1979, Kim Thúy could not herself have expected or predicted that by 2010 she would be receiving the highest literary distinction in Canada, the Governor General's Literary Award, for *Ru*, her French-language debut novel. Since that prestigious recognition of her first foray into literary writing, Kim Thúy has published six more books and collaborated on two others, for which her collective sales have topped 700,000 worldwide, including translations into twenty-nine languages in nearly forty countries. Her four novels have been nominated fifteen times and have won eight prizes in addition to the Governor General's award, and her 2017 cookbook, *Le Secret des Vietnamiennes*, also won three awards and was nominated for another. Confirmation of her rising international fame came in 2018, when Kim Thúy was one of the finalists for the Swedish New Academy Prize in Literature, created during the year that the selection process for the Nobel Prize for Literature was suspended. She is, without question, the best-selling and most critically acclaimed Vietnamese immigrant writer in Canadian literary history.

The road to that success, however, was not a straightforward one. Kim Thúy was not fluent in French when she arrived in Granby, Quebec, nor did she have an easy time obtaining first an undergraduate degree in translation and then a law degree from the University of Montreal. By 1995, she passed the Quebec bar, and, as a representative for the Stikeman Elliott law firm, she was posted back to Viet Nam.

She decided to leave the legal profession in 1998 but remained an additional year abroad at the Canadian Consulate in Saigon. Upon returning to Quebec, Kim Thúy swerved yet again and became a restaurateur, opening Ru de Nam, a venture that she pursued for five years and that served to cement her status as an ambassador of Vietnamese cuisine and a notable figure in Montreal's cultural and media milieus.

Although she began publishing only after this array of educational and career experiences, Kim Thúy's energy, approachability, and charismatic media presence are undeniable factors in her literary success over the past decade. Her atypical trajectory has enhanced her relatability and bolstered her capacity to present her ideas effectively in both French and English. She possesses an exceptional ability to put others at ease, visible most recently in the television series that aired beginning in late 2019 on Radio-Canada's ARTV, called *La Table de Kim*. The hour-long episodes present groups of intellectuals and cultural figures who join Kim Thúy for congenial discussions over a meal served in her home, showcasing in the process a savvy fusion of the author's talents as chef, cultural commentator, and entertaining literary figure. This series, in its third season as of 2022, is not the first time Kim Thúy has used her notoriety to highlight others' talents and expertise, of course. The author has also collaborated on a number of other projects, including two important books on autism, born of her own experience as the mother of an autistic son: *L'Autisme expliqué aux non-autistes* in 2017, followed two years later by *L'Estime de soi et l'Autiste*, both published with Trécarré. In 2019, she came out with the beautiful illustrated poem *Le Poisson et l'oiseau*, for which Rogé did the two-page watercolour spreads. Rogé's progressive introduction of red and yellow expresses visually the titular creatures' increasing sense of respect and appreciation for each other's differences and abilities and enhances the impact of Kim Thúy's simple but moving text. The book is a tribute to the value of unity in diversity, where the red fish and the yellow bird recall the colours of the Vietnamese flag, suggesting the country's history of separation and reunification, even as the fable itself offers an intentionally universal truth.

Both prior to and following the exodus after Viet Nam's reunification in 1975, many Vietnamese expatriates and refugees succeeded in building new lives for themselves and their families in Canada and elsewhere. However, of those who have written about their experiences, relatively few have published in French. Still, it is important to note that Kim Thúy's work does not spring out of a vacuum. When Kim Thúy published *Ru* in 2010, her novel entered into dialogue with a corpus of literature in French by authors with connections to Viet Nam. The first texts belonging to this corpus appeared in 1913: a collection of poetry, *Mes heures perdues* by Nguyen Van Xiem, and an anthology of short narratives, *Contes et légendes du pays d'Annam* by Le Van Phat.[1] With a symbolic tip of the hat to these two writers, many such collections – poetry and short narratives – subsequently appeared, produced by some of the leading francophone writers with ties to Viet Nam, such as Pham Van Ky and Pham Duy Khiem, who published in both Hanoi and Paris.[2]

It is, in fact, significant that the first publications in French were poems, on the one hand, and folktales and legends, on the other. In traditional Vietnamese society, poetry was synonymous with literature and, in fact, improvised, fixed-form poetic composition in Chinese was an integral part of the exams for the mandarinate.[3] In addition, folktales and legends reveal a parallel tradition of oral storytelling while offering glimpses into local culture. Hoai Huong Nguyen and Anna Moï are two contemporary writers who have also published poetry and collections of legends and short fiction, respectively, continuing a long tradition.[4]

The twin impulses of poetic expression and storytelling come together in what is known in Viet Nam as the *truyện*, or verse romance: a long-form, narrative poem. The best known of these is Nguyễn Du's *The Tale of Kiều* (*Truyện Kiều*) from the early nineteenth century, considered by many to be Viet Nam's national poem.[5] Based on a Chinese novel, this text is elevated to the level of masterpiece by Nguyễn Du's lyrical talents. As Alexander Woodside has written, "To the Vietnamese people … *The Tale of Kiều* is much more than just a glorious heirloom from their literary past. It has become a kind of continuing emotional laboratory in which all the great and timeless issues of personal morality and political obligation are tested and resolved (or left unresolved) for each new generation."[6]

What also matters here is that this text and other long-form verse narratives like it prepared the way for the prose novel in Viet Nam, a genre introduced by the French colonizers that would vie for literary credibility with Vietnamese traditions. Its adoption by writers in what was then French Indochina would signal a break with the past that accompanied the transformation of Vietnamese society from pre-modern to modern industrial with its new social classes, Western science, and by extension new literary genres. Novels first appeared in Vietnamese in the late nineteenth century while the first long prose narratives in French from the pens of Vietnamese writers date from the early 1920s, when, for example, Nguyen Phan Long's *Le Roman de Mademoiselle Lys* was published.[7] The rise of the novel thereafter coincided with the wrenching of the Vietnamese from their past, a traumatic process with few contemporary parallels.

The novels produced in the last hundred years show many characteristics that bind them together as a corpus. Many texts are linked directly to history, such as the trilogy of novels by Ly Thu Ho set during the violent period of armed conflict in Viet Nam from the 1930s to the 1970s that explore its effects on her fictional characters.[8] Other novels include references to events and circumstances that anchor a narration in a documented historical context. Pham Van Ky sets his first novel, *Frères de sang*, in the tumultuous period just after World War II in Viet Nam, while Kim Lefèvre stands as witness to events in Viet Nam from 1940 to 1960 in her novel/autobiography.[9]

Likewise, Vietnamese culture serves as a platform for references to certain local customs and practices, such as the Confucian hierarchy in a small village in Pham Van Ky's novel and the full chapters on Tết, the lunar new year, in others. These kinds of presentations highlight cultural differences and conflict in many texts, including in such novels as Truong Dinh Tri and Albert de Teneuille's *Bà-Đầm* (the Vietnamese transcription of the French word *madame*), a novel depicting the doomed marriage of a Vietnamese man and a French woman, which resonates with a similar involvement at the centre of Pham Duy Khiem's *Nam et Sylvie*.[10] Linked to the emphasis on culture and cultural differences is the construction of an implied reader as francophone "other" through explanations of vocabulary words using parentheses, footnotes, or the French translation within the text a few lines later, or through cultural references to, for example, the legendary Trưng sisters in Tran Van Tung's *Bach-Yên ou la fille au coeur fidèle* and Ly Thu Ho's *Printemps inachevé* or to the poet Nguyễn Du in Nguyen Duc Giang's *Vingt ans*.[11] Often, descriptions of everyday life, festivals, houses, schools, and philosophical outlooks are contrasted consciously with French culture. The cultural emphasis in the novels also reinforces the narrative threads of assimilation and its risks, life between worlds, being from nowhere, *métissage*, exile, and life in diasporic liminal zones as spaces of creativity and possibility that may resonate strongly in francophone literatures generally.

Women characters may also play prominent roles in the novels in French with ties to Viet Nam. Tran's tragic diary, a text within a text, recounting her rape by a French soldier, lies at the heart of Ly Thu Ho's *Printemps inachevé*, illuminating the novel's title, and a community of women is all that remains after the war's end in 1975, at the close of her *Le Mirage de la paix*. The transition of Vietnamese culture and society surfaces in the conflict between a mother and her daughter who wants to marry for love in Tran Van Tung's *Bach-Yên ou la fille au coeur fidèle*, while a constellation of woman characters represents what is at stake in leaving the past and tradition behind in Trinh Thuc Oanh and Marguerite Triaire's *En s'écartant des ancêtres*.[12]

The autobiographical mode figures prominently, too, in Vietnamese francophone novels. Writing from France, Pham Van Ky imagines, through his first-person narrator, his own return to his village after a decade in Paris in *Frères de sang* – a way of filtering his own experience through a fictional lens. Adolescent reflections on life choices, education, and the future in Hoang Xuan Nhi's *Heou-Tâm* and Nguyen Duc Giang's *Vingt ans* recall the novelists' own lives.[13] Some writers, like Nguyen Van Nho in his *Souvenirs d'un étudiant*, play with the line between life writing and fiction.[14] Similarly, at a reading in Paris in 1989, Kim Lefèvre referred to her then recently published autobiography *Métisse blanche* as a novel ("roman"), reinforcing her own in-betweenness as the child of a French father she never knew and a Vietnamese mother who raised her, thus expanding the cultural and linguistic *métissage* of previous texts to include the complexities of her own biracial status as protagonist. However, Lefèvre was not the first to make such a move in Vietnamese francophone literature. Bach Mai, in fact, casts a biracial protagonist in her *D'Ivoire et d'opium*, the first Vietnamese francophone novel to be published in Canada.[15] Dubbed a "roman documentaire" [documentary novel] by its author, the first-person narrator, Michelle Melville, recounts her return to Southeast Asia as part of a crew filming a documentary on elephants in the Golden Triangle area of northwest Thailand, an itinerary that eventually leads to Vietnamese refugee camps on the Thai-Cambodian border. Interspersed in the text are the actual photographs that Bach Mai took herself or had taken in 1981 of her own CBC-sponsored trip to the region of her birth as part of a film crew. Michelle is thus the double of the author herself, and that narrative tension refracts that of the liminal, floating status of the Eurasian protagonist. Michelle's return is also left in limbo, incomplete and floating, in that she is unable to obtain permission from the Vietnamese government to visit her mother, who remains in Saigon. She writes, "J'intériorisais naturellement les deux versions de la vie. Elles étaient en moi, me transformaient en un personnage rempli de contrastes, d'une sensibilité à fleur de peau, aux sentiments extrêmes. L'endroit et l'envers en une seule face. Serpent à deux têtes. Dualité qui n'arrêtera jamais de me tirailler au plus profond de moi-même ... Étrangère, Eurasienne" [I naturally internalized the two versions of life. They were inside me and transformed me into an individual full of contrasts, overly sensitive and subject to extreme emotions. The inside and the outside on the same side. A snake with two heads. A duality that will never stop gnawing at the deepest part of myself ... A foreign woman, a Eurasian].[16] This passage from the first Vietnamese francophone novel published in Canada and in Quebec encapsulates anew many of the key questions of the corpus.[17]

Kim Thúy's narrative texts, too, resonate strongly with the work of her predecessors. She sets all four of her novels published thus far in documented historical frames. In the opening lines of *Ru*, the first-person narrator tells of her birth in Saigon during the 1968 Tết Offensive, during what is known in Viet Nam as the American War, to the sounds of firecrackers and machine guns.[18] The eponymous narrator of *Mãn* sets up a dual cultural context at the outset of her story through what becomes a series of Vietnamese words and their French translations as cues for episodes set primarily in Viet Nam and Quebec (with forays to New York and Paris). *Vi*'s eponymous narrator, too, uses place names from Viet Nam and beyond, as well as the names of organizations (such as the United Nations), historical heroes (the Trưng sisters), and "a comfortable place to rest one's head," for example, to organize her account. Kim Thúy's most recent novel, *Em* – the title of which is the Vietnamese word for younger brother or sister (commonly used as a pronoun for "I" or "you" by an interlocutor up to a generation younger or older, respectively) – chronicles the American-organized evacuation of mixed-race or *métis/se* children out of Viet Nam in 1975 during the month just before the fall of Saigon. Thúy's storylines are in this way deliberately grounded in historical and geographic realities, like those of her predecessors.

Her first-person narrations lend themselves to autobiographical readings as well, and indeed, many of the events recounted in *Ru*, for example, parallel Kim Thúy's own experiences, such as the departure by boat in the late 1970s,[19] the transition in a refugee camp in

Southeast Asia, and life overseas in Quebec with the challenges of a new language, culture, and weather. Her novels are in many ways all the more compelling for their similarity to her own life story. Similarly, Thúy's published exchange of emails with the Swiss writer Pascal Janovjak flirt with the line between autobiography and authorial invention.[20] In addition, the explanations of cultural and linguistic differences also recall many novels of the past as does the construction of a francophone implied reader as other. Finally, all her protagonists are strong woman characters.[21]

At the same time, Kim Thúy's novels extend and transform the primary threads of the Vietnamese francophone corpus with their emphasis on the contemporary dilemmas of Vietnamese exiles living in Quebec. Her originality surfaces, too, in her unique perspective as a person who escaped by boat and her detailed rendering of that harrowing journey as well as in her emphasis on food and cooking with all its metaphorical overtones, reinforced by her presentation of select recipes in *Le Secret des Vietnamiennes*.[22] The physical presentation of her novels with their fragmentary narratives, their juxtapositions of many brief "chapters" and blank, silent spaces, may reflect through their format the necessity of cobbling together a life in exile and the traditional emphasis placed on the female virtue of *vô hình*, discretion and silence. Writing itself breaks that silence, and in this, Kim Thúy joins her female contemporaries such as Anna Moï, Minh Tran Huy, Hoai Huong Nguyen, Bach Mai, and the late Linda Lê[23] among the foremost voices in the contemporary Vietnamese francophone novel.

Vietnamese authors who emigrated to Canada, or those among the 1.5 or second-generation descendants of Vietnamese immigrants and refugees,[24] represent but one of many groups whose presence and cultural contributions have enriched their host societies over the past half century. Scholars and observers of Quebec's literature and culture have wrestled with the influence of such "new" voices and with how they have inflected the overall tendencies of Quebec's literary milieu since their emergence as a recognizably distinct phenomenon in the 1980s. The Haitian-born, Quebec immigrant writer Robert Berrouët-Oriol is credited with the first use of the term *écriture migrante* in 1986 in the multilingual and transcultural magazine *Vice Versa*.[25] The rapid adoption and theoretical exploration of the term by other Quebec critics – among whom one must include Pierre Nepveu and Simon Harel as two of the earliest and most often cited[26] – found no immediate parallel among English-language literary criticism, which was dominated instead by the rise of postcolonial theory at the time. In order to situate Kim Thúy's work with respect to this broader historical and critical context, it seems useful to offer a sketch of the main approaches to and nomenclature for literature by and about immigrants, beginning with a thumbnail history of Quebec's cultural evolution and its literary traditions within which immigrant stories found expression and that were, indisputably, also changed by those stories.

Most historians agree that Quebec society changed rapidly after the election of Jean Lesage in 1960, transforming itself from a traditional, Catholic, homogenous, and deeply insular collective consciousness into a more modern, secular, cosmopolitan, and yet linguistically and culturally distinct "imagined community," signalled notably by the move away from citizens calling themselves "French Canadian" in favour of the adjective "Québécois," even as Quebec sought to raise its international profile by hosting major events such as Expo '67 and the 1976 Summer Olympics in Montreal.[27] This Quiet Revolution, as it has been called, was both supported and reflected in the province's literary milieu, where a number of writers, filmmakers, journalists, and intellectuals sought to define, buttress, and further develop a sense of Quebec's identity, particularly in opposition to that of English Canada and an English-speaking elite that had held on to privileges and political and economic power to the detriment of the region's French-speaking majority more or less since the British victory on the Plains of Abraham in 1759. Although a number of French Canadian historians and intellectuals had since Canadian Confederation in 1867 sounded the clarion call of nationalism – or "l'appel de la race," to recall Lionel Groulx's 1922 novel bearing that title[28] – the significant socioeconomic transformations in the 1960s and 1970s provided a crucible for the development of a renewed sense of Quebec's distinct identity. This identity was rooted in the people's history and the survival of the French language but also oriented by a resistance to anglophone influence born of a sense of having been oppressed and of a desire for "decolonization," in an echo of the independence movements that had swept through former European colonies worldwide as well as of the civil rights movement in the United States. The influence of such global events and ideas can be seen in the manifesto of the Front de libération du Québec (FLQ) and in the writings of its thought leaders like Pierre Vallières, whose comparison of the situation of French Canadians with that of African Americans in the 1950s and 1960s still creates controversy to this day.[29] In sum, a growing nationalist sentiment among Quebec's francophone majority went hand in hand with a sense of global solidarity, expressed in poems like Michèle Lalonde's "Speak White," first written and performed in 1968 but principally remembered from her iconic performance of it during the cultural happening that was the 1970 Nuit de la poésie, and in the lyrics to songs as familiar as Gilles Vigneault's 1964 anthem "Mon pays"[30] and Robert Charlebois's 1968 hit "Lindberg," which couches a love affair with international air travel in *joual*, a form of spoken French unique to Quebec, brandished as a marker of working-class identity beginning in the 1960s.

The election of the separatist Parti Québécois in 1976, the 1977 passage of Bill 101 (known as the Charter of the French Language), the failure of Quebec's first referendum on sovereignty-association in 1980, and its refusal to sign on to Canada's Constitution Act of 1982 were all salient moments for the renewed nationalism that infused Quebec's political and literary discourse during the Quiet Revolution period and beyond. These political and legal milestones both expressed and affected Quebec's distinct identity and aspirations, but they occurred during a time of increasing demographic diversity and migration that was simultaneously transforming the social fabric of Quebec and the rest of Canada, along with many other countries around the world. According to a 2016 overview of 150 years of immigration produced by Statistics Canada, by the 1970s and 1980s, Asian and Caribbean immigrants to Canada far outstripped those of European origins, and, after several additional waves of arrivals in the intervening decades, over 20 per cent of Canada's total population was made up of immigrants by 2011.[31] Canada has a long history of accepting immigrants and refugees, including some 60,000 Vietnamese refugees at the end of the 1970s, among whom were Kim Thúy and her family.[32] Although Quebec signed administrative agreements with Canada in 1978 and again in 1991 with respect to its authority to control immigration to the province, its emphasis on French language acquisition and cultural assimilation was a significant factor in the experience of immigrants to the province and, somewhat perversely, also made it a hotbed for reflections on diversity (or a lack thereof) in a country that had promoted an official policy of multiculturalism since 1971. To cite but one example, Italian immigrant writer Marco Micone's 1980 reworking of Lalonde's poem "Speak White" as "Speak What" generated an immediate polemic because it was perceived, in its foregrounding of an immigrant perspective, as critical of Quebec's nationalistic zeitgeist and the Charter of the French Language that imposed French language learning on new arrivals and their children.[33] It was in this climate of federal-provincial tensions and of the assertion of Quebec's distinct cultural and linguistic identity that Kim Thúy arrived and received her education. While one might be hard pressed to detect any direct commentary on national and provincial identity politics in her writings, it is not a stretch to say that the experience of immigrating to and being welcomed by Quebec were crucial formative experiences for her, not least because it meant she learned French instead of English in school.

In this, Kim Thúy was far from alone. However, it is notable that the recognition and classification of immigrant and refugee experiences as expressed in literary and cultural works in Quebec was different, and one is tempted to say distinct, from the debates generated within and by postcolonial scholarship elsewhere. To return to the intellectual discourse on migrant voices and transculturality advanced by the contributors to *Vice Versa*, we would be remiss if we did not mention French immigrant writer Régine Robin, whose novel *La Québécoite* is frequently cited as a pioneering example of *écriture migrante* in Quebec and who was an active participant in the discussions launched by her Haitian immigrant peers like Berrouët-Oriol. As Robin puts it, highlighting her identification with the *Vice Versa* cohort, "Nous voulions un vrai métissage culturel, une imprégnation des cultures, un processus de passage, de mouvement, de métamorphose. Nous étions vraiment les penseurs et les initiateurs, au Québec, des réflexions sur les identités plurielles, sur la transculture" [We wanted a real cultural *métissage*, a fertilization of cultures, a process of passing, of movement, of metamorphosis. We were truly the thinkers and initiators, in Quebec, of reflections on plural identities, on transculture].[34] In a 1992 article published in *Québec Studies*, a few years after proposing the concept of *écriture migrante*, Berrouët-Oriol and his collaborator Robert Fournier would advance "l'hypothese selon laquelle le pays de l'historien Lionel Groulx est en *devenir transculturel*" [the hypothesis that the country of historian Lionel Groulx was in the process of *becoming transcultural*].[35] This process has been fostered and expressed by several distinct generations of migrant writings, identified and supported by statistics, which the authors defined as "un microcorpus d'œuvres littéraires produites par des *sujets migrants*: ces écritures sont celles du corps et de la mémoire;

elles sont, pour l'essentiel, travaillées par un référent massif, le pays laissé ou perdu, le pays réel ou fantasmé constituant la matière première de la fiction" [a microcorpus of literary works produced by *migrant subjects*: these writings are those of the body and of memory; they are, in the main, permeated by a massive referent, the lost or departed country, the real or imagined country constituting the source material of fiction].[36]

The increasing influence and centrality of *écriture migrante* within Quebec's publishing milieu gave rise to a proliferation of critical analyses, following the path blazed by Nepveu and Harel in the late 1980s. These include *Ces étrangers du dedans: Une histoire de l'écriture migrante au Québec (1937–1997)*, published in 2001 by Clément Moisan and Renate Hildebrand, which Moisan followed up on in 2008 with his monograph *Écritures migrantes et identités culturelles*; Daniel Chartier's 2003 *Dictionnaire des écrivains émigrés au Québec, 1800–1999*; and Susan Ireland and Patrice J. Proulx's 2004 collaboration, *Textualizing the Immigrant Experience in Contemporary Quebec*. Notwithstanding this accumulation of research and its moves to expand the canon of Quebec literature, a certain discomfort with the attention accorded to the phenomenon must simultaneously be noted. This uneasiness emerged as early as 1996 when Monique Larue published her short but controversial essay *L'Arpenteur et le navigateur* in which a conversation with an imaginary Quebec-born, or *Québécois de souche*, writer reveals deep-seated fears about a loss of identity and opportunity resulting from the perceived popularity of the new literary voices and visions of immigrants. Needless to say, in a decade marked by the outcome of Quebec's second referendum in 1995 – that the province remain part of Canada, after which the then premier of Quebec Jacques Parizeau pointed the finger at "money and ethnic votes" – such reactions to the province's increasingly diverse population and cultural productions were as politically regrettable as they were increasingly socially unacceptable.[37] Perhaps fortunately, this period of tensions between the *Québécois de souche* majority and Quebec's so-called "cultural communities" occurred while Kim Thúy was working as a lawyer in Viet Nam after passing the bar exam. She thus did not witness the at times acrimonious debates firsthand, which is perhaps one reason why to this day she is able to speak in overwhelmingly positive terms about the welcome she and her family received and about her love for the language and culture of Quebec.[38]

Kim Thúy's return to Southeast Asia in the 1990s means she also missed a crucial period for the growing community of immigrant and diasporic writers publishing in French in Quebec. Marie Carrière and Catherine Khordoc's jointly penned 2015 article for *The Oxford Handbook of Canadian Literature,* "For Better or Worse: Revisiting *écriture migrante* in Québec," and Subha Xavier's 2016 monograph, *The Migrant Text: Making and Marketing a Global French Literature*, both offer a solid overview of the critical impasses and theoretical debates surrounding the notion and phenomenon of *écriture migrante* during this period. Some twenty years after the term first appeared in *Vice Versa*, both of these studies bear witness to the persistence of migrant writings that have so changed the complexion of Québec's literary landscape that one wonders "whether Québécois literature can be understood and fully imagined without this notion of the migrant coming into play."[39] Several scholars, reflecting on this state of affairs, have pointed to issues of essentialism and stereotyping, institutional recuperation, and ghettoization of migrant writing, including Simon Harel, whose 2005 title, *Les passages obligés de l'écriture migrante*, highlights the issue of normativity; Daniel Castillo Durante, whose *Les dépouilles de l'altérité* was published the preceding year with the same editor; and more recently, Régine Robin in her 2011 essay collection, *Nous autres, les autres*.[40] For Carrière and Khordoc, "the point of écriture migrante as a critical category has been to allow the study of forms of writing that thematize notions of exile and migration, of belonging and identity, without necessarily enclosing them in a ghetto cordoned off from the mainstream Québécois literary corpus."[41] Xavier sums up the issues with the category by saying it "fell into trouble as a prejudicial marker of otherness that could not contain the variety of works that fell within its alleged parameters."[42]

If Xavier recognizes some of the issues, and some limits to the usefulness of *écriture migrante* as a catch-all category, she nonetheless translates the phrase and proposes the idea of the "migrant text" as a way to reinvigorate the international English-language critical landscape that has been grappling with postcolonial theory since the 1970s.[43] Quebec's role as the place of first publication of Tunisian-French essayist and writer Albert Memmi's famous *Portrait du colonisé* with its preface by Jean-Paul Sartre is not often as well recognized as the French-Caribbean locus of fellow francophone intellectuals Aimé Césaire and Frantz Fanon, and later thinkers like Edouard Glissant, who rejected the idea of postcolonialism because he observed the rise of new forms of colonization in the form of multinational corporate interests. Despite obvious early contacts with the postcolonial theoretical enterprise, Quebec's cultural trajectory and critical nomenclature seemed largely to sidestep postcolonial debates until the turn of this century.[44] In 2003, to cite but one example, Vincent Desroches guest-edited a special issue of *Québec Studies* devoted to the question of the postcoloniality of Quebec literature, claiming that "l'intérêt des théories postcoloniales est précisément qu'elles nous fournissent de nouveaux outils pour critiquer l'essentialisme, la prétention à l'universel, le discours monologique à l'œuvre dans la construction des idéologies impérialistes, colonialistes, et nationalistes, pour approcher, enfin, les multiples composantes d'un tissu culturel hétérogène et évoluant très rapidement" [the interest of postcolonial theories is precisely that they provide us with new tools to critique essentialism, the pretention to universality, the monologic discourse at work in the construction of imperialist, colonialist, and nationalist ideologies, in order to approach, finally, the multiple constitutive elements of a heterogeneous and very rapidly evolving cultural landscape].[45] In his presentation of the issue, Desroches tempers any overzealous theoretical application by clearly recognizing Quebec's complicated status as a white settler society: while its minority linguistic and religious status within Canadian Confederation indisputably created conditions of oppression and economic inferiority for Quebec's French-speaking majority, it is nonetheless simultaneously true that the Indigenous peoples living within its borders are still "les seuls colonisés sans équivoque" [the only unequivocal colonized people].[46] Considering Quebec literature from within a postcolonial framework is thus a complexly layered enterprise, which is perhaps why Carrière and Khordoc note that "in Québec as well as France, there is still resistance to postcolonial and transnational approaches to literature."[47]

For her part, Xavier also reminds readers that even foundational postcolonial thinkers like Edward Said and Homi Bhabha themselves display both evolution and impasses in their respective theories of the role of exile and hybridity in the postcolonial experience, not the least of which is that "postcolonial theory is not free of the nefarious links between criticism and the colonial enterprise."[48] Such issues lead Xavier in the direction of situatedness and the strategic exploitation of identity in the marketplace of ideas. As she puts it, "No theory of the migrant text can exclude the market considerations that have made this type of literature especially viable today … These are novels that capitalize on ethnic heritage, especially when it carries a seal of marked otherness, saddling writers with the expectations and hopes of their communities of origin as well as those of their new countries." This issue of "market considerations" is also at the heart of debates sparked by the 2007 publication in *Le Monde* of the "Manifeste pour 'une *littérature-monde*' en français," signed by over forty French, Québécois, and global francophone writers and intellectuals.[49] Ostensibly desirous of thinking beyond categories like French and francophone in favour of a greater recognition of "the realities of migration, globalization, cosmopolitanism, and multilingualism,"[50] proponents of a *littérature-monde* preached abolishing the centre-periphery relationship of France to the literary production of the rest of the French-speaking world. However, in practice, the importance of Paris has proven a persistent publishing and marketing reality, even if French literary prize selection committees are becoming more open to writers from elsewhere.[51]

So, how do all of these categories and debates help us better situate the work of Kim Thúy? First, it must be recognized that her literary career began after the critical conversations about *écriture migrante*, postcolonial theory, and *littérature-monde* were already underway – or, indeed, were a thing of the past. Kim Thúy's life, to put it another way, paralleled and participated in this history, but she did not add her voice to it until the landscape was already mapped, if not always agreed upon. This is important because in many ways, Kim Thúy benefited from the increasing acceptance and popularity of stories and textual forms, especially autofictional or semi-autobiographical first-person narration, by literary voices from elsewhere. Moreover, by the time Kim Thúy's first novel appeared, there were well-oiled institutional structures in place primed to support and showcase French-language works by foreign-born or first-generation immigrants publishing in Quebec: among these, we can count grants from the Conseil des arts et des lettres du Québec that began in the 1990s,[52] a decade that also saw the founding of the International Association for Quebec Studies (AIEQ) with its seed grants to fund international speaking tours for Québec authors and creators,[53] not to mention the opportunities for national support and recognition for translations of literary works between Canada's two official languages, as well as individual and publishers' funding provided by the Canada Book Fund and the Canada Council for the Arts.

Beginning in the 1990s, then, Quebec publishers, many of which receive some federal and/or provincial government support, were generally increasingly open to migrant texts and were able to sustain a market that did not depend on Paris or even an international francophone readership, although international distribution became more readily accessible than before with the rise of online ordering and e-books worldwide. By 2009, the year Kim Thúy published *Ru*, she was thus quickly able to reach a public eager for new faces and stories, and her rapid rise to best-selling-author status in both Quebec and France was certainly bolstered by the mechanisms supporting Quebec's literary market and the worldwide marketing of migrant texts, as well as by relatively rapidly available English-language versions by award-winning translator Sheila Fischman. In total, *Ru* has been published in twenty-six languages and even more editions worldwide to date. Although Kim Thúy is not one of the case studies Xavier chooses for her book *The Migrant Text*, it is clear that her works display what Xavier is talking about when she speaks of "how migrant texts position themselves at the nexus of commercial and cultural capital."[54]

A widespread conviction among publishers and critics alike that immigrant stories matter and express something important about our globalizing world, coupled with a growing public consciousness of increasing diversity, afforded Kim Thúy's spare but poetically beautiful novels, inspired by personal experiences as a refugee, a measure of immediacy and relevance that made them each best sellers virtually overnight. As Pamela Sing puts it, Kim Thúy's "success is due more to *how* she writes about exile than to the fact that exile is at the heart of her writing."[55] The author's presence and presentation of her work also continue to fuel public interest, for she is adept at media appearances and not shy about telling her story and showing how the autobiographical is related to if not the direct inspiration for her writing. One thing that Kim Thúy makes clear when speaking about her writing, however, is that there is a difference between an immigrant story and a refugee story. Notwithstanding critics' identification of her writing as part of *écriture migrante*, diasporic, transnational, or exilic literature,[56] Kim Thúy reminds us that "refugee and immigrant are very different," because "a refugee is someone ejected from his or her past, who has no future, whose present is totally empty of meaning."[57] That experience has indelibly inflected her literary voice, and continues to do so, for her fourth novel *Em* again addresses the experiences of children who were taken or uprooted from Viet Nam at the close of the war during Operation Babylift. This mass displacement, which the author herself learned the full details of only long after the fact, resonates deeply with her own emotional trajectory, as she indicates in an extended interview conducted prior to *Em*'s publication, included in this volume.

All of the chapters we assembled for this first scholarly book devoted to Kim Thúy's work offer insights into how her writing enchants and educates, both exciting and eluding the desire of her reader to uncover its secrets. While our contributors cover Kim Thúy's fictional and semi-autobiographical works as well as her recent cookbook, we do not discuss her writings on autism or her non-book publications and television projects, so there is still much to discover and discuss. Our approach has therefore been to introduce Kim Thúy's *oeuvre* in a way that invites readers in and opens up areas of cultural and linguistic knowledge that help us to understand the author and her texts.

Our chapters are organized in thematic sequences, rather than following the order of publication of Kim Thúy's work, because we think this allows readers to see how thematic or formal threads play out in and connect different texts over the course of her career to date. In "*Récits* and *Recettes*: Preserving and Recreating Culture and Identity through Writing and Cooking," Jack A. Yeager builds on this introduction to show how the characteristics that identified the Vietnamese francophone novel emerge in Kim Thúy's second novel, *Mãn*. Spinning out of the cues of Vietnamese words and their French translations, the narrative follows the uprooting and displacement of the eponymous narrator from postwar Viet Nam to Quebec, told through a parallel move away from the traditional Vietnamese female virtue of discreet silence with cooking and writing as imaginative practices that reflect the protagonist's creation of a new identity in exile based on her discovery of a voice and her own agency. The narrator embeds the stories of fellow exiles into her own, preserving their lives and legacies as well, affirmed by the act of storytelling itself.

In chapter 2, "Keeping Secrets: Kim Thuy's Representations of Vietnamese Foodways," Amy Reid explores what she terms the "elusive" representation of Vietnamese food culture in what purports to be a cookbook, *Le Secret des Vietnamiennes*. She further demonstrates how cooking is linked to displacement, loss, nostalgia, memory, magic, and sensuality as illustrated in the stories Kim Thúy tells in the cookbook as well as through examples from *Ru*, *Mãn*, *Vi*, and *À toi*, passages of which are quoted in *Le Secret*. In setting her own texts in dialogue, Kim Thúy creates a kind of complicit intertextuality, connected to Reid's contention that the writer in exile "conjures" secrets but does so "in order to keep them," generating a sense of unsatisfied hunger doubled by an open-ended potential.

In "Poetics of Silence and the Act of Writing in Kim Thúy's Narrative Works," using the Asian value placed on silence as her point of departure, Nguyễn Giáng Hương examines how non-speaking, non-writing moments reveal the ways that other forms of communication – looks, gestures, and cooking, for example – surface in *Ru*, *Mãn*, and *Vi*. The absence of any dialogue in all three novels in favour of interior monologues demonstrates how silence operates beyond articulation, providing glimpses of the abstract outside the representational capacities of language. Silence could itself be simply another way of writing. It is up to the reader to discover the various meanings of silence and, as Nguyễn Giáng Hương shows, to understand how Kim Thúy's writing is connected to a "Far Eastern poetics based on the aesthetic of silence."

In 2011, in a surprising move, Kim Thúy and Swiss-Slovak author Pascal Janovjak collaborated on an email exchange published under the title of *À toi*, a book unique in Kim Thúy's *oeuvre* because of its use of the second-person pronoun characteristic of letter writing. In chapter 4, "Epistolarity, Exchange, and Transdiasporic Identities: Writing *À toi*," Juliette M. Rogers suggests that the co-authors' innovative use of the epistolary genre simultaneously reinforces and dismantles recent theories on transnational and transcultural identity formation, with the result being the emergence of a transdiasporic alternative. Although there is a well-known tradition of immigrant correspondence seeking to preserve ties with distant family, Rogers shows how *À toi* departs from that tradition in that the "virtual" correspondents had met only once before they started writing each other, thus giving rise to emails that introduce their histories, memories, and identities. Despite their differences, Kim Thúy and Pascal Janovjak share experiences of mobility, fluidity, hybridity, and *métissage*, which Rogers highlights as constitutive elements of what she calls their transdiasporic identity formation.

In her contribution to this volume, "Post-Migratory Identities: Changing Masculinities in Kim Thúy's *Vi*," Ashwiny O. Kistnareddy offers a contrasting reading of the author's third novel by investigating how men are portrayed and their masculinities expressed before and after the experience of migration. In examining the grandfather, the father, and the brothers in Vi's family, Kistnareddy detects contrasts between these male characters whose social positions, successes, and treatment of women vary from one generation to the next. According to Vietnamese tradition, the husband or first-born male offspring must officially be the head of both the household and the business, despite the fact that in reality women play a significant role in both spheres. However, whereas previous generations would follow choices imposed by their parents, the experience of migration permits a shift in the performance of masculinity, particularly for Vi's eldest brother Long, who develops a more flexible identity in Quebec, having learned from his father's mistakes. In this way, Kistnareddy shows how gender roles and traditional values can be inflected by the refugee experience.

Miléna Santoro's chapter, "Kim Thúy's Many Mothers," embraces all of the author's Vietnamese-born female narrators and characters who experience displacement, cultural differences, and identity issues as refugees or immigrants. What helps them weather these hardships is often a mother figure, or even several women who play a maternal role, demonstrating how motherhood and mothering can be affective and relational, rather than merely biological. While literary exploration of the mother-daughter relationship is far from new, *Ru*, *Mãn*, *Vi*, and *Em* offer a distinct perspective on the theme, because, through the eyes of her narrating daughters and orphan protagonists, Kim Thúy paints portraits of sacrifice and filial piety clearly rooted in Vietnamese culture and affected by the legacies of conflict and migration. Santoro's chapter explores the historical and cultural contexts that inform how Kim Thúy's characters grapple with the forces that challenge their sense of identity, family ties, and cultural traditions, even if at times some desire an escape from such constraints.

The final chapter of this volume is a condensed version of two interviews Miléna Santoro conducted with Kim Thúy, as well as a virtual class visit the author made to an upper-division seminar at Georgetown University, between June of 2019 and March of 2020. The exchanges cover a broad array of topics, including questions of language, family, memory, cultural differences, refugee stories, food, and, of course, writing. She also discusses the inspiration for *Em*, which at the time was a work in progress. The overarching pursuit of beauty is at the heart of everything Kim Thúy does, and so it seems fitting to include a conversation about "chasing beauty" at the end of this volume devoted to her writing.

Our brief afterword offers a consideration of, and perhaps a conversation-starting reflection on, how the publication of *Em* in 2020 preserves and further develops thematic threads from her earlier works. This novel, as well as Kim Thúy's television series, deserve sustained critical attention. Others will surely take up this challenge in due course. We are indebted to Kim Thúy for her generosity in supporting this project, with not only with her blessing but also her active collaboration. As a final gift, she offered us a previously unpublished text, "Les mots au milieu des mots," with which we have chosen to conclude the volume. Given that Kim Thúy has given no sign of slowing down her creative output, we feel it only fitting that she be given this last, or perhaps first, word on her writing to come. With a film adaptation of *Ru* in production, and so many other projects in preparation, Kim Thúy's work will continue to offer rich sources of reflection. We hope the research presented here inspires future readers and scholars to embark on that journey.

NOTES

1 Nguyen Van Xiem, *Mes heures perdues*; Le Van Phat, *Contes et légendes du pays d'Annam*.

2 Pham Van Ky, *L'homme de nulle part*; Pham Duy Khiem, *Légendes des terres sereines*. For more information on these writers and those who follow, see the references listed below in note 17 in addition to Yeager, *The Vietnamese Novel in French*.

3 Mandarins were the civil servants of traditional, pre-modern Viet Nam and were chosen by an elaborate system of examinations. The last of these were administered in the 1910s.

4 In addition to her novels, Hoai Huong Nguyen has published two collections of poetry thus far: *Parfums* (2005) and *Déserts* (2009). Anna Moï has published *Nostalgie de la rizière* (2012), a compilation of two earlier volumes, *L'Écho des rizières: Nouvelles* (2001) *and Parfum de pagode: Nouvelles* (2004), in addition to several novels, an essay, and a kind of memoir/return narrative, *Le pays sans nom: Déambulations avec Marguerite Duras* (2017).

5 See Nguyễn Du, *The Tale of Kiều, a Bilingual Edition of Truyện Kiều*.

6 Ibid., xi.

7 Nguyen Phan Long, *Le Roman de Mademoiselle Lys*.

8 Ly Thu Ho, *Au milieu du carrefour*; *Le mirage de la paix*; *Printemps inachevé*.

9 Pham Van Ky, *Frères de sang*; Lefèvre, *Métisse blanche*.

10 Truong Dinh Tri and Albert de Teneuille, *Bà-Đầm*; Pham Duy Khiem, *Nam et Sylvie*.

11 Tran Van Tung, *Bach-Yên ou la fille au coeur fidèle*; Ly Thu Ho, *Printemps inachevé*; Nguyen Duc Giang, *Vingt ans*.

12 Trinh Thuc Oanh and Marguerite Triaire, *En s'écartant de ancêtres*.

13 Hoang Xuan Nhi, *Heou-Tâm*.

14 Nguyen Van Nho, *Souvenirs d'un étudiant*.

15 Bach Mai, *D'ivoire et d'opium*.

16 Ibid., 150. Translation by Jack A. Yeager. See also Yeager's article "Bach Mai's Francophone Eurasian Voice."

17 For more on Vietnamese francophone literature, see, for example, works by Nathalie Huynh Chau Nguyen, Karl Ashoka Britto, Sharon Lim-Hing, Ching Selao, Lily Chiu, Leslie Barnes, and Nguyễn Giáng Hương, the author of a recent book on the novels of this corpus as well as a contributor to this volume.

18 Thúy's works have been published in many editions. In this volume, when her works are quoted, the editions referred to (both French and English) are noted.

19 We are aware that the expression "boat people" is controversial and is rejected by some refugees. However, because Kim Thúy herself uses this expression, we will do so as well, but with quotation marks to indicate this is an expression that is not universally accepted even if it is still in common usage.

20 Thúy and Janovjak, *À toi*.

21 In a Zoom appearance sponsored by the Alliance Française de Milwaukee, Kim Thúy mentioned that a Spanish journalist has talked about "la force des femmes" in her novels. "Presentation and Discussion with Canadian Writer and Foodie Kim Thúy," Alliance Française de Milwaukee, 2 July 2020.

22 While food, cooking, and meals may figure in the work of other Vietnamese francophone writers, Kim Thúy carries these tropes to a new level of importance in her work. See Thúy, *Le Secret des Vietnamiennes*. Linda Lê does, however, make effective and original use of cooking, recipes, and their relation to culture in her novel *Les trois parques*.

23 Linda Lê passed away in May of 2022, a sad event marked by many obituaries. See, for example, Leclair, "Mort de Linda Lê."

24 Chan defines the 1.5 generation of immigrants from Viet Nam as those "who come at a young age who retain their ability to speak, if not always to read and write, the ancestral language as well as Asian values and

norms" and who "perform a unique bridging function, given their ability to understand both their elders and their American-born peers ... They mediate not only between different generations in their families, but between American and Vietnamese ways of life and thought as well" (Chan, *Vietnamese American 1.5 Generation*, xiv). Of course, the qualifier second-generation, or 2.0, designates the first generation born in the host country after immigration.

25 Berrouët-Oriol, "L'effet d'exil du champ littéraire québécois."

26 See Nepveu's chapter "Écritures migrantes" in *L'écologie du réel* and Harel's *Le voleur de parcours*.

27 The concept of the "imagined community" comes from Anderson, *Imagined Communities*. For recent reconsiderations of the Quiet Revolution and its lasting effects, see the essays in Pâquet and Savard, *Brève histoire de la Révolution tranquille*, and Paquin and Rioux, *La Révolution tranquille 60 ans après*.

28 For the 1986 English translation, the less controversial title *The Iron Wedge* was adopted.

29 In June of 2020, a CBC journalist, Wendy Mesley, had to apologize and had her show canceled for twice referencing the title and ideas of Vallière's provocative 1967 essay, *Nègres blancs d'Amérique*. See "Wendy Mesley Disciplined for Use of 'Offensive Language' on 2 Occasions," CBC News, 25 June 2020, https://www.cbc.ca/news/canada/wendy-mesley-disciplined-1.5627424.

30 "Je mets mon temps et mon espace / À préparer le feu, la place / Pour les humains de l'horizon / Et les humains sont de ma race" (Gilles Vigneault, "Mon pays"). For a full performance history of the song and its importance in Quebec, see Thomas, Willis, and Plouffe, "Mon Pays."

31 The summary highlights the immigrant influx as follows: "World events also led to the massive movement of refugees and migrants from different parts of the world to Canada. Examples include the arrival of 60,000 boat people from Vietnam, Cambodia and Laos in the late 1970s; 85,000 immigrants from the Caribbean and Bermuda (for example, Jamaica, Haiti, and Trinidad and Tobago) in the 1980s; 225,000 immigrants from Hong Kong over the 10 years leading up to its return to China by the United Kingdom in 1997; and 800,000 immigrants from the People's Republic of China, India and the Philippines in the 2000s" (Statistics Canada, "150 Years of Immigration in Canada").

32 See Government of Canada, "Canada: A History of Refuge."

33 In "Speak What," we read, "imposez-nous votre langue / nous vous raconterons / la guerre, la torture et la misère / ... nous sommes cent

peuples venus de loin / pour vous dire que vous n'êtes pas seuls" [Impose your language on us / we will tell you of / war, torture and poverty / … we are a hundred peoples come from afar / to tell you that you are not alone] (Micone, "Speak What," 85). Translation by Miléna Santoro. For a discussion of the relationship of Micone's poem to its source, and its controversial reception, see Plamondon, "Les manifestes québécois, acteurs et témoins d'un champ en évolution," 69–70. The immigrant children who learned French after 1977 because of the 1977 Charter of the French Language are sometimes known as the Children of Bill 101.

34 Robin, *Nous autres, les autres*, 279. Translation by Miléna Santoro.

35 Berrouët-Oriol and Fournier, "L'émergence des écritures migrantes et métisses au Québec," 9. Translation by Miléna Santoro.

36 Ibid., 17. Translation by Miléna Santoro.

37 Parizeau resigned on 31 October 1995, in the fallout from his comments.

38 See, for example, "Kim Thúy: Fan finie de la francophonie – Les visages de la francophonie," a clip produced by Quebec's Ministère des relations internationales for a 2020 Facebook campaign highlighting la Francophonie (Facebook, 10 July 2020, https://www.facebook.com/watch/?v=518330808939206).

39 Carrière and Khordoc, "For Better or For Worse," 622.

40 It bears noting that in the postface to the 1993 paperback edition of *La Québécoite*, Robin was already leery of "la tentation du ghetto, y compris d'un ghetto chic, celui de l'altérité sympathique" [the temptation of the ghetto, including the chic ghetto, that of likeable otherness] (quoted in ibid., 627). Translation by Miléna Santoro.

41 Ibid., 623.

42 Xavier, *Migrant Text*, 12.

43 Ibid., 50–68 ("The Migrant Undercurrents of Critical Theory").

44 For other explorations of postcolonial theory's applicability within Canadian and Quebec contexts, see Moura, *Littératures francophones et théorie postcoloniale*; Maclure, *Récits identitaires*; and Moss, *Is Canada Postcolonial?*

45 Vincent Desroches, "Présentation: En quoi la littérature québécoise est-elle postcoloniale," 7. Translation by Miléna Santoro.

46 Ibid., 5.

47 Carrière and Khordoc, "For Better or For Worse," 633. See also Hargreaves, Forsdick, and Murphy, *Transnational French Studies*.

48 Xavier, *Migrant Text*, 57. See Said, *Orientalism* and *Reflections on Exile and Other Essays*; and Bhabha, *The Location of Culture*.

49 Le Bris et al., “Manifeste pour ‘une littérature-monde’ en français.” See also the follow-up book edited by Le Bris and Rouard, *Pour une littérature-monde*.

50 Xavier, *Migrant Text*, 35.

51 See Collins, “The *Littérature-monde* vs. the Parisian Publishing Empire.”

52 Conseil des arts et des lettres du Québec, “Programmes pour les artistes,” accessed 29 November 2022, https://www.calq.gouv.qc.ca/aide-financiere/programmes-daides-financiere/artistes.

53 Kim Thúy was supported by the AIEQ funding program for international “tournées d’auteur” (speaking tours for authors) to travel eight times to six countries between 2011 and 2019 (information courtesy of the Association internationale des études québécoises).

54 Xavier, *Migrant Text*, 80.

55 Sing, “Kim Thúy: A Gentle Power,” 182.

56 See Britto, “Kim Thúy: A Way with Words.” For a discussion of the distinctions between migrant, exilic, and transnational literatures, see Paterson, “Identité et altérité,” in addition to Carrière and Khordoc, *Migrance comparée*, and Xavier, *Migrant Text*.

57 Quoted in Bethune, “Kim Thúy on How ‘Refugee Literature’ Differs from Immigrant Literature,” n.p. See also Kurmann and Do, who assert that “refugee writing is decidedly *not* immigrant writing” (“Children on the Boat,” 231).

1

Récits and *Recettes*

Preserving and Recreating Culture and Identity through Writing and Cooking

Jack A. Yeager

> I write not only because it brings me pleasure, but also out of fear – fear that if I do not tell a new story, I cannot truly live.
>
> Viet Thanh Nguyen

Fictional Vietnamese narratives from exile written in French may recall the country, culture, and people left behind by relating the historical and political circumstances of departure from the homeland, sometimes through memories of specific events from the past. Characters remembering a culture may, too, focus on recollections of more private moments and of the routines of day-to-day life: the celebration of Tết or lunar new year, preparing and sharing a meal, a marriage or funeral, an emotional involvement, school days, or, as is often the case in Vietnamese francophone novels, the fact of learning French. Some writers with roots in Viet Nam may distance the experience of exile altogether, but most do not, to the extent that even work that seemingly does not refer to the writer's own displacement may still do so by suggestion, allusion, or image.[1]

In her work, Kim Thúy chooses to be open about her origins and ongoing ties to Viet Nam. Her 2013 novel *Mãn* is firmly attached to the country of her birth, as are her three other fictional narratives, *Ru* (2009), *Vi* (2016), and *Em* (2020). Furthermore, she sets her story of escaping from Viet Nam by boat against the known historical backdrop of war and its aftermath in Southeast Asia. Her version of dislocation and displacement, however, reveals a unique perspective, most apparent in the novel's connection to Quebec, where Kim Thúy began her life overseas, far from Southeast Asia.

At first glance, *Mãn* seems to resemble a dictionary because of its layout: Vietnamese lexical items and their French translations on the left side of the page with paragraphs of what might be taken for definitions on the right.[2] What Kim Thúy has done, however, is break up her continuous, first-person narrative, told by the eponymous protagonist, with Vietnamese words that may have been spoken had the story she tells been recounted orally in her first language. The presence of the Vietnamese language suggests that she may have imagined her story in her native language and chosen to retell it in that of her adopted province and culture. The evocation of a dictionary alludes to this kind of translation, of course, but also to the power of words with their connotations and overtones, and to definitions, explanations, and various usages with examples and illustrations. The novel uses the words to inspire, recall, and recount the push and pull of immigration, life between worlds, and the potential of connections through friendship and love. The "dictionary" then serves as guide to a story that pivots on certain key words. Their power in combination – sentences, paragraphs, pages of prose – constructs a story that embodies the power of storytelling itself with Mãn as narrator, protagonist, and cultural interface.[3]

Apparent references to Kim Thúy's own lived experience – escaping by boat, resettling in Montreal, learning French, cooking in and expanding her new husband's Vietnamese restaurant, writing a cookbook, becoming a television personality – suggest an autobiography *en filigrane*, a characteristic of many texts in the Vietnamese francophone corpus. The ideas that emerge in this narrative resonate with others in the work of such writers as Pham Van Ky, Ly Thu Ho, and Linda Lê that focuses on displacement, exile, living abroad, seismic life shifts. Pham Van Ky's first-person narrator in his first novel, *Frères de sang* (1947), returns to a Viet Nam in post–World War II upheaval after a decade earning his doctorate in Paris. Ly Thu Ho's trilogy of novels – *Printemps inachevé* (1962), *Au milieu du carrefour* (1969), and *Le mirage de la paix* (1986) – spans forty years of war and violence that freed the Vietnamese from the French only to see the country descend subsequently into a civil conflict that pitted family against family. The dual narrators of Linda Lê's *Calomnies* (1993) refer obliquely to an unnamed former colony torn apart by war and evoke their lives in exile in France. In a move simultaneously autobiographical and fictional, Lê casts her female narrator as a novelist living in Paris who is attempting to learn the truth about her genealogical origins.[4]

The autobiographical mode resonates with the use of history as backdrop in *Mãn*. Early in the novel, for example, in writing about the man who would become her husband, the narrator includes the words *thuyền nhân* – that is, "boat people" – and refers to his itinerary as a refugee in Thailand before arriving in Montreal, a reflection of the author's own passage through Malaysia (*Mãn*, 14). A reference to "deux fils ennemis" [enemy sons (7)] tells us of families torn apart in a war that set North and South against each other (*Mãn*, 28). The division of Viet Nam at the seventeenth parallel, following the Geneva Accords in 1954, reinforces the notion of the fratricidal war and the eventual reunification of Viet Nam at its close (*Mãn*, 98).[5] References to colonialism, the war for independence from the French, and the colonial educational system that taught students to say "nos ancêtres, les Gaulois" deepen the recognizable historical backdrop (*Mãn*, 27). The use of documented historical events as a *toile de fond* also aligns this text with those of Vietnamese francophone writers such as those mentioned above, as well as Nguyen Tien Lang in his novel *Les Vietnamiens I: les chemins de la révolte* (1953), in which the protagonist, a former mandarin, is arrested and imprisoned as a traitor by the nationalists fighting for independence from the French. In *Le domaine maudit* (1961), Cung Giu Nguyen casts Loan, the daughter of the owner of a tea plantation attempting to restore and maintain the family estate, against the background of civil war in Viet Nam.[6] This role of history in fictional narratives links Kim Thúy's *Mãn* to the work of her predecessors.[7] Though her references are infrequent, they are nonetheless powerful not only for those familiar with this historical period but also, more importantly, for those who lived through it or know someone who did.

Within the framework of history and paralleling the autobiographical narrative mode are the cultural explanations in *Mãn* prompted by many of the Vietnamese words in the lexicon of Kim Thuy's fictional text. In an interview she has mentioned her didactic goals[8] in writing, and in fact, the examples abound. So frequent are these cultural insights that they may be presented in categories.

At the top of the list is the Vietnamese language itself, highlighted most obviously in the "dictionary" format presenting Vietnamese words and their French translations. Near the beginning, in the third section five pages into the novel, the narrator learns the days of the week in French while readers learn their equivalents in Vietnamese (*Mãn*, 10–11). Halfway through the text she coaches her friend Julie, and the reader, in the phonemic tones of Vietnamese (*Mãn*, 65–6). Readers also become aware of the French loan words transcribed into Vietnamese: for example, the Vietnamese word for birthday cake, *bánh gatô*, from *gâteau* combined with the classifier for bread, cake, and noodle, all flour-based (*Mãn*, 69); or the word *cao su* from the French *caoutchouc*, meaning rubber (*Mãn*, 82); or *va-li* from *valise*, suitcase (*Mãn*, 134).[9] In the section on jade, the narrator mentions that the value of the stone increases in its changing shades of colour and that the Vietnamese word *xanh* means both green and blue (*Mãn*, 88–9).[10]

The presentation of language leads naturally to expansions on cultural characteristics, such as Vietnamese attitudes toward gender, filtered by the narrator. Cafés, she declares, are primarily masculine spaces (*Mãn*, 16), and a male heir is crucial in perpetuating a family name and line (*Mãn*, 23), alluding to the patriarchy sanctioned by Confucianism. When the protagonist meets her future husband for the first time in the company of her mother, the latter asks her daughter to serve tea; in a clear reference to a gender hierarchy, she says, "Je n'ai pas regardé le visage de cet homme, même lorsque j'ai déposé la tasse devant lui. Mon regard n'était pas requis, seul le sien comptait" (*Mãn*, 14) [I did not look at the face of the man even when I set the cup in front of him. My gaze wasn't required, it was only his that mattered (6)]. Traditionally, a go-between facilitates marriages arranged by parents for their children (*Mãn*, 14), and the new wife would live with the husband's family to be at the beck and call of her mother-in-law and otherwise remain invisible, anticipating the needs of her husband and his mother. This virtue is taught to young girls by their mothers, as in the case of Mãn's mother: "Elle a surtout appris comment devenir souple, indécelable, voire invisible" (*Mãn*, 24) [What she learned above all was how to become flexible, imperceptible, invisible even (17)]. Echoing the experience of her mother, the narrator later writes in the section *vô hình* (invisible), "J'ai appris très vite à être invisible et utile afin d'être oubliée, afin que personne ne puisse me faire de reproches, afin que personne ne m'atteigne" (*Mãn*, 102) [I learned very quickly to be at once invisible and helpful so that I'd be forgotten, so no one could criticize me, so no one could attack me (97)]. Adolescent girls wear white *áo dài* at school, a sign of their innocence (*Mãn*, 20), and would never be seen drinking coffee in public. The narrator writes that their eventual weddings, too, are marked by certain rituals: gifts are offered wrapped in red paper for luck; guests who will wish the couple happiness are given carefully prepared betel – a word whose Chinese characters are written twice, each one inscribed inside the other, to convey double happiness. Prayers of respect are offered at the ancestral altar, and gold, spherical earrings are worn by the bride as a symbol of her deflowering and the children to come, which are also assured by the partaking of bird's nest soup (*Mãn*, 48–56). The narrator also emphasizes the importance of family as the foundation of identity, and in fact, patronymic pronoun use in Vietnamese is a constant reminder of familial relationships and the respect due elders. As Mãn explains, "la langue vietnamienne impose une posture dès le premier contact: le plus jeune des deux interlocuteurs doit respect et obéissance au plus âgé et, inversement, ce dernier doit conseils et protection au plus jeune. Si quelqu'un écoutait une conversation entre les deux, il serait capable de deviner que, par exemple, le jeune est le neveu d'un des frères aînés de sa mère. De même, si la conversation se tenait entre deux personnes sans lien familial, il serait également possible de déterminer si le plus vieux est moins âgé que les parents de l'autre" (*Mãn*, 15) [the Vietnamese language imposes a relationship from the very first contact: the younger of the two interlocutors must respect and obey the elder, and conversely, the elder must give advice and protection to the younger. If someone were to listen to a conversation between them, he would be able to guess that, for example, the younger one is the nephew of one of his mother's older brothers. Similarly, if the conversation were taking place between two people with no family ties, it would be possible as well to determine whether the elder is younger than the parents of the other (8)]. In the same vein, in first-time encounters, the names of home villages and information about family trees are exchanged "parce que nous croyons fermement que nous sommes ce que nos ancêtres ont été, que nos destins répondent aux gestes des vies qui nous ont précédés" (*Mãn*, 53) [because we firmly believe that we are what our ancestors have been, that our destinies respond to what we have done in the lives that came before us (47)]. The departed are lamented by "pleureuses professionnelles" (*Mãn*, 66) [professional mourners (60)], and the souls of those without a proper burial are doomed to wander (*Mãn*, 67).

It goes without saying that explanations such as these construct an implied reader who is not only French-speaking but also outside the culture of the narrator. Cultural difference and distance between narrator and implied reader are emphasized both by the explanations themselves and by the use of the first-person plural from the perspective of insider, seen in the example above and as well as elsewhere in the novel.[11] The division also captures another that is manifest in many francophone narrative texts, not simply the ones with roots in Viet Nam: duality, life between worlds, and belonging, with its implications of citizenship.[12]

These issues, too, surface multiple times in *Mãn*, from the beginning of the novel. In referring to her future husband, Phương, who, as we recall, also left Viet Nam with others in a boat, Mãn writes, "Il était de ceux qui ont vécu trop longtemps au Vietnam pour pouvoir devenir canadiens. Et, à l'inverse, qui ont vécu trop longtemps au Canada pour être vietnamiens de nouveau" (*Mãn*, 14) [He was one of those who had lived too long in Vietnam to become Canadian. And conversely, who have lived too long in Canada to be Vietnamese again (7)]. The observation captures the tension of belonging/not belonging and sets the stage for others. When Phương gets up to leave, "sa démarche vers la porte était celle d'un homme incertain, perdu entre deux mondes. Il ne savait plus s'il devait franchir le seuil avant ou après les femmes" (*Mãn*, 15) [his steps to the door were uncertain, like those of a man lost between two worlds. He no longer knew if he was supposed to cross the threshold before or after a woman (8)]. He forgets proper usage of pronouns in Vietnamese and the respect they imply, randomly calling Mãn's mother elder sister (*Chị*), auntie (*Cô*), and great-aunt (*Bác*). As Mãn points out, the last would have impressed her mother the most, because it would have placed her at the rank of his own parents (*Mãn*, 29–30).[13]

These tensions reverberate with others, such as the shift from traditional pronoun use to the use of "comrade" under the Communists (*Mãn*, 29) the trauma of a country divided in two at the seventeenth parallel, two different ways of eating a custard apple in the North and in the South (*Mãn*, 98), the opposition of East and West, Canada and Viet Nam (and their weather differences [*Mãn*, 36]), the wandering souls between life and death. These tensions are captured aesthetically as well in the novel itself, between autobiography and fiction, similar to the way Kim Lefèvre plays with this difference in her 1989 autobiography *Métisse blanche*, a text she herself has called a novel – another way of evoking her own multifaceted identity.[14] Even the cover of the first French edition of *Mãn*, showing two nested bowls, with the inner one tipped so that its edge touches the inside of the one below, portends the dual tensions to come. At the same time, a pair of chopsticks poised at the left, held by a hand outside the frame, also tells us how the pieces of wood are inseparable in their function as a utensil for eating. Finally, the lotus combines the fragrance of its flower and the stench of the stagnant water where it grows, also inseparable (*Mãn*, 34).

The threads of hybridity, or *métissage*, mainstays in Vietnamese francophone literature, run throughout *Mãn*.[15] In this text, however, hybridity surpasses the cultural and linguistic implicitly emphasized in the explanations in the novel to include the suggestion that Mãn herself is biracial. In a section titled *trắng* (white), she writes, "Moi, je n'ai jamais su qui était mon géniteur. Les mauvaises langues soupçonnent qu'il est blanc, grand et colonisateur puisque j'ai le nez fin et la peau diaphane. Maman me disait souvent qu'elle avait toujours désiré cette blancheur pour moi" (*Mãn*, 34) [As for me, I never knew who my father was. Mean-spirited gossips suspect that he is white, tall and a colonizer because I have a delicate nose and luminous, pale skin. Maman often told me she'd always wanted that whiteness for me (27)], comparing her whiteness to that of a *bánh cuôn*, a thin round pancake made of rice flour used for what are often called in the West fresh spring rolls. In the section on family, Mãn mentions that some in her village remembered that she did not resemble her mother's brothers and sisters and also that "On enviait mes jambes effilées, mais on craignait l'histoire irrégulière dissimulée derrière mes courbes trop prononcées" (*Mãn*, 53) [They envied my slender legs, but they feared the scandalous story hinted at by my overly pronounced curves (47)]. The suggestion of racial mixing puts Mãn in dialogue with several other protagonists, notably the novelist in Lê's *Calomnies*, Kim Lefèvre in her autobiography/novel, and Bach Mai's first-person Eurasian narrator in *D'ivoire et d'opium* (1985), the first novel in French from Quebec with ties to Viet Nam. This uncertainty of origins is full of potential in *Mãn* and opens up possibilities for the narrator. Likewise, the gesture of throwing her personal documents overboard to hide her identity paves the way a few pages later to cast doubt on her origins, which pivots on the notion of duality. Whether Mãn is *métisse* or not, her mother claims that wrapping her daughter in a *bánh cuôn* during her nap would ensure that her skin be comparable to the reflection of light off snow and to the lustre of porcelain. Furthermore, the mother also knows the secret of how to "occidentaliser" [Westernize (27)] her daughter's nose, making it larger (*Mãn*, 34). This is why she named her daughter Mãn, meaning perfectly fulfilled with nothing left to desire – someone whose every wish is granted, the narrator writes with a tinge of irony. Uncertainty reinforces the idea of being unanchored, from nowhere, Asian but with light skin and a thin nose, between night and day, in "territoires aux frontières invisibles" (*Mãn*, 28), a border zone.[16] *Mãn* shares such uncertainty, displacement, and dislocation with the larger corpus of Vietnamese francophone novels.

Culture and race intersect in the mother's claim that she has a technique for whitening her daughter's skin with a rice-flour pancake. In fact, Vietnamese culture as it manifests in food and cooking is central in *Mãn*, clearly reflecting the primacy of preparing and sharing a meal, as announced by the cover photograph noted above. The emphasis on food deepens the mode of cultural explanation.[17] Among the first words in the dictionary are *dừa* (coconut), and how it is prepared (*Mãn*, 10);[18] *ớt hiểm* (hot pepper), and how mothers teach their daughters their secret recipes, whose goals may include the seduction of their husbands (*Mãn*, 12); and *chuối* (banana), with the idea of learning recipes and the details of their techniques, such as measuring water for rice using the first joint of the finger, transforming a hot pepper into an inoffensive flower with a knife, or cutting into a mango in the direction of the fruit's fibres (*Mãn*, 12–13). Mãn writes, "Les mères enseignaient à leurs filles à cuisiner à voix basse, en chuchotant, afin d'éviter le vol des recettes par les voisines, qui pourraient séduire leurs maris avec les mêmes plats. Les traditions culinaires se transmettaient en secret, tels des tours de magie entre maître et apprenti, un geste à la fois, selon le rythme du quotidien" (*Mãn*, 12) [When mothers taught their daughters how to cook, they spoke in hushed tones, whispering so that neighbours couldn't steal recipes and possibly seduce their husbands with the same dishes. Culinary traditions are passed on secretly, like magic tricks between master and apprentice, one movement at a time, following the rhythms of each day (4)].[19] Food and how it is prepared are thus immediately associated with secrecy, sensuality, and certain skills.

The comparison of the narrator's skin to the *bánh cuôn* is accompanied by a description of the delicate task of making it (*Mãn*, 34). *Yến* (swallow) occasions an explanation of the rarity and special power of the soup made from its nest (*Mãn*, 56); likewise the healing qualities of a chicken soup, *gà tân*, made with lotus seeds, carefully shelled ginkgo nuts, and dried goji berries, simmered for hours over low heat (*Mãn*, 38–9). Mãn's soup, made for her ill husband, leads to a reflection on balancing tastes and flavours: "On croit que les goûts qui nous plaisent trop facilement doivent être modérés parce qu'ils nous abîment, alors que la saveur amère rétablit l'équilibre. J'aurais pu ne pas séparer chacune des graines de lotus en deux pour éliminer les germes, puisque certains les boivent en infusion pour faciliter leur sommeil. Mais je voulais éviter les extrêmes, les goûts extrêmes, les sensations extrêmes" (*Mãn*, 39) [It's believed that we should cut back on tastes we enjoy too easily because they're bad for us, while a bitter taste restores the balance. I could have avoided separating the lotus seeds in two to eliminate the germs, which may be drunk in infusions to bring on sleep. But I wanted to avoid extreme tastes, extreme sensations (32)]. This reaction, from a character who lived through the trauma of war in her birth country and left under the direst of circumstances to end up in a place far from where Vietnamese culture was ingrained in her, catches our attention. In fact, the notion functions as a kind of leitmotif in the novel, seen in the balance of two baskets carried on a wooden stick across her mother's shoulder (*Mãn*, 31) or the balance of flavours in a special dish made for Tết, the most important holiday on the Vietnamese calendar (*Mãn*, 54). Mãn discerns the same "équilibre en bouche" in French cuisine that she knows from Vietnamese cuisine, which she then compares to similar features in Québécoise cuisine as well as the Cajun cooking of Louisiana (*Mãn*, 9).[20] At Mãn's engagement party, the colour red is meant to wish the newlyweds the good luck they will need to find the "équilibre permettant à deux personnes de construire une seule et même vie, qui devra à son tour en soutenir d'autres" (*Mãn*, 48) [the balance that allows two individuals to build a single shared life, one that will support others in turn (42)], in the section titled *hạnh phúc* (happiness).

The emotional charge of food, suggested in the mother's and daughter's sharing of cooking secrets, emerges elsewhere in *Mãn*. The young Vietnamese student hired by Phương to help his wife in the kitchen of the restaurant eventually earns his high school diploma with Mãn's help and moves on to a job in an electronics factory, returning to the restaurant on weekends to help out his former tutor in the kitchen. At the factory he meets Bạch, a newly arrived refugee and former seamstress adept at soldering circuit boards. Confiding to Mãn his having fallen in love with Bạch at first sight, he takes her leftovers from the restaurant in what is nothing less than a form of seduction, introduces her to his aunt with whom he lives, and proposes (*Mãn*, 47). Even the preparation of Mãn's Vietnamese banana cake suggests anthropomorphic liaisons: "Les cinq heures de cuisson à feu doux obligeaient le pain à jouer un rôle de protecteur envers les bananes et, inversement, ces dernières lui livraient le sucre de leur chair. Si l'on avait la chance de manger ce gâteau fraîchement sorti du four, on pouvait apercevoir, en le coupant, le pourpre des bananes gênées d'être ainsi surprises en pleine intimité" (*Mãn*, 71) [Five hours' baking at a low temperature forced the bread to play a protective role for the fruit as the bananas slowly delivered up the sugar in their flesh. Anyone lucky enough to taste that cake freshly baked could see, when cutting it, the crimson of the bananas embarrassed at being caught in the act (64–5)] – a blush-worthy passage.

Food, too, for Vietnamese refugees in this novel unsurprisingly provides a connection to the distant homeland. When Mãn first arrives at her husband's restaurant, it reminds her of the places she would eat on the streets of Hanoi that served one thing, a specialty, typical of the Old Quarter with its original street names derived from what was primarily sold in the shops on it – shoes, silk, or in this case, soup with medicinal herbs (*Mãn*, 38). One of Mãn's first tasks is to begin expanding the menu beyond one single dish. With each town having its specialty, she decides to reproduce first that from Chợ-Lớn, "le grand quartier chinois de Saigon" (*Mãn*, 41–2) [the big Chinese neighbourhood in Saigon (34)], well known to readers of Duras (*Mãn*, 41–2). Mãn's success is immediate. The clients in the restaurant represent in their changing demographics the very waves of immigration, beginning with single men, Phương's friends, awaiting the arrival of their wives and families, finding a home in the place that serves food whose tastes transport them back to Viet Nam: "Semaine après semaine, les clients amis de mon mari avaient des regards de plus en plus expressifs chaque fois qu'il recevaient leur assiette ou leur bol" (*Mãn*, 42) [Week after week, clients who were friends of my husband received their plate or their bowl with ever-greater anticipation (35)]. For a customer from the coastal town of Rạch Giá, she makes its fish noodle soup with pork and shrimp caramelized with shrimp eggs. "Des larmes ont coulé sur sa joue lorsque j'ai arrosé son bol d'une petite cuillerée d'ail mariné au vinaigre" (*Mãn*, 42) [Tears ran down his cheeks when I sprinkled his bowl with a small spoonful of pickled garlic (35)], a typical condiment on restaurant tables in Viet Nam. "En mangeant cette soupe, il m'a susurré qu'il avait goûté sa terre, la terre où il avait grandi, où il était aimé" (*Mãn*, 42) [Eating that soup, he murmured that he had tasted his land, the land where he'd grown up, where he was loved (35)]. As the regulars start bringing their friends and colleagues, lines begin to form. Mãn's daily specials are in demand as the customers opt for something other than the bowl of Tonkinese soup, most likely the family version of *phở*, the restaurant's original offering: "Un seul choix par jour. Un souvenir à la fois, car il me fallait beaucoup d'efforts pour ne pas laisser les émotions déborder des limites de l'assiette" (*Mãn*, 43) [Just one dish per day. One memory at a time, because it took me a lot of effort not to let my emotions overflow the plates (36)], she writes. The synergy of these interacting emotional threads creates an original and moving coherence in *Mãn*, sustained till the end of the novel.

At the Salon du livre while on a book tour in Paris, Mãn meets Francine, who introduces her new friend to her younger brother Luc, also a *chef de cuisine* in his own restaurant. They, too, know Viet Nam from the colonial period and after, when their father was a chief surgeon at a hospital in Saigon where he had also built an orphanage for handicapped children (*Mãn*, 82). The family left on the last plane out of the city in 1975, when Luc was barely a year old. The immediate connection between Mãn and Luc, based initially on their nostalgic memories of Saigon and reactions to more recent changes in the city, mirrors that of the young student and the refugee Bạch in Montreal as well as the instant friendship Mãn experiences upon meeting Julie at the restaurant for the first time (*Mãn*, 54), and Mãn discovers new horizons of desire, signalled by the appearance of the word *yêu* (love) in the lexical itinerary (*Mãn*, 89). At home she and her husband never kiss (*hôn*) in public, and their intimate moments are referred to indirectly using the Vietnamese adjective *gần* (near). Whether or not they would make love depended solely on him: "Il suffisait que mon mari se tourne vers moi pour que je comprenne mon devoir d'épouse. Il suffisait qu'il soit heureux pour que nous le soyons tous. Nous étions un couple sans histoires ni disputes" (*Mãn*, 102) [My husband just had to turn towards me and I would understand my wifely duty. It was enough for him to be happy for all of us to be. Our marriage was uneventful, undramatic (96)]. By contrast, Luc awakens within her feelings she had never known – or permitted herself to know, in keeping with the traditional value of *vô hình*. At his behest, Mãn prepares a caramelized fish with ingredients they have purchased in the 13th arrondissement for his and Francine's mother that transports the latter back to Saigon, where she would make it once a month when the family was living there. Past and present collide through the sensations of taste and smell created by Mãn (*Mãn*, 96–101).

Food, too, brings syntheses of Vietnamese and French cuisine and more, new combinations of Vietnamese and Western cooking methods, techniques, ingredients, and tastes. Philippe, a pastry chef, is hired by Julie to reinvent Vietnamese desserts at the restaurant using butter, milk, chocolate, and vanilla (*Mãn*, 69). With a sleight of hand, he lightens the "air costaud" [frightening, sturdy and uncouth [look] (64)] of Mãn's banana cake with a whipped foam of caramel made from unrefined sugar: "Il avait ainsi marié l'Est et l'Ouest" (*Mãn*, 70) [Thus he married East and West (64)]. It is a salient example of syncretic cooking, developed in Philippe's having "embelli et ennobli" (*Mãn*, 72) [enhanced and ennobled (66)] the well-known dessert *chè*, made from various sweet combinations of such ingredients as mung beans, tapioca, black-eyed peas, gelatin cubes, longans, mango, lychees, and coconut milk. The combinations are endless, leaving the way open for Philippe's own inventions (*Mãn*, 72). Julie also convinces her younger friend to offer classes in Vietnamese cuisine including tasting menus, another kind of East-West connection (*Mãn*, 60). Working with other Western chefs, Mãn discovers the balance of flavours in other cuisines, mentioned earlier, while introducing her collaborators to new juxtapositions influenced by Viet Nam, such as grilled or pan-fried salmon and green mango salad with ginger, or a marinade mixing fish sauce and maple syrup for baby back ribs (*Mãn*, 79–80).[21] Lengthy descriptions of the preparation of certain dishes resemble recipes: *bánh xèo*, a crepe made with rice flour and turmeric stuffed with vegetables and pork, shrimp, and/or chicken (*Mãn*, 128–9), called "happy pancake" on some Western menus; *cá kho*, the caramelized fish prepared for Francine and Luc's mother (*Mãn*, 96); and *bánh chung*, rice cakes wrapped in banana leaves and steamed overnight for Tết, whose fragrance when prepared abroad reminds many of that time of year back "home," in Viet Nam (*Mãn*, 54), offer further examples of the intertwining threads of this text.

These passages resonate naturally enough, too, with the cookbook Mãn writes, *La Palanche*, named for the restaurant, as many cookbooks written by restaurant chefs are. The word itself – *palanche* in French, *đòn gánh* in Vietnamese – refers to the long, flat, narrow piece of wood carried across the shoulders with a basket hanging at either end.[22] Carrying one is a balancing act in itself, requiring some skill, but it obviously reinforces the leitmotif of equilibrium in many contexts in *Mãn*, those of tastes and flavours, of words and phrases, of double happiness, of connections, of collaborations, of cross-cultural communication, of bridges. Often carried in those baskets are fruits, vegetables, or all that is needed for an entire *phở* restaurant on a sidewalk or at the edge of a street. The *palanche* and two baskets, *cái đòn gánh và đôi thúng*, are also a metaphor for Viet Nam itself, according to an old saying – a long country, narrow through the centre with a fertile, rice-producing delta at either end.[23] All these overtones are captured in a single word.

The cookbook is a critical success, publicized by word of mouth through the restaurant's considerable clientele and heavily in mass media outlets thanks to Julie's connections. Favourable reviews lead to a television show, the occasion for Mãn's collaborations with other chefs beyond Philippe, thanks again to Julie (*Mãn*, 76–9). The trajectory of Mãn from refugee to restaurant owner and chef, to cookbook author to television celebrity with invitations to the Salon du livre and to cooking demonstrations in Paris (*Mãn*, 128–9) seems like legend itself, and the breaking of the secrecy of her own culinary heritage, "parler à voix haute," demonstrating her agency, stands in stark opposition to her upbringing and cultural origins in the private, female, "intimiste" space of the home and the kitchen where, as we know, she learned the feminine virtue of *vô hình* (*Mãn*, 102–3), along with secret family recipes (*Mãn*, 12). At the same time, speaking publicly participates in the project I once termed "initiating" readers into Vietnamese culture,[24] as we see in these examples, while setting forth the narrator's personal history as exemplary rather than simply anecdotal. Indeed, Vietnamese family stories often carry larger implications, recalling the family as building block of society, each one reflecting another as well as the hierarchy of the village, the region, and the overall society beyond, according to Confucianism and the principle of filial piety.

In a similar way, each recipe has a story behind it: "Chaque recette était portée par une histoire" (*Mãn*, 79).[25] Hồng, Mãn's friend and fellow Vietnamese immigrant, is one such example; her picture and story accompany a recipe for tomato soup with parsley. When Hồng was nine, she was arrested and imprisoned for having tried to escape by boat with her father and elder brother. Once captured, her father told her not to identify him; she was to tell the police officers that she and her brother were travelling alone. Separated by sex, Hồng and her brother managed to remain connected discreetly, touching hands in a hollowed-out space under the corrugated metal partition between the male and female sides of the prison. Their father did not reveal his identity to the guards, thinking that his children would be freed because of their ages, "grâce à leur innocence et à leur solitude" (*Mãn*, 77) [thanks to their innocence and their loneliness (71)]. And indeed, they were released. Hồng's last memory of her father is of a soup he was able to share with her surreptitiously, a clear bouillon with a piece of tomato and a single stem of parsley floating on the surface. She had never had anything as delicious as that soup, and for years afterward she tried to replicate the recipe, without success, "incapable de reproduire le souvenir indélébile mais fuyant de ces quelques gorgées" (*Mãn*, 78) [she never managed to reproduce the indelible but elusive memory of those few sips (72)]. A version of this soup is included in the cookbook in memory of her father, who never returned home (*Mãn*, 76–8).

In a section announced by the words *ảo tưởng* (illusion), Mãn writes that Hồng had met her Québécois husband in a café in Saigon where she worked as a waitress. Seeing his Canadian passport, she agreed to join him later in Quebec to get her daughter away from the smell of tobacco and of the sweat of the male hands that groped her during her shift. "Il était amoureux d'elle, amoureux de son séjour au Vietnam, où ses mille dollars lui permettaient de vivre l'expérience de l'amour éternel" (*Mãn*, 62) [He was in love with Hồng, in love with his time in Vietnam, where his hundred dollars were worth a million dongs, where a thousand dollars let him live the experience of eternal love (56)] – an unusual luxury for someone who cuts grass for a living. The relationship unravels quickly after Hồng's arrival in Montreal, her life "un tunnel sombre" (*Mãn*, 62) [a dark tunnel (56)] in Mãn's retelling, full of verbal and physical abuse that Hồng suffers in silence. In an alignment of the planets, she replaces her lazy, abusive husband behind his mower one day and meets Julie while cutting her grass – in the section titled *cỏ* (lawn) (*Mãn*, 63) – and then gets to know her on several return trips. Julie suggests to Phương that he hire Hồng at the restaurant, and she accepts: "Au début, Hồng gardait ses distances. Je n'entendais que ses gestes, qui étaient d'une efficacité inouïe" (*Mãn*, 64) [At first, Hồng kept her distance. I only heard her moving around, efficient, extraordinary (58)], yet another example of *vô hình*.

What speak for themselves, however, are the bruises scattered over her body, usually covered by her long sleeves and dark pants. Rescued from her alcoholic husband, she and her daughter come to live at the restaurant with Mãn and her family, to become part of a newly invented extended family that now includes Mãn's mother, recently arrived from Viet Nam. The cookbook is published during Hồng's daughter's first year in medical school (*Mãn*, 75).

Two aspects of this story demand commentary. The first is that Hồng's story resembles that of the *con gái*, a staple of colonial and war novels and memoirs from Viet Nam: the adolescent or young woman who may have had a child out of wedlock with a foreigner. The word in Vietnamese simply means daughter or girl; in French, however, it is transformed into mistress or concubine. Jean d'Esme's novel *Thi Ba, fille d'Annam* (1920) and Kim Lefèvre's autobiography *Métisse blanche* (1989) provide examples of the *con gái*.[26] While the lineage of her daughter is never mentioned, Hồng's place in society as a single mother reverberates with the women, many of whom worked in bars and cafés and were involved with foreign soldiers particularly during the colonial period, the war of liberation and the American War in Viet Nam. In this case, the smell of the sweaty hands on Hồng's clothes when she returns home at midnight speaks volumes. As a kind of war bride analogous to her sisters, she fears being sent back to Viet Nam more than anything else and lives under that constant threat from her husband. Thus, "elle avançait la tête en première en écartant ses nuits, en faisant abstraction des coups, en utilisant son corps comme bouclier pour protéger sa fille contre la menace de se faire renvoyer au Vietnam, où elle ne croyait plus avoir des points de repère désormais" (*Mãn*, 75) [She pushed forward headlong, ignoring her nights, disregarding blows, using her body as a shield to protect her daughter from the threat of being sent back to Vietnam, where she thought she would no longer fit in (69)], splitting to observe herself, a well-known defence mechanism among battered women.

In addition, Hồng's story is embedded in the cookbook in the same way that many other texts contribute to the creation of the novel itself, including the longer version of Hồng's story. Phương's would be another (*Mãn*, 14–16) as well as that of the young student who works with Mãn in the kitchen, her "frère soleil" (*Mãn*, 46) [sun brother (39)], as she calls him and whom she tutors (*Mãn*, 44–6). Bạch's story emerges in conjunction with the encounter with her young "Cyrano" (*Mãn*, 47) and their subsequent marriage. Luc and Francine's connections to Viet Nam figure in the Paris visit (*Mãn*, 82–104), and the story of Jean Pierre, a regular restaurant customer, and his Vietnamese wife, Lan, adds another dimension to the harrowing escapes by boat and to cross-cultural relationships (*Mãn*, 112–13). Mãn's mother's story of her parents expands these family histories (*Mãn*, 89–90).

Well-known poems (woven into hats from Huế, for example; *Mãn*, 57), songs (the paradoxical lotus; *Mãn*, 80), legends (the origin of the practice of chewing betel; *Mãn*, 50–1), fairy tales (the woodcutter in the moon; *Mãn*, 93), and even an allusion to *Peter and the Wolf* (*Mãn*, 108) layer the text, as do references to personal letters, notebooks, emails, cooking courses, good wishes on papers attached to a tangerine tree for Tết (*Mãn*, 137), and even *dictées*. More abstract "texts" – facial wrinkles (*Mãn*, 120–1), a scar (*Mãn*, 125), an impression inscribed on a bed (*Mãn*, 127), a photograph (*Mãn*, 119), dog tags (*Mãn*, 139), beauty marks on one body (*Mãn*, 133) and corresponding tattoos on another (*Mãn*, 142), bruises (*Mãn*, 75), all of which suggest, imply, tell stories – reinforce the novel's resonances and expand its metaphorical readings. The diversity of both voices and forms adds to the distinct originality of *Mãn*.

Writing and cooking align in Kim Thúy's novel, supported by a network of images and references. In the section on family, genealogy, and identity, "un regard vierge" (*Mãn*, 53) [a neutral gaze (47)] appears in parallel with "une page blanche" (*Mãn*, 53) [a blank page (47)], suggesting potential and possibility, reinvention and by extension creativity, a moment when, in a Québécois context, Mãn does not have to explain why she looks different from other members of her family. In this passage, the conventional "page blanche" is nuanced and reinvented as well, no longer a clue to her ancestral lines (*Mãn*, 53). When they first meet, Luc holds Mãn's hand "trop longtemps" (*Mãn*, 85) [too long (79)], "cette seconde de trop" (*Mãn*, 86) [that second too long (80)], prompting a reflection on *bàn tay* (hand) and writing. When paper and ink were scarce during the war, pupils would still manage to write, and their work was graded on content as well as form, "car la calligraphie traduisait aussi bien l'idée que l'intention et le respect. Toutes ces années d'entraînement où j'avais une tache d'encre mauve sur les phalangettes m'avaient dotée d'une écriture fine et constante, que j'aime utiliser de temps à autre pour ne pas perdre la souplesse dans les pleins et la légèreté dans les déliés" (*Mãn*, 86–7) [because calligraphy translated idea and intention as well as respect. All those years of training when I had a mauve ink stain on my fingers had left me with fine and steady handwriting that I like to use now and then so I won't lose flexibility in the downstrokes and lightness in the upstrokes (80–1)]. In one reading, with writing and cooking in dialogue, we could say that the presentation of food on a plate is as important as its taste, its original combination of known flavours and something new, the juxtaposition of, say, *sirop d'érable* and *nước mắm* or a flower fashioned from a fiery *ớt hiểm*. However, the passage also refers clearly to literary texts, elevating what might seem to some, mistakenly, to be the banal practice of cooking. And in a subtle tip of the hat to the arc of Vietnamese literature, Kim Thúy alludes as well to a past in Viet Nam when poetry and "literature" were synonymous, before the advent of the prose novel brought by a colonial power – prose now, too, poetically transformed and thus in its own way grounded in an imagination with roots in Viet Nam. With a hand for writing, storytelling then becomes its own meta-thread in *Mãn*, with the cookbook mirrored *en abyme* within the outer framing story.

However, this passage that seems on the surface to be about handwriting also recalls one earlier in the novel, a reference to what is considered Viet Nam's national poem, a verse romance titled *Truyện Kiều*, or *The Tale of Kiều*, by Nguyễn Du (1765–1820).[27] In his historical introduction to the late Huỳnh Sanh Thông's beautiful English translation with the poem in *quốc-ngữ*, the Romanized version of Vietnamese, published on facing pages, Alexander Woodside writes, "Western readers who are curious about Vietnam and the Vietnamese may well gain more real wisdom from cultivating a discriminating appreciation for this one poem than they will from reading the entire library of scholarly and journalistic writings upon modern Vietnam which has accumulated in the West in the past two decades. As a vivid transcript of Vietnamese approaches to the dilemmas of the human condition, *The Tale of Kiều* has survived in, and gained new strength from, hundreds of different contexts."[28] Nearly forty years later, Kim Thúy's own lines affirm Woodside's judgment then and his prescience: "*Truyện Kiều* [est] l'histoire d'une jeune fille qui s'est sacrifiée pour sa famille. Certains disent que, aussi longtemps que ce poème de plus de trois mille vers continuera d'exister, aucune guerre ne pourra faire disparaître le Vietnam. C'est peut-être pour cette raison que, depuis plus d'un siècle, même un Vietnamien analphabète peut en réciter des strophes entières" (*Mãn*, 25) [*Truyện Kiều* [is] the story of a girl who sacrificed herself to save her family. Some say that as long as the poem, with its more than three thousand lines, still exists, no war can make Vietnam disappear. Maybe that is why, for more than a century, even an illiterate Vietnamese has been able to recite entire stanzas (18)]. Mãn's maternal grandfather required his children to learn the poem by heart, "parce que l'auteur dépeignait, entre autres, la pureté et l'abnégation, deux couleurs essentielles à l'âme vietnamienne" (*Mãn*, 25) [because … the poet depicted, among other things, purity and selflessness, two shades essential to the Vietnamese soul (18)]. In contrast, her mother always insisted on the importance of the poem's opening lines, which remind readers that in the wink of an eye, everything in life may change, be turned upside down, in the confrontation of Destiny and Talent (*Mãn*, 25).

In his own introduction to the poem, Huỳnh Sanh Thông, MacArthur Fellow, director of the Southeast Asian Refugee Project within the Council on Southeast Asia Studies at Yale, and founding editor of *The Vietnam Forum*, explains how the poet transformed his Chinese model: "Nguyễn Du has reduced the number of incidents and personae, condensing the longish novel into a spare poem of 1,627 couplets which, through the magic of his art, springs to life as a world revolving around a creature of fiction that has become a person of flesh and blood in the minds and hearts of most Vietnamese: Kiều."[29] There is no better explanation for the poem's sustained popularity, cited spontaneously to interpret daily events, to understand reversals of fortune, to inspire courage.

The reference to this important Vietnamese text thus participates in Kim Thúy's novel as another embedded story, but it is also as a touchstone. As Mãn declares, as long as this poem continues to exist so will Viet Nam and by extension the Vietnamese people. And, as she adds, it is perhaps for this reason that even Vietnamese who cannot read and write are able to recite verses from the poem, telling its compelling and unforgettable story. The act of recounting, retelling, remembering is paramount in itself and exactly what this novel does with its embedded and layered narratives; Mãn as protagonist, narrator, and scribe speaks for others. In *Retour à la saison des pluies* (1990), the sequel to *Métisse blanche*, Kim Lefèvre tells of encountering one of her old schoolmates from the Couvent des Oiseaux in Paris who gratefully tells her "Vous avez parlé pour moi" [You spoke for me].[30] And as the author Amy Jo Burns said in an interview, "Our stories may be lived in isolation, but they gather meaning when they are shared."[31] The very gesture of telling recalls and preserves a culture, its people, and its history and resonates harmonically with spontaneous citations of *Truyện Kiều*. Kim Thúy's novel, too, stands as testimony, in dialogue with those writers with roots in Viet Nam writing abroad. For those destined to write, as Viet Thanh Nguyen also affirms, the act of telling stories is life itself.[32]

NOTES

1 A pertinent example would be Linda Lê's first novel, *Un si tendre vampire* (1987), set in France and Italy with French characters.

2 In his review of *Mãn*, Karl Britto makes a similar observation. He writes, "The headings become a dictionary of both abstract concepts and everyday objects out of which the story is generated. The bilingual nature of each heading recalls both the exilic trajectory along which the narrator has traveled, and the long and often painful history shared by France and Vietnam" ("Kim Thúy: A Way with Words," 2).

3 *Tự điển* (or the more modern *từ điển*), or dictionary, is included in the lexicon. See Kim Thúy, *Mãn* (Paris: Liana Levi, 2013), 59. All subsequent references to this edition will appear in the text in parentheses. Passages from *Mãn* in English are from the 2014 Fischman translation and will appear in square brackets, with the page numbers in parentheses.

4 In many of her prose narratives up to 1997, Linda Lê strongly alludes to Viet Nam without ever naming it. In a private conversation, Carole Salmon aptly dubbed this narrative strategy "unnaming" (personal communication, October 2012).

5 Mentioning the production of mines in the tropical forest reinforces the ever-present dangers during the war (*Mãn*, 31).

6 Loan's struggle to save the family tea plantation may be easily set in dialogue with Claire Denis's film *White Material* (2009), in which the daughter-in-law struggles to save the family's coffee plantation. One might also include in this conversation Marguerite Duras's *Un barrage contre le Pacifique* (1950) with a mother trying to protect her land from the sea in order to grow rice.

7 For more on historical background in the novels, see Yeager, *The Vietnamese Novel in French*, 91–123 (chap. 5).

8 Thúy, "Habiller le vécu de mots et d'images," 171.

9 In *Em*, Kim Thúy devotes nearly an entire chapter to these loan words (*Em*, 36–7). Mãn also references the appropriation of the baguette in

a gesture similar to adopting words from the French language (*Mãn*, 42). In the late afternoons in Hanoi, women sell small baguettes for *bánh mì* (sandwiches) on the curbs of the streets in the Old Quarter.

10 Hernández also notes the importance of language in *Mãn* in "L'oeuvre de Kim Thúy," 323.

11 For more on the implied reader constructed as francophone other, see Yeager, *The Vietnamese Novel in French*, 53–60. The use of the first-person plural subject pronoun is interesting for another reason here. In Vietnamese there are two such pronouns, *chúng ta* and *chúng tôi*. The former includes the person/s addressed while the latter does not; clearly the pronoun that would be used here were the text in Vietnamese is the latter.

12 The idea of belonging is perfectly captured in the opening pages of Ying Chen's *Les Lettres chinoises* (1993) at the moment when Yuan, the main character, arrives in Vancouver from China on his way to Montreal to pursue university studies and writes to his fiancée, Sassa, in Shanghai: "je pourrais dire que c'est aujourd'hui, bien plus qu'à d'autres moments de ma vie, que je ressens un profond besoin de reconnaître mon appartenance à mon pays. C'est important d'avoir un pays quand on voyage. Un jour, tu comprendras cela: quand tu présentes ton passeport une dame aux lèvres serrées, quand tu te retrouves parmi des gens dont tu ignores jusqu'à la langue, et surtout quand on te demande tout le temps de quel pays tu viens. Pour pouvoir vivre dans un monde civilisé, il faut s'identifier, c'est cela" [I could say that it's today much more than any other moment in my life that I feel a deep need to recognize my belonging to my country. It's important to have a country when you travel. One day you will understand that when you present your passport to a woman with pursed lips, when you find yourself among people whose very language you don't know and especially when people ask you all the time what country you are from. In order to be able to live in a civilized world, you need to have an identity, that's it] (Chen, *Les Lettres chinoises*, 9–10). Translation by Jack A. Yeager.

13 This "forgetting" of culture recalls the uncertainty of the protagonist of Doan's *Retour* when she returns to Viet Nam after many years in France.

14 Lefèvre said this during a reading at the Nhà Việt-Nam (Viet Nam House) in Paris shortly after her book appeared in early 1989. See Yeager, "Blurring the Lines."

15 For more on this field, see Bacholle-Bošković, *Linda Lê, l'écriture du manque*; Barnes, *Vietnam and the Colonial Condition*; Britto, *Disorientation*; Ching Selao, *Le Roman vietnamien francophone*; Chiu,

"Alter/Native"; Lim-Hing, "Vietnamese Novels in French"; O'Riley, "Discerning the Empire's Other"; Nguyễn Giáng Hương, *La littérature vietnamienne francophone*; Nathalie Huynh Chau Nguyen, *Vietnamese Voices*; and Pears, *Remnants of Empire in Algeria and Vietnam*.

16 In the Fischman translation, the entire passage reads as follows: "They crept between two lines of fire, careful not to set foot on one boundary or the other, invisible and changing depending on the time" (21).

17 See also Sing, "Migrance, sensorium et translocalité," and Lohka, "Senteurs de l'ailleurs," as well as Amy B. Reid's piece in this volume, for example.

18 The following three words illustrate the importance of tones in Vietnamese: *dừa* with a falling tone, indicated by the grave accent, means, of course, coconut; *dưa* with a level tone, indicated by no diacritical mark, means melon; and *dứa* with a rising tone, indicated by the acute accent, means pineapple. The consonant and vowel sounds remain the same in all three. The soft, uncrossed "d" (as opposed to "đ") is sometimes rendered in English as "dz," reflecting a Northern pronunciation.

19 This oft-quoted passage recalls an important scene in Ly Thu Ho's *Le Mirage de la paix* (118–19), in which an aging female character representing tradition teaches two younger female characters how to make chicken pâté, passing on a family recipe. See Yeager, "La politique 'intimiste,'" 143.

20 After Mãn meets Julie, the latter prepares a whole range of Québécois dishes for her new friend to try, from Montreal's famous smoked meat to *tourtière* to *pouding chômeur* (*Mãn*, 54).

21 Mãn decides to spare her collaborators the strong tastes of *mắm tôm* (fermented shrimp paste) and green guava with salt and chili pepper (*Mãn*, 79).

22 The word *đòn gánh* is spelled *đòn gách* [*sic*] in the novel, a typographical error.

23 Lê Thánh Khôi, *Le Viêt-Nam*, 19.

24 Yeager, *The Vietnamese Novel in French*, chap. 4.

25 This phrase is omitted from the Fischman translation. It means "Each recipe was carried by a story" (translation by Miléna Santoro).

26 Esme, *Thi Ba, fille d'Annam*; Lefèvre, *Métisse blanche*. These questions also arise in Kim Thúy's first novel, *Ru*, in the references to the *métis* orphans of Vietnamese mothers and American GIs and in the scene when a cyclo driver in Danang mistakes the narrator as the escort of her "white" husband (Liana Levi edition, 2010, 90, 87). Kim Thúy also explains the French use of the term *con gái* in *Em*, 37.

27 Nguyễn Du, *The Tale of Kiều, a bilingual edition of Truyện Kiều.* This famous text is known under various titles – including the original, *Đoạn trường tân thanh* (A new cry from a broken heart), and the title under which it was engraved and printed later in Hanoi, *Kim Vân Kiều tàn truyện* (A new version of the tale of Kim, Vân, and Kiều) – but as Huỳnh Sanh Thông points out in his introduction to the bilingual edition, "To millions of Vietnamese it is known as *The Tale of Kim, Vân and Kiều* (*Truyện Kim-Vân-Kiều*), as *The Tale of Kiều* (*Truyện Kiều*), or simply as *Kiều.* A perfect example of the long narrative poem in six-eight verse, it has also stood unchallenged since its publication and dissemination in the second decade of the nineteenth century as the supreme masterwork of Vietnamese literature. And through its pervasive popularity, little short of adulatory worship, among both scholars and illiterates and in all spheres of life, its author, Nguyễn Du, has achieved a status seldom equalled by a writer in his or her own country. The only other example that readily comes to mind is Alexander Pushkin, for *Eugene Onegin*" (Huỳnh Sanh Thông in Nguyễn Du, *Tale of Kiều*, xx). Fitzpatrick also mentions the passage on the *Truyện Kiều* in her review of *Mãn* ("Kim Thúy's *Mãn* Is a Story of Realism," n.p.).

28 Woodside in Nguyễn Du, *Tale of Kiều*, xi.

29 Ibid., xxi.

30 Lefèvre, *Retour à la saison des pluies*, 23.

31 Burns, "Author Amy Jo Burns on Her Debut Novel 'Shiner.'" See also "Chasing Beauty," p. 155, in this volume.

32 Viet Thanh Nguyen, "Ideas That Won't Survive."

2

Keeping Secrets

Kim Thúy's Representations of Vietnamese Foodways

Amy B. Reid

In 2017, Kim Thúy published *Le Secret des Vietnamiennes*, a beautiful book that combines recipes with photographs, family anecdotes, excerpts from her writing, and short essays by Thúy and by two of her friends.[1] The interweaving of practical information (how to prepare various dishes or the right wine to pair with Vietnamese cuisine) with tidbits of personal information and, significantly, photos of her family and friends raises the question: What *secret* is Thúy sharing, or, more to the point, which secrets is she keeping? This chapter examines Thúy's elusive representation of Vietnamese foodways in her writing. While the primary focus will be on her works *Ru* (2009), *Mãn* (2013), *Vi* (2016), and, to a lesser extent, *Em* (2020),[2] I will also consider her cookbook as a model for the aura of secrecy that surrounds descriptions of food in her prose.

Images of food appear throughout Thúy's work and have attracted the attention of readers and critics alike. While memories of the scents, flavours, and practices of Vietnamese cooking form a recurrent motif in her writing, the variety among these references is even more significant than their frequency. One of the consequences of Thúy's literary style, where fragments of fiction and memory exist in a state of emulsion (suspended together, without really breaking down the boundaries between), is that it is difficult to generalize about how she represents something as omnipresent as food; each page brings another shift in perspective. At times Thúy's descriptions suggest an exotic *ailleurs* or the seduction involved in preparing and sharing a meal, at others the suffering and sense of loss born of exile and want. In *Ru*, for example, which begins with the dangers faced by those, like Thúy, who left Viet Nam during the exodus of the 1970s and highlights the challenges faced by immigrants adapting to life in Quebec, images of food are often linked to hunger and dislocation, to nostalgia and mourning. In contrast, for the immigrant protagonist of *Mãn*, who finds a path to professional success as a restaurateur, foods linked to specific places both trigger positive memories for her customers and serve as an aphrodisiac in her relationship with a French chef. While *Vi* provides powerful images of food insecurity in postwar Viet Nam, the novel also explores food's participation in an erotic economy. While I aim to identify patterns of representation common to each of Thúy's works, I am in no way suggesting that Thúy's writing about food is one-dimensional – quite the contrary.

Given the richness of this motif, it is no surprise that the critical response has been equally diverse, with some reading it as a marker of cultural authenticity and others a feature that makes the work more accessible or appealing to Western readers. Thus, for Pamela Sing, "Mãn cherche à nous server 'le' – ou peut-être serait-il plus juste de préciser 'son' – Vietnam sur le plateau: Ses gens, sa nourriture, sa langue, ses croyances, ses rues et ses gestes d'affectation, tous racontés sous l'angle de leurs aspects gustatifs, olfactifs et tactiles" [*Mãn* attempts to serve us Vietnam – perhaps it would be better to say "her" Vietnam – on a platter: its people, food, language, and beliefs, its streets and its affectionate gestures, all told from the angle of how they taste, smell, and feel].[3] In "Des affects plein l'assiette: Migration, nourriture et agentivité chez Kim Thúy," Marie-Christine Lambert-Perrault draws on Sing's analysis, as well as that of Ching Selao, to explore shifts in the representation of foodways across Thúy's work and how this reflects her immigrant narrators' "alignment" with their adoptive home, concluding that this "contributes to the favorable reception" of the author's writing.[4] This is echoed, as well, by Eileen Lohka, who, in "Senteurs de l'ailleurs: mémoire culinaire chez Kim Thúy," suggests that Thúy's representation of Vietnamese foodways frames the feminine subject within a web of social and family connections that effectively extends an invitation to the reader by opening "la sphère socio-culturelle québécoise à l'altérité" [Quebec's sociocultural sphere to alterity].[5] Jennifer Howell, on the other hand, reads Thúy's depictions of foodways as speaking to/for an emergent Việt Kiều, or Vietnamese diasporic, identity. She holds up Thúy's work as representative of a trend among "writers of the 1.5 generation" – those who left Viet Nam for the West as children – to attend to the regional differences in traditional Vietnamese cooking and thereby "more effectively represent the trans/national" reality of the Vietnamese diaspora.[6]

For my part, I aim to build on the insights of these different critics to tease out what undergirds the air of secrecy with which Thúy surrounds many of her images of Vietnamese cooking. In opposition to the practice of sharing kitchen secrets, as suggested by the title of Thúy's cookbook, I argue that Thúy mainly conjures secrets in order to keep them: first soliciting and then toying with her readers' curiosity. I am interested in the tropes she uses in her descriptions of food – from references to magical fairy tales to the deployment of metonymy, paradox, and ellipses – because of how they allow her to simultaneously draw attention to and *keep* secrets. While this emphasis on secrets does gesture toward an Orientalist discourse that associates Asian women with silence, secrecy, and desirability,[7] I want to read this not as an unavoidable repetition of a cliché but as a knowing and ironic response. It reflects Thúy's negotiation of the tension between the imperative of representing immigrant success and resistance to the reader's objectifying gaze. The result is an approach to representation that values keeping secrets, whether about the self or foodways – a way of writing that alludes to but does not reveal significant details.

Lohka draws attention to this dimension of Thúy's style, seeing it as an extension of Vietnamese idiom and its reliance on litotes – a modesty about naming things explicitly.[8] In my reading, however, it is less a reflection of stylistic hesitancy or linguistic *pudeur* than a strategy designed to entice readers and tease at our desire to know. With evocative allusions to unfamiliar ingredients and laborious preparations, to aromas and textures that link the exotic and the erotic, Thúy offers the reader images of desire, sometimes of its satisfaction and at others its frustration. While readers of *Ru* may in turn be horrified by the description of the "biscuits imbibés d'huile à moteur" (*Ru*, 13, 15) [biscuits soaked in motor oil (3, 5)][9] eaten during the perilous crossing from Viet Nam to Malaysia or find comfort in their own familiarity with the Canadian staples, such as Minute Rice or an omelette with maple syrup, that leave Thúy's immigrants hungry and perplexed (*Ru*, 31, 33), my interest lies primarily in evocations of what might be called "authentic" Vietnamese foodways: the preparation of and ingredients for traditional dishes, and the transmission of these recipes and other kitchen secrets from one generation to the next. More specifically, I focus on what is left out of these descriptions and on the tropes used to *keep* kitchen secrets. While there is a significant overlap between the passages about Vietnamese foodways that I discuss, they fall into four broad categories: food as metonymy for place; food as magic potion; food as labour of love; and culinary secrets and intimacy. Before turning to Thúy's fiction, however, I first return to *Le Secret des Vietnamiennes*, which establishes well the paradigm of keeping, rather than sharing, secrets.

Le Secret des Vietnamiennes is designed more as a photographic coffee-table book than as a practical cookbook, and this is central to its appeal.[10] While including information about ingredients that might not be familiar (or easily available) to some home cooks, whether in Quebec or elsewhere in North America, and a context for the preparation and serving of Vietnamese food (as is typical in other cookbooks focused on a regional or national cuisine), Thúy's book allots far more space to photographs and anecdotal text than to recipes. All told, the book presents a modest number of recipes: fifty-nine, which, at a page each, comprise just under a third of the book.[11] The book opens with simple versions of dipping sauces – for example, Thúy's *nước mắm chua* calls for sugar, water, fish sauce, and either lime juice or vinegar, but no garlic or hot pepper (33) – and offers recipes ranging from an easy-to-make *corrosol*, or soursop, smoothie (160) to more complicated dishes, such as a *ragoût de porc au caramel*, or *thịt kho* (136). Of *Le Secret*'s 196 pages, almost half are dedicated to photographs: there are ninety full pages of photos (including the inside and outside cover). These include forty-nine full-page photographs of food (thirty-three are of just food and sixteen focus on food but also include a fragmentary image of a person, whether an arm or a blurred or obscured face); fourteen pages of images of Vietnamese street scenes (comprised of four two-page spreads, plus three pairs of facing pages that juxtapose related images of markets and goods); twenty-five full-page portraits of individuals, mostly women, sometimes in pairs, but also one group shot of four men; and one page featuring a collage of snapshots. In addition, one page features a photographic border with a picture of eight people from the author's family. The front matter credits Gilles Dufour with the photos of Viet Nam and Sarah Scott with those that illustrate some of the recipes, as well as with the portraits of Thúy's family. There are several keepsake family pictures included too, notably a black and white portrait of the author's maternal grandparents, Lý Quí Phát and Lê Kiêm Gương, featured at the start of the book (1). Filling out the volume are thirty-five pages of text. Much of the writing is fairly typical for regional cookbooks, describing the noodles, herbs, vegetables, and fruits that distinguish Vietnamese cooking, for example (see "La Base" [17–29]), but there are also suggestions for the wine and music to pair with Thúy's recipes (see "Les accords mets vietnamiens-vin" [171–4] and "Les accords mets vietnamiens-musique" [179–81], signed respectively by two of the author's friends and collaborators). The book also offers numerous anecdotes about Thúy's family, some presented alongside photographic portraits, others highlighted in red italics as an epigraph at the start of a section (e.g., 7, 11). There are also brief excerpts from *Ru* (31), *À toi* (136), *Mãn* (115), and *Vi* (79).

Each of the cookbook's main sections is introduced by a pair of photos of a member of Thúy's family, whether a sister, an aunt, or Thúy herself. These photos are significant not just because they provide the scaffolding for the book, marking divisions between sections, but because of how they present the photographic subjects as possessing secrets unshared. While a couple of Scott's portraits have the subject posed looking squarely at the camera, with a gaze that connects directly with the viewer (e.g., *grande soeur 3* [14] and *tante 5* [62]), in at least one of each of the seven pairs of portraits the subject's eyes are averted, either looking thoughtfully off to the side, like *tante* 4 (44), or, more often, as if caught in the middle of a laugh, like *grande soeur 3* (16). Both of the individual portraits of the author, which are used to introduce the section on desserts and snacks, show her laughing and turned away from the camera (144, 146; the first of these also appears on the front cover). In this way, the photos that so effectively draw the reader into the book also produce a pattern that reflects ironically on the Orientalist trope of the beautiful and enigmatic Asian woman suggested by the book's title.

This teasing quality of the portraits, and the nod to Orientalism, is also amplified by the number of photographs that include fragmentary or out-of-focus images of (primarily female) bodies in images centred on food or scenery; as noted above, sixteen of the forty-nine full-page photographs of food in the book also include fragmented or blurred images of people. These are often photographs by Scott suggesting food preparation but also include some of Dufour's images of Viet Nam and local colour. Images by Scott include one of a hand apparently scattering chopped herbs on top of a bowl of sweet and sour soup (56) and another in which two hands slice lotus stems (98). A two-page display by Dufour shows, on the left, a cropped image of a woman standing by a display of grilled meat and, on the right, two hands grilling meat over a flame (122–3). The proliferation of these fleeting and partial images of bodies in motion is hard to ignore as one leafs through the book; they leave the viewer with unanswered questions and hungry for more detail.

Among these, however, one photograph stands out for the carefully constructed and enigmatic way in which it brings together images of food, a woman's body, and poetry: the photo by Scott that accompanies the recipe for a stir-fry of chayote, pork and shrimp, or *su su xào* (72–3). The image is focused on a bowl of the dish, on the hand that cradles the vibrantly coloured red and green bowl, and on a single shrimp suspended above the bowl by a pair of chopsticks. The woman's body, which forms the backdrop for the food, is slightly blurred and cropped; we see only one of her shoulders, parts of her hands, and, primarily, the lacy front of her blue and white dress. The bottom of her face appears in the top right of the photo; though her eyes are not in the image, she seems to gaze down over the bowl she's holding to an open book and a poem, the text of which is also somewhat out of focus and upside down for the viewer. While there is no title given for the poem, it appears to be "Je suis revenue à la maison," from the 2015 bilingual French and Arabic collection *Le Rapt* by Maram Al Masri, a Syrian-born poet based in France. While the explicit purpose of the image is to illustrate the recipe on the facing page, the image is structured by a series of secrets, where vibrant colour alludes to fragrance and taste, and where the poetry of one woman alludes to the writing of another, both of whom foreground the presence of their mother tongues – Arabic and Vietnamese, respectively – in the books they publish in French. For me, this image, with its metonymic representation of food as object of desire but also of the ambiguous position of the immigrant reader/writer, provides a visual model for understanding how Thúy plays with revealing and keeping secrets in her representation of Vietnamese foodways.

FOOD AS METONYMY FOR HOME

A primary function of the evocation of Vietnamese food in Thúy's writing is as metonymy for the missing home, a stand-in for what was lost during the refugee exodus and for what cannot be found when the narrator returns to Viet Nam decades later. As the eponymous narrator of *Vi* puts it, "J'ai tenté de rattraper quelques bribes des vingt ans du Vietnam derrière le rideau de fer en traînant autour des tables-restaurants" (*Vi*, 102). [I tried to seek out some fragments of Vietnam's twenty years behind the Iron Curtain by hanging around restaurant tables (92)]. When the narrator of *Ru* returns for work to the Viet Nam she left as a child, her foreignness is linked to her embodiment of a different relationship to food; a waiter tells her pointedly that she is "trop grosse pour être vietnamienne" (*Ru*, 86) [too fat to be Vietnamese (77)].

In *Mãn*, however, food seems to possess the power to collapse spans of time and space. The narrator, who runs a small restaurant with her husband, revels in how food is doubly linked to time travel: her return in memory to places from her past allows her to create food that transports her customers back home to the Viet Nam they had left years before.

> Je leur servais le même petit-déjeuner à tous, mais le changeais chaque matin au rythme de ma visite virtuelle des rues du Vietnam ... Il suffisait donc que je retourne dans ma tête à Chợ Lớn, le grand quartier chinois de Saigon, pour avoir l'idée de leur préparer les boulettes de porc haché enveloppant un petit morceau de côte levée, cuites à la vapeur dans un mince filet de sauce tomate ... L'un [des clients] était originaire de Rạch Giá, une ville côtière où l'on a inventé une soupe-repas au poisson poché avec des vermicelles, rehaussée de porc et de crevettes caramélisés dans les œufs de crevettes. Des larmes ont coulé sur sa joue lorsque j'ai arrosé son bol d'une petite cuillerée d'ail mariné au vinaigre. En mangeant cette soupe, il m'a susurré qu'il avait goûté sa terre, la terre où il avait grandi, où il était aimé. (*Mãn*, 41–2)

> [I served the same breakfast to everyone, but I changed what was on offer every morning to the rhythm of my virtual visit to the streets of Vietnam ... So I only had to go back mentally to Chợ Lớn, the big Chinese neighbourhood in Saigon, to get the idea of preparing pork meatballs wrapped around a small piece of sparerib, steamed in a trickle of tomato sauce ... One of the men came from Rạch Giá, a coastal town where a meal-in-a-bowl – a poached fish with vermicelli, embellished with shrimp eggs and caramelized pork – had been invented. Tears ran down his

> cheeks when I sprinkled his bowl with a small spoonful of pickled garlic. Eating that soup, he murmured that he had tasted his land, the land where he'd grown up, where he was loved. (34–5)]

The matter-of-fact description at the start of the passage – "il suffisait donc" [I only had to] – gives way to a more magical, more secretive experience: a bit of sparerib hidden in a meatball, steamed with a slight hint of tomato. In the end, a recipe "invented" in a town on the border between land and sea, and recreated worlds away, brings tears to the eater's eyes, the intensity of his experience only hinted at – "susurré" – in a secretive murmur.

A similar magic is invoked in Thúy's most recent novel, *Em* (2020), where the author conjurs *phở* as not just the marker of Vietnamese identity but the *sine qua non*, what makes someone Vietnamese. She opens the passage titled "*Phở*" with two absolute statements that distinguish Vietnamese emigrants from those living in the country: "Aucun Vietnamien vivant au Vietnam ne prépare un bouillon de *phở* à la maison. Or tout Vietnamien vivant à l'extérieur du Vietnam a préparé ou mangé un *phở* maison au moins une fois. Car les Vietnamiens expatriés ne peuvent pas sortir de chez eux et aller au kiosque à *phở* au coin de la rue" (*Em*, 123) [No Vietnamese living in Vietnam makes *phở* broth at home. But every Vietnamese living outside Vietnam has prepared or eaten a homemade *phở* at least once, since expatriate Vietnamese can't just leave the house and go to a *phở* kiosk on the street corner (123)]. After listing the usual ingredients for the soup, she describes the cauldrons typically used to prepare the broth, each imparting a unique flavour developed over decades of use, such that there is an almost limitless number of recipes representing the individual tastes and the authentic identities of each cook and each eater (*Em*, 124).[12] In this way, she redefines Louis, one of the novel's central characters, first introduced as a biracial orphan – "Un petit garçon encore né sans nom" (*Em*, 61) [Another little boy born with no name (54)] – who survives on the street by eating others' leftover *phở*, as not marginally but essentially Vietnamese: "Louis était la somme de tous ces clients" (*Em*, 125) [Louis was the sum of all those clients (125)]. It is the soup that magically makes the individual and, collectively, the people.

Elsewhere, however, Thúy cautions her readers – her non-Vietnamese readers, specifically – against the assumption that food provides an authentic connection to place. She ironizes this when Vi's brother gets a job at a Japanese restaurant in Quebec: "Il faisait voyager les convives jusqu'à Kobé, un endroit où il n'avait jamais mis les pieds. Sa manipulation acrobatique des ingrédients lui accordait une identité japonaise. D'un côté, les clients nourrissaient leurs rêves d'exotisme. De l'autre, mon frère Long se dirigeait vers la réalisation de ses rêves" (*Vi*, 51–2) [He transported the diners all the way to Kobe, a place where he'd never set foot. His acrobatic manipulation of the ingredients lent him a Japanese identity. While his clients were realizing their dreams of exoticism, my brother Long was making his way towards the realization of dreams of his own (42–3)]. Here, Long's performance, his "acrobatic manipulation" of food, stands in for the Orientalist sleight of hand that elides differences between Japan and Viet Nam. At the same time, as a *mise-en-abyme* of a reader's voyeuristic presence at the table, the anecdote undercuts any impulse Thúy's readers may have to enjoy the descriptions of Vietnamese food in her writing. As we read her books, the vignette suggests, we cannot or ought not simply indulge our "dreams of exoticism."

FOOD AS MAGIC POTION

And yet, in other places, Thúy seems to encourage precisely that impulse. Near the start of *Mãn*, for example, the narrator describes the transmission of culinary secrets from mother to daughter in terms that suggest the magic of a fairy tale:[13]

> Les mères enseignaient à leurs filles à cuisiner à voix basse, en chuchotant, afin d'éviter le vol des recettes par les voisines, qui pourraient séduire leurs maris avec les mêmes plats. Les traditions culinaires se transmettaient en secret, tels des tours de magie entre maître et apprenti, un geste à la fois, selon le rythme du quotidien. Dans l'ordre naturel, les filles apprenaient donc à mesurer la quantité d'eau pour le riz avec la première phalange de l'index, à tailler les "piments vicieux" (*ớt hiểm*) avec la pointe du couteau pour les transformer en fleurs inoffensives, à éplucher les mangues de la base à la pointe pour ne pas contredire le sens des fibres … (*Mãn*, 12, ellipsis in the original)

> [When mothers taught their daughters how to cook, they spoke in hushed tones, whispering so that neighbours couldn't steal recipes and possibly seduce their husbands with the same dishes. Culinary traditions are passed on secretly, like magic tricks

between master and apprentice, one movement at a time, following the rhythms of each day. In the natural order, then, girls learned to measure the amount of water for cooking rice with the first joint of the index finger, to cut "vicious peppers" (*ớt hiểm*) with the point of the knife to transform them into harmless flowers, to peel mangoes from the base to stem so they won't go against the direction of the fibres … (4)]

Here the familiar (daughters learning from mothers) is defamiliarized, reframed as witches casting spells that seduce, apparently by transforming dangerous peppers into flowers. While I want to note that this passage, like another I will discuss below, ends enigmatically with an ellipsis (an allusion to what is left unsaid, to secrets unspoken), it actually contains one of the few true culinary secrets passed on in Thúy's fiction: how best to peel a mango.

The link between food and fairy tales is made repeatedly across Thúy's body of work. In *Ru*, for example, she describes the salted grilled meat that women prepared for their husbands, prisoners in reeducation camps, as "une potion magique" [a magic potion], first suggesting that the preparation of the dish helps to keep the missing men alive, even if only in memory, and then confessing that she herself continues to protect both her sons and tradition in this way: "En souvenir de ces femmes, je prépare de temps à autre cette viande rissolée pour mes fils, afin de préserver, de répéter, ces gestes d'amour" (*Ru*, 44) [In memory of those women, I cook that browned meat for my sons now and then, to preserve, to repeat, those gestures of love (35)]. Similarly, in *Mãn* the narrator hints at the magical attributes of a dish she prepares when her husband is sick:

> Quand mon mari est tombé malade la première fois, je lui ai préparé ce plat, qui exigeait une cuisson douce du poulet avec des graines de lotus, des noix de ginkgo et des baies de goji séchées. Selon les croyances, une portion de l'éternité est retenue dans le lotus alors que le ginkgo fortifie les neurones, car ses feuilles ont la forme du cerveau. Quant aux gojis, leurs vertus médicinales sont attestées dans les livres depuis le temps des empereurs et des princesses. Les bienfaits de ce plat doivent probablement provenir aussi de l'attention consacrée à la préparation. En plus des longues heures de cuisson lente, il y a la coquille des noix de ginkgo à craquer avec fermeté mais tout en retenue, afin de préserver la

chair tendre entière. De même, il faut retirer le germe vert des graines de lotus pour enlever le goût amer. (*Mãn*, 39)

[When my husband fell sick for the first time, I prepared a dish for him that involved gently cooking chicken with lotus seeds, ginkgo nuts and dried goji berries. According to certain beliefs, a portion of eternity stays behind in the lotus, while the ginkgo strengthens the neurons, since its leaves are shaped like brains. As for the goji berries, books attesting to their medicinal virtues have existed since the days of emperors and princesses. The benefits of the dish are likely due to the attention devoted to its preparation. In addition to the long hours of slow cooking, the shell of the ginkgo must be cracked firmly but with restraint, to protect the whole of the tender flesh. And the green germ must be removed from the lotus seeds to get rid of their bitter taste. (32)]

The passage begins with a list of ingredients and a caution about how the recipe requires a delicate touch: "une cuisson douce" [gently cooking]. At its heart, however, it conjures images of a fairy-tale kingdom, a place of secretive beliefs, the mythical time of emperors and princesses. It is also important to note that here – as so often in Thúy's writing – what we have is an evocation of the preparation of food, rather than of its eating. No discussion of taste or aroma, but an emphasis on cooking as devotion, both as a means to cure her ailing husband and as a laborious process: note the verb "exiger" [literally "to require," but translated by Fischman as "involved"] in the first line, the "longues heures de cuisson" [the long hours of slow cooking], the paradox of a firm and restrained hand to crack the ginkgo, and the careful removal of the bitter germ.

While in these passages the magic potion is prepared to protect a loved individual, in other places, as in the passage about *phở* from *Em* cited above, Thúy makes a connection to the broader question of cultural survival. In *Ru*, for example, the ritualized preparation of a lotus-infused tea produces a magical tonic capable of preserving an identity steeped in tradition. The anecdote begins with the accidental death of one old woman, who drowns in a septic pond filled with catfish: "Elle est morte dans la fosse septique familiale ... derrière sa hutte, entourée de poissons-chats à la chair jaune, à la peau lisse, sans écailles, sans mémoire" (*Ru*, 48) [She died in the family's septic tank, her head plunging in a hole full of excrement between two planks, behind her hut, surrounded by smooth-skinned, yellow-fleshed bullheads, without scales, without memory (39)]. The significance of this image of apparently meaningless sacrifice is recuperated in the following segment, which casts "les femmes au dos arqué" [women with bent backs] – the long-suffering women who symbolize Vietnamese cultural survival in Thúy's novel – as engaged in a metaphoric battle for the soul of the nation.

> Après le décès de cette vieille dame, tous les dimanches, j'allais au bord d'un étang à lotus en banlieue de Hanoi, où il y avait toujours deux ou trois femmes au dos arqué, aux mains tremblantes, qui, assises dans le fond d'une barque ronde, se déplaçaient sur l'eau à l'aide d'une perche pour placer des feuilles de thé à l'intérieur des fleurs de lotus ouvertes. Elles retournaient le jour suivant pour les recueillir, une à une, avant que les pétales se fanent, après que les feuilles emprisonnées avaient absorbé le parfum des pistils pendant la nuit. Elles me disaient que chaque feuille de thé conservait ainsi l'âme de ces fleurs éphémères. (*Ru*, 49)
>
> [After the old lady died, I would go every Sunday to a lotus pond in a suburb of Hanoi where there were always two or three women with bent backs and trembling hands, sitting in a small round boat, using a stick to move across the water and drop tea leaves into open lotus blossoms. They would come back the next day to collect them one by one before the petals faded, after the captive tea leaves had absorbed the scent of the pistils during the night. They told me that every one of those tea leaves preserved the soul of the short-lived flowers. (40)]

The literary inscription of the narrator's own devotion – her weekly pilgrimage in honour of the woman who died – creates a *mise-en-abyme* that frames and extends the ritual practice of other women, anonymous and multiple, whose repetitive gestures preserve the "soul" of the lotus flowers, which, as the national flower, are emblematic of Viet Nam itself. This image of a never-ending pattern – note Thúy's use of the imperfect throughout, and the faceless women who are always there and who, paddling a round-boat,[14] place and collect tea leaves, one by one, day after day – depicts Viet Nam as timeless and eternal but also contingent upon the repetition of magical gestures.

FOOD AS A LABOUR OF LOVE

This brings us to a related theme that emphasizes the time-intensive preparation of foods as a gauge of devotion and, ultimately, a tool for seduction, at times again echoing an Orientalist discourse that links the exotic and self-abnegation. Already in the passages above, references to magical attributes are paired with phrases that underscore the effort necessary to create a special dish. In *Ru*, magic and a filial devotion verging on obsession come together in the description of the dish of roast pork and rice ritually prepared by the narrator's aunt for her father, where pork sliced so thin it appears ground is served in bowls remarkable for their translucence and topped with a small dollop of imported butter (*Ru*, 76). But Thúy's narrators also tell of women who use culinary secrets more pragmatically as a means to attract and keep a man. This is underscored in *Vi*, which explains in great detail not only how the narrator's mother patiently plots the seduction of the man she eventually marries but also how she passes on her strategic use of food to her future daughter-in-law. When Vi recounts how her mother and father met, the story hinges on a culinary secret: the exotic and rare coffee she brings him each morning, made with beans extracted from the scat of wild civets. While her social position, emblematized by her dark skin and acne scars (*Vi*, 18), had kept him from noticing her – "Même si elle était debout à quelques pas de lui … elle restait invisible à ses yeux" (*Vi*, 19) [Even if she was standing just a few steps away … she remained invisible to his eyes (10–11)] – one sip of the exotic potion is all it takes: "Étonné du goût distinct et soyeux du café, il a tourné les yeux vers ma mère. Elle lui en a confié le secret en lui montrant une petite boule difforme sertie de grains, ramassée dans les environs des plantations à Buôn Mê Thuôt. Ces boules provenaient des civettes sauvages qui rejetaient les grains tout entiers après avoir mangé et digéré les cerises de café mûres … Mon père est devenu instantanément un adepte" (*Vi*, 21) [Astounded by the unusual, velvety taste of the coffee, he turned his eyes in my mother's direction. She revealed to him the secret, showing him a small misshapen ball dotted with seeds, gathered nearby from the plantations at Buôn Mê Thuôt. Those balls came from wild civets that excreted the seeds whole after having eaten and digested ripe coffee cherries … My father became an instant convert (12)]. The magical effect of her coffee is instantaneous, but highlighting this distracts from the effort she put into her plot, elaborated over more than a year, not to mention the labour of those who scoured the plantation grounds for civet scat. The sharing of that particular secret led to their wedding, but maintaining the marriage required additional and repeated sacrifices, also linked to food. Thus the narrator notes that while her mother carefully avoided the apartment where her husband met his lovers, she ensured that the servants prepared the right foods for his trysts (*Vi*, 27–8) and also continued to serve dishes at home that she painstakingly prepared for him alone, as an offering, "une offrande" (*Vi*, 41).

While Vi's mother's obsequious attention to her husband's tastes was not sufficient to ensure his fidelity in Viet Nam, she employs the same strategy in Quebec to try to keep her son Long from straying from his wife, Hoa, by silently, secretly, plying him with food: "S'il arrivait trop tard trop souvent, elle lui préparait ses plats préférés. Elle l'appelait au travail sans insister, sans mentionner qu'une famille l'attendait, sans lui rappeler de résister au désir. Elle livrait tout simplement les plats à Hoa et espérait entendre un rire ou deux à travers les murs" (*Vi*, 123) [If he arrived too late too often, she prepared his favourite dishes. She called him at work without making demands, without mentioning that a family was waiting for him, without reminding him that he should resist his desires. She simply brought the dishes to Hoa, and hoped to hear a laugh or two through the walls (113–14)]. Even before Long and Hoa marry, she passes on to her daughter and her future daughter-in-law the secret of demonstrating love through food and self-abnegation:

> [Les amis de Long] ne soupçonnaient pas que chaque bouchée renfermait des heures de travail, d'humilité et d'obéissance de la part de Hoa. Elle devait subir les ordres précis de ma mère concernant la cuisson du riz pour la farce, qui doit se faire en deux temps, la taille des cubes de saucisson vietnamien une fois cuit, le bon dosage de champignons shiitake dont le parfum doit accompagner sans envahir … Hoa supportait tous les excès de ma mère en silence, même lorsque j'étais seule avec elle à retirer la pellicule des arachides une à une. Patiemment, elle me montrait comment rouler une bouteille vide sur les graines pour les concasser sans les émietter." (*Vi*, 57–8, ellipsis in the original)

> [They did not suspect that each mouthful involved hours of work, humility, and obedience on the part of Hoa. She had

> to follow my mother's strict orders concerning the two stages of cooking the rice for the stuffing, the size of the Vietnamese sausage cubes once they were cooked, the proper quantity of shiitake mushrooms, whose scent must enhance without being invasive ... Hoa endured in silence all my mother's demands, even when I was alone with her, peeling the skins off peanuts, one by one. Patiently, she showed me how to roll an empty bottle over the nuts in order to crush them without reducing them to powder. (48–9)]

Although the passage stresses Hoa's long-suffering obedience, it begins with the fact that her efforts remained a secret to those who ate the dishes she prepared – just as the culinary secrets passed from mother to daughter-in-law, and between sisters, are kept from the readers. The passage names but carefully avoids revealing any secrets: not the right way to cook rice or the right amount of shiitake mushrooms to add; not how to use a bottle to crack and peel peanuts. Ultimately, all that is not explained in this cooking lesson is underscored by the ellipsis in the middle, which alludes to other secrets, unimaginable and untold.

CULINARY SECRETS AND INTIMACY

Curiously, this aura of secrecy prevails as well when Thúy draws attention to the significance of sharing food. Take, for example, Vi's description of the start of her relationship with Vincent, a passage where food and seduction are linked in a more positive light and where the reader is still left out of the secret:

> Le lendemain, [Vincent] est venu me chercher pour le petit-déjeuner chez l'élégante Mme Simone Đài, qui servait des crêpes au sucre et jus de lime, du yaourt maison et des croissants, appelés "cornes de buffle" par les serveurs. A midi, il m'a fait découvrir les arachides rôties à la sauce de poisson que les "locaux" mangeaient avec du riz. Le soir, j'ai pédalé à côté de lui jusqu'à Hồ Tây, où les jeunes amoureux partageaient des escargots cuits dans des herbes médicinales. En moins de vingt-quatre heures, j'ai constaté que Hanoi se révélait beaucoup plus grande que les quinze rues et les six adresses que je fréquentais au quotidien. (*Vi*, 106–7)

> [The next day he came to fetch me for breakfast at the elegant Mme Simone Đài's, where crepes were served with sugar and lime juice, along with homemade yogurt and croissants, called "buffalo horns" by the waiters. At lunchtime, he introduced me to peanuts roasted in fish sauce, which the "locals" ate with rice. In the evening, I pedaled at his side to Hồ Tây, where young lovers shared snails cooked in medicinal herbs. In less than twenty-four hours I saw that Hanoi was much more than the fifteen streets and six addresses that I frequented from day to day. (97)]

Here, in a return to the earlier trope of using food as a metonymy for home, place and time are linked through food such that the city (and its blending of French and Vietnamese traditions) would seem to be restored, thereby suggesting a synecdoche that links the city to the budding relationship between Vincent and Vi. But note the way in which the passage distinguishes between observing and experiencing Vietnamese foodways: crepes are served, rather than tasted; the "locals" eat peanuts with fish sauce and rice; and young lovers share escargots cooked in unspecified "medicinal herbs." These are things Vi "discovers" and "notices" as she moves through the city but that she does not actually describe. It is perhaps implied that she eats, but the phrasing strategically avoids making that explicit; the young lovers who share escargots are presumably not Vi and Vincent. As a result, the reader, like Vi herself, is kept on the margin; we share in the vicarious experience of *watching* others eat, not that of enjoying a meal, per se. That experience is kept secret.

Secrets are centred, too, even in passages where Thúy lingers over the description of a shared meal. Thúy's description of Vietnamese fondue, or hot pot – a dish where foods and friends are joined by communal cooking around a single pot – gestures toward a sense of home and family and offers food as sign of both devotion and the erotic dynamic of the relationship between Vi and Vincent.

> Au retour des fêtes, Vincent a atterri à Hanoi deux jours après moi. Je nous ai préparé une fondue vietnamienne le soir même avec un bouillon clair dans lequel nous avons fait cuire des tranches de poulet, de bœuf, de porc, ainsi que des crevettes et des palourdes. La partie favorite de Vincent était le panier de

> verdure qui accompagnait les viandes. Sa "mère vietnamienne" m'avait aidée à trouver les rhizomes de nénuphar, les jeunes pousses de bambou, les liserons d'eau, les fleurs de bananier, les fleurs de courge, les ocras, les champignons de paille … et une sorte de mimosa pudique dont le goût et la texture lui plaisaient tout particulièrement. Ce plat était plus goûteux s'il était dégusté en groupe puisque le bouillon s'enrichissait lorsqu'une grande quantité d'ingrédients y cuisaient. Alors même si j'aurais préféré garder Vincent juste pour moi, je l'ai partagé avec nos amis présents à Hanoi. L'amitié éphémère mais intense, entre expatriés formait une famille sans pareille. (*Vi*, 127–8, ellipsis in the original)
>
> [After the Christmas holidays, Vincent landed in Hanoi two days after me. I prepared us a Vietnamese fondue that evening, with a clear bouillon in which we cooked slices of chicken, beef, and pork, as well as clams and shrimp. Vincent's favourite part was the basket of greens that accompanied the meats. His "Vietnamese mother" had helped me to find the water lily rhizomes, the young bamboo shoots, the water spinach, the banana flowers, the squash blossoms, the okra, the straw mushrooms … and a kind of shy mimosa with a taste and texture he particularly liked. This dish was tastier if it was eaten in a group, because the bouillon was richer when a large quantity of ingredients was involved. And so, even though I would have preferred to keep Vincent all to myself, I shared him with our friends who were in Hanoi. The ephemeral but intense friendship with expatriates made for a very special family. (118–19, ellipsis in the original)]

There are many things to notice in this passage, including the long list of ingredients that suggests excess and an exotic palate (five different proteins, as well as eight different flowers or vegetables). More significantly, the passage also shifts from sharing food to sharing Vincent, a move that suggests food as metonymy not only for home but for a lover.

This is, without a doubt, one of the more extended descriptions of a shared dish in Thúy's writing – and the most complete if you simply count up the ingredients listed. But it is also markedly lacking in descriptives: of the seven adjectives used in the passage (*vietnamienne*, *clair*, *favorite*, *plus goûteux*, *présents*, *éphémère*, et *intense*), none actually describes the dish shared ("Vietnamese" simply names the dish, while "clear," "favourite," and "tastier" do not do much to conjure a sensual experience for the reader: they are empty adjectives). The strongest adjectives in the passage, *éphémère* and *intense* ("ephemeral" and "intense"), are not only applied to the abstract notion of friendship but also bound in an oppositional relationship, thus constituting an enigmatic paradox, a secret. Finally, I want to consider the ellipsis in the middle of the passage: "les champignons de paille ... et une sorte de mimosa pudique" [the straw mushrooms ... and a kind of shy mimosa]. Thúy's insertion of the pause just before the final ingredient points to the value of the flower as a secret both erotic and culinary, an item she hesitates to include in the list and one she cannot accurately name: "a kind of shy mimosa," or sensitive plant. While it is significant that this type of plant – better known as *Mimosa pudica* – recoils from touch,[15] we have no inkling of why the taste and texture of the plant appeal so much to Vincent. One might connect this back to the sociolinguistically conditioned use of litotes identified by Lokha,[16] but ultimately, all we know is that Vincent's adoptive mother helped Vi to find the flower. The narrator's hesitancy underlines the secret she modestly keeps – one more secret that tantalizes and eludes readers.

WHY KEEP CULINARY SECRETS?

To conclude, references to Vietnamese foodways in Thúy's writing are frequent and diverse; Thúy offers up food as, in turn, metonymy for place and love; a magic potion that protects and even creates the people; a symbol of devotion and of self-abnegation; and suggestive of intimacy. But mostly, food is wrapped in an air of secrecy, of secrets passed on, perhaps, but generally kept from the reader.[17] While I am inclined to agree with Lambert-Perrault that the evocations of Vietnamese foodways contribute to the positive reception of Thúy's writing in Quebec (and elsewhere),[18] I think that is due less to what she reveals than to how she keeps her secrets. Even as Thúy cautions readers against falling for the sleight of hand that seems to provide an "authentic" experience of Asian cuisine (Japanese in the example with Vi's brother Long; Vietnamese throughout Thúy's work), the author toys with her readers' desire to be let in on the secret, whetting our appetites but deferring delivery. But why?

One path toward answering that question begins with the popular reception of Thúy's work, which often focuses on the author at the expense of her writing. The burden of representation is evident in magazine reviews that blur the distinctions between fiction, autofiction, and autobiography. For example, Jean-Yves Girard, who interviewed Thúy for *Châtelaine*, draws an explicit equation between author and narrator, declaring flat out – and erroneously – that *Ru* is an "autobiography." After marvelling at the author's optimism – "jamais on ne sent chez [Thúy] la moindre amertume ni l'ombre d'un reproche à la vie" [never with Thúy does one sense the least bit of bitterness or the shadow of a reproach to life] – he concludes, "Pour certains, elle représente l'immigration réussie" [For some, she represents immigrant success].[19] Martine Laval, in a 2010 review of *Ru* published in the French magazine *Télérama*, also blurs the distinction between the author and her work as she evokes both Scheherazade and Salomé to conjure an image of Thúy "dressed in words": "La romancière ... se dévoile, mais avec grâce, pudeur. Elle opère surtout une mise à nu de ses souvenirs éparpillés dans le temps et l'espace ... Elle fouille sa mémoire, touche les empreintes d'une histoire commune comme on effleure tendrement des cicatrices sur une peau ... Elle s'est habillée de mots. A fait sienne la langue française. S'est mise au centre d'un récit et nous raconte mille vies" [The novelist ... unveils herself, but with grace, modesty. Most of all, she manages to lay bare her recollections, scattered across time and space ... She searches through her memory, touches the traces of a collective story as one might tenderly touch scars on skin ... She has dressed herself with words. Has made the French language her own. Has put herself in the centre of a tale and tells us of a thousand lives].[20] The terms and tropes Laval draws on to praise Thúy's work – from the evocative paradox created by the juxtaposition of the words "se dévoile" and "mise à nu" ("unveils" and "lay bare") with the author's "pudeur" (modesty), to the mimetic image of seeking hidden truths in someone's scars – harken both to an all too familiar Orientalist discourse and to the reader's desire to discover secrets. And as I have tried to show in my reading of Thúy's descriptions of Vietnamese foodways, we see these same tropes and figures strategically deployed in *Ru*, *Mãn*, *Vi*, and, albeit to a lesser extent, *Em*.

While Thúy's ability to bespeak the immigrant experience poignantly is central to both the success and the significance of her work, as critics including Jennifer Howell argue so effectively, that she does so also reflects the expectation that narratives of the immigrant experience conform to models of adaptation, success, and gratitude. In "Refugee Gratitude: Narrating Success and Intersubjectivity in Kim Thúy's *Ru*," which traces the tensions that shape Thúy's writing, Vinh Nguyen suggests both the implications of the "good refugee" narrative and Thúy's awareness of and resistance to those pitfalls. Building on the work of David Palumbo-Liu and Yen Le Espiritu, Nguyen notes that "the success narrative can become regulatory and punitive and, as a result, easily lends itself to appropriation by revisionist, nationalist, and neo-imperialist forces."[21] He later concludes, specifically about Thúy's *Ru*, that "the narrator is aware [in this candid moment] of how her past becomes a spectacle for white, mainstream consumption. As she performs this ethnic minstrelsy, however, she is not only catering to the desires and expectations of a particular audience hungry for stories of trauma, but also rendering the traumatic past for herself in a particular way that can be accommodated by the present."[22] Nguyen's linking of the readers' "desires and expectations" to their hunger is not inconsequential. I agree with Nguyen that Thúy's work fills the hunger of North American (Western) readers for narratives of success and gratitude that allay our sense of collective guilt for the human consequences of Western military and economic exploitation; I would further emphasize that she does so in part through her alluring representation of Vietnamese foodways.

By wrapping her descriptions of the preparation and sharing of food in an aura of secrecy, the author both heightens our appetite for the secrets she claims to hold and resists self-exposure, gesturing toward the autobiographical but refusing to fully indulge the reader's (voyeuristic) desire, whether for a story of immigrant success or the revelation of culinary secrets. In a 2017 *HuffPost Québec* piece about her cookbook *Le Secret des Vietnamiennes*, Thúy in fact admits as much. When Samuel Larochelle asks Thúy how she was able to convince her family to allow her to share the family secrets – "Les recettes vietnamiennes sont des secrets sensibles et jalousement précieux, transmis de génération en génération dans la discretion. Comment as-tu convaincu ta famille de divulguer vos secrets?" [Vietnamese recipes are significant secrets, jealously treasured, transmitted discreetly from generation to generation. How did you convince your family to divulge your secrets?][23] – the author responds suggestively, "D'abord, le livre ne révèle pas tant ces secrets" [First off, the book doesn't fully reveal those secrets]. Ultimately, the real secret of Thúy's writing is not what she reveals but how she tantalizes us with the image of the secrets she keeps.

NOTES

1 The cookbook was translated and published in English as *Secrets from My Vietnamese Kitchen* (Random House, 2019), a title with significantly different connotations. In this chapter I will refer to the original French-language edition and title.

2 References to Kim Thúy's novels are to the Libre Expression editions and quotations will be cited in the text with page numbers in parentheses. The sole exception is for *Ru*, where citations refer to the 2014 Stanké pocket edition.

3 Sing, "Migrance, sensorium et translocalité," 285, cited in Lambert-Perrault, "Des affects plein l'assiette," 81. Here and below, translations of quotations from secondary materials, unless otherwise indicated, are my own.

4 Lambert-Perrault, "Des affects plein l'assiette," 89; Ching Selao, *Le Roman vietnamien francophone*.

5 Lohka, "Senteurs de l'ailleurs," 193.

6 Howell, "À chaque recette, son histoire," 72–3.

7 Said, *Orientalism*.

8 Lohka, "Senteurs de l'ailleurs," 186.

9 All English versions of excerpts from Thúy's novels *Ru*, *Mãn*, and *Vi* are from the translations by Sheila Fischman and appear in square brackets, including parenthetical page references.

10 See, for example, Samuel Larochelle's 11 June 2017 piece for *HuffPost Québec*, which opens with a reference to the appeal of the photographs: "Certains livres de recettes sont élaborés avec un tel souci esthétique qu'ils sont à la fois pratiques et magnifiques. Le livre de Kim Thúy va plus loin encore. La nourriture étant l'un des moyens prisés des Vietnamiens pour exprimer leur affection, on sent à travers les pages de cet ouvrage une ode aux saveurs et aux odeurs. On découvre grâce au travail de la photographe Sarah Scott – et quelques sublimes photos d'archive – des extraits d'une culture fascinante, sa beauté, sa richesse, ses nuances et son âme. On jouit d'un accès privilégié à la famille de la plus célèbre Vietnamienne du Québec, à ses tantes et à sa mère, à la vie qui défile sur leurs visages, marqués par une histoire que l'écrivaine nous dévoile bribe par bribe, dans

ses romans et dans ses recettes" [Some cookbooks are put together with such attention to aesthetics that they are at once practical and magnificent. Kim Thúy's book goes further still. Since food is one of the primary ways for the Vietnamese to express their affection, readers sense in the pages of this work an ode to flavours and scents. Thanks to the work of photographer Sarah Scott – and several sublime archival photos – we discover bits of a fascinating culture, its beauty, its richness, its nuances, and its soul. We enjoy a privileged access to the family of the most famous Vietnamese woman in Quebec, to her aunts and her mother, to the life visible on their faces, marked by a history that the writer reveals to us bit by bit, in her novels and in her recipes]. (Larochelle, "'Les secrets des Vietnamiennes': Kim Thúy concocte un livre culinaire … touchant," n.p.)

11 For comparison, Linh Nguyen's *Lemongrass, Ginger and Mint: Vietnamese Cookbook* presents 83 recipes, with recipes accounting for more than 60 per cent of the book's 208 pages, and Mai Pham's *The Best of Vietnamese and Thai Cooking: Favorite Recipes from Lemon Grass Restaurant and Cafes* presents 131 recipes, which similarly comprise more than 60 per cent of the book's 274 pages.

12 Thúy goes so far as to stipulate that there are at least "twenty-four to the power of twenty-four" possible variations for the broth, a number so large it defies vocabulary, although I'm tempted to see it as an amplification of the scale of human genetics, with twenty-four being one more than the twenty-three pairs of human chromosomes (*Em*, 124).

13 Reading food blogs about Viet Nam, the same tropes of fairy tales and secrets are repeated (sometimes alongside quotes from Thúy); for example, *Le Guide du Mangeur averti*'s post from 24 August 2013 includes a passage from Thúy's *Mãn* and cites Linh, the author of another blog (*Baguettes et traditions*), who asserts, "La culture populaire vietnamienne est avant tout une culture qui se transmet oralement. Les femmes, en charge … de nourrir le pays, ont transmis à travers les siècles des dictons dans une tradition orale qui a donné à la nourriture un rôle d'allégorie qui perdure encore aujourd'hui … [P]ersonne ne s'étonne que la maîtresse de maison consacre beaucoup de temps et de labeur à la préparation des repas" [Vietnamese popular culture is primarily transmitted orally. The women responsible … for feeding the country have handed down across the centuries the sayings of an oral tradition that bestows upon food an allegorical role that persists until today … [N]o one is surprised that the mistress of the house dedicates much time and labour to preparing meals]. The post then concludes: "Chaque plat est un souvenir, un lien avec leur famille, un lieu ou un événement lié au Vietnam. Les recettes et les tours

de main sont des secrets qui se transmettent de mère en fille" [Each dish is a memory, a link to their family, a place, or an event connected to Vietnam. The recipes and tricks are secrets transmitted from mother to daughter]. (Une Mangeuse Avertie [pseud.], "La touchante sensibilité.")

14 Woven round-boats are frequently cited as a symbol of Vietnamese tradition and ingenuity. See, for example, "Charting Their Own Course," on the National Geographic website, which notes the boats' origin in resistance to French colonialism and the challenge of steering a craft that tends "to spin in circles."

15 *Encyclopaedia Britannica*, s.v. "mimosa," accessed 29 October 2022, https://www.britannica.com/plant/mimosa.

16 Lohka, "Senteurs de l'ailleurs," 186.

17 Curiously, Marie-Josée R. Roy seems to acknowledge something similar in a piece publicizing *La Table de Kim*, a TV show Thúy hosted where guests discussed current events while eating a meal; six episodes of the program aired on ICI ARTV in 2019. Writing in *Le Journal de Montréal*, Roy cautions viewers that while the program is premised on a shared meal, it is not about food, per se: "Ne cherchez toutefois pas les recettes dégustées sur le site Internet de l'émission, et n'espérez pas de conseils culinaires, même s'il est question de bouffe; ce n'est pas là le mandat d'ICI ARTV, ni l'objectif poursuivi par Kim Thúy et ses collègues" [But don't expect to find the recipes of dishes sampled on the show's website, and don't expect any cooking tips either, even if food is discussed; that is not the purpose of ICI ARTV, nor the goal of Kim Thúy and her colleagues]. (Roy, "ICI ARTV: La table d'amitié de Kim Thúy," n.p.)

18 Lambert-Perrault, "Des affects plein l'assiette," 89.

19 Girard, "Les joies de Kim Thúy," n.p.

20 Laval, "*Ru* de Kim Thúy," n.p.

21 Nguyen, "Refugee Gratitude," 1; Palumbo-Liu, *Asian/American*; Espiritu, "Thirty Years AfterWARd."

22 Nguyen, "Refugee Gratitude," 7.

23 Larochelle, "Les secrets des Vietnamiennes," n.p.

3

Poetics of Silence and the Act of Writing in Kim Thúy's Narrative Works

Nguyễn Giáng Hương

Silence is usually associated with the limit of the speakable or to the impossibility of describing extreme emotions. As the opposite of silence, the term *logos* is a fundamental concept derived from a Greek word variously meaning "speech" or "word." In Heraclitus's works, *logos* became a philosophical term that signifies a principle of order and knowledge. Then, the term was applied in the field of rhetoric by Aristotle to refer to "reasoned discourse" or "the argument," for he considered it one of the three modes of persuasion alongside *ethos* and *pathos*. According to this concept of *logos*, language means reason and knowledge. However, words lost their supremacy in the nineteenth century during the Romantic era. Hölderlin, Mallarmé, and Rimbaud consider language an obstacle to expression. European authors in the twentieth century continued to doubt the role of speech because of its limitations in the face of the fullness of the world. Rilke, Joyce, and Borges used their writing itself to question the power of speech.[1]

In the East, silence as the opposite of speech has always been valued in ancient philosophy. According to Laozi, "One who knows does not speak; one who speaks does not know."[2] In other words, silence is considered by Laozi as the only recourse to one who has true knowledge of the Dao. The Dao possesses multiple connotations and could be the equivalent of the Greek *hodos* (way) but also of the Greek *logos*.[3] But the Dao cannot be named or articulated because to speak of the Dao is, in some sense, to lessen or deny its absolute power. In Taoist doctrine, ways of knowing become inseparable from ways of being: in being with the Dao, one knows the Dao. Then emptiness becomes an abstraction of silence; it pushes people to seek the truth or the fullness of meaning and encourages us to reach wisdom. Therefore, the Taoist master advocates experience and condemns the limited and rigid character of speech. The Taoist master only accepts the use of speech for its evocative and allusive functions, as François Jullien explains: "Dans sa condamnation catégorique de la parole, le sage taoïste rejoint l'expérience mystique la plus universelle, de même que dans son acceptation contrainte de la parole – comme pis-aller, comme moyen frauduleux et néanmoins nécessaire –, puisque *aussi* il parle. Ce qui est peut-être le plus original est la façon dont le Sage chinois se montre conscient du caractère purement allusif et fictif du langage auquel il recourt. Le seul langage possible est un langage 'forcé'" [The Taoist wise man connects to the most universal mystical experience in his categorical condemnation of the spoken word, as well as in his compelled acceptance of the word – as a last resort, as a fraudulent and nonetheless necessary means – given that he perforce *also* speaks. What is perhaps most original is the way in which the Chinese Sage shows his consciousness of the purely allusive and fictitious character of the language he resorts to. The only possible language is a "compelled" one].[4]

Consequently, we will apply the philosophical and Taoist point of view on the relation between silence and verbalization in the analysis of Kim Thúy's texts. In fact, silence is omnipresent in Kim Thúy's novels *Ru*, *Mãn*, and *Vi*. Throughout these works of fiction, there is virtually no dialogue, with some exceptions in *Mãn* and *Vi*. Interior monologue dominates Kim Thúy's writing, conveying the narrator's thoughts, emotions, and memories. This silence marks the break between the past and the present, between the South and the North of Viet Nam, and between family members. But at the same time, the emptiness associated with silence is filled by many other things. Without dialogue, communication comes in other forms. Kim Thúy's characters exchange their emotions with one another through looks, with affectionate gestures, and especially by cooking and sharing traditional meals. Moreover, Kim Thúy questions not only silence in the narrative but also the use of silence as a method of writing. Silence is conceived as going beyond speech, a textual gap in which readers have to find the true meaning; words are used only to evoke. Therefore, this chapter analyzes both the silence in Kim Thúy's novels as a particular way of communication and the link between her writing and a Far Eastern poetics based on the aesthetic of silence.

THE NARRATIVE OF SILENCE: BETWEEN EMPTINESS AND FULLNESS

The novels *Ru*, *Mãn*, and *Vi* are written in the form of an interior monologue, composed by a flow of thoughts. Characters in the protagonist's entourage appear in different moments of the narrative, but no one speaks out or talks to one another. As such, Kim Thúy deliberately renounces verbal communication among her fictional characters. Readers have the impression that they are wandering in the narrator's internal world and hearing only the narrator's intradiegetic voice recounting stories and expressing her subjective emotions. Thúy's most recent novel, *Em*, is composed of separate histories linked by Louis's and Emma-Jade's destinies. Dialogue is almost absent in this work, too.

At first glance, silence is perceivable as a limitation, or even as something harmful. In *Ru*, silence appears in the form of a disability and refers to the narrator's son's autism: "Je n'ai pas crié ni pleuré quand on m'a annoncé que mon fils Henri était emprisonné dans son monde, quand on m'a confirmé qu'il est de ces enfants qui ne nous entendent pas, qui ne nous parlent pas, même s'ils ne sont ni sourds ni muets" [I didn't cry out and I didn't weep when I was told that my son Henri was a prisoner in his own world, when it was confirmed that he is one of those children who don't hear us, don't speak to us, even though they're neither deaf nor mute].[5]

The parallelism "ni sourd ni muet" [neither deaf nor mute] is repeated in the next chapter, when the narrator looks to define her sense of identity. The extreme sadness when she learns that her son is autistic evokes memories of the little girl on her first day in Canada. Or inversely, in an overflowing love for her son, she associates one of her most remarkable memories with her son's experience. Thus, she seeks to integrate his muteness into herself: "J'étais comme mon fils Henri: je ne pouvais pas parler ni écouter, même si je n'étais ni sourde ni muette" (*Ru*, 23) [I was like my son Henri: unable to talk or to listen, even though I was neither deaf nor mute (8)]. Like some people with autism, she was able neither to talk nor to hear when she saw snow, Canadian landscapes, and Canadian people for the first time. Her brain was paralyzed and fell into emptiness because of her losing "points de repère" (*Ru*, 23) [points of reference (8)]. Then, in parallel with having an autistic child, from that day on, she felt like a disabled person herself – a deaf-mute, to be precise – which she manifests through being a self-effacing girl: "elle avait oublié que j'étais sourde et muette" (*Ru*, 41) [She had forgotten I was a deaf-mute (20)]. This self-portrait reveals the difficult acculturation of a little girl who arrives in a totally new country without speaking the language, without knowing the local customs and climate. The more her mother pushes her to integrate into the host society, the less she feels at ease, and she ends up shutting herself away, refusing to communicate. Communicative verbs, including "écouter" (*Ru*, 23) [to listen to], "parler" (*Ru*, 23, 38) [to speak], "répéter" (*Ru*, 25) [to repeat], "comprendre" (*Ru*, 25) [to understand], "raconter" (*Ru*, 69) [to recount], and their negative forms, appear often in the first half of *Ru*, as well as how verbal communication torments the narrator's mind. The medical examination by the Canadian delegation when the doctor verifies her sex without asking her (*Ru*, 37) is as uncomfortable as her experience at the military garrison of anglophone cadets where she feels completely lost among irritated teenagers and does not understand anything (*Ru*, 39).

In *Mãn*, silence represents first and foremost the absence of emotions. The absence is revealed by the eponymous title itself: "Voilà pourquoi je m'appelle Mãn, qui veut dire 'parfaitement comblée' ou 'qu'il ne reste plus rien à désirer,' ou 'que tous les vœux ont été exaucés.' Je ne peux rien demander de plus, car mon nom m'impose cet état de satisfaction et d'assouvissement" [That's why my name is Mãn, which means "perfectly fulfilled," or "may there be nothing left to desire," or "may all wishes be granted." I can ask for nothing more because my name imposes on me that state of satisfaction and satiety].[6] Her name means "fullness," but ironically, she does not know the richness of desire. Mãn has a fully satisfied identity imposed on her by her own name, but she has no right to have dreams or hopes. She exists and has to accept the situation, whatever it is. The narrative of *Mãn* is clearly recounted by the interior voice of the protagonist, but in the narrative itself, the heroine is completely self-effacing and hardly ever speaks. Exceptionally, she utters a few words to her fiancé at the beginning of the novel (*Mãn*, 18). However, this limited and unstitched dialogue cannot break the silence that reigns throughout the narrative; rather, it emphasizes the weight of silence. In the dialogue, the heroine's fiancé, talking to her, pronounces only one simple sentence at a time, while she replies to him with a nominal sentence and then by silence textually represented by ellipses. Through his simple sentences, the man announces only essential information: there are squirrels in

Montreal where he lives, he is leaving Viet Nam the following day, he will send her the papers for the marriage and, in exchange, he requests her to confirm that they will have children; she acquiesces with the brief affirmative form "oui." It is a conversation empty of emotions but enough for an engagement for life, constituted not only by an arranged marriage but also by an expatriate life. The high contrast between this scant verbal exchange and the important decision that creates a turning point in their lives, especially in hers, is particularly revealing of the fatality and unstable life of many Vietnamese people: like him – a refugee; or like her – a person who comes from the poor countryside in Viet Nam. Silence continues to dominate their marriage and even becomes useful in maintaining it as well as their routine life at the restaurant. Mãn and her husband form "un couple sans histoires ni disputes" (*Mãn*, 102) [[the] marriage was uneventful, undramatic (96)] because they refrain from expressing every emotion or feeling. Even when it comes to sexual relations between husband and wife, words are completely removed: "Il suffisait que mon mari se tourne vers moi pour que je comprenne mon devoir d'épouse" (*Mãn*, 102) [My husband just had to turn towards me and I would understand my wifely duty (96)]. Their married life is strongly assured by a nonverbal compromise about responsibilities toward each other: she understands her husband's needs and tries to satisfy him; he respects her personal space when she cooks and her education of their children.

The question of silence is clearly enunciated at the outset in *Vi*: "J'avais huit ans quand la maison a été plongée dans le silence" [I was eight years old when our house was plunged into silence].[7] That year, the autodiegetic narrator's two elder brothers would turn seventeen; this means that they would have to join the war the following year. The anticipation and the fear of impending death that follows joining the army is expressed not in words but with the mother's tears and the pain she expresses with every move she makes: "À partir de ce jour d'anniversaire, que nous n'avons pas célébré, ma mère pleurait chaque matin devant ce calendrier. J'avais l'impression qu'elle se déchirait en même temps qu'elle arrachait la feuille du jour. Le tic-tac de l'horloge qui d'habitude nous endormait au moment de la sieste de l'après-midi sonnait soudainement comme celui d'une bombe à retardement" (*Vi*, 7) [Beginning on that birthday, which we didn't celebrate, my mother cried every morning in front of the calendar. It seemed to me that she was being torn apart each time she ripped off that day's page. The tick-tock of the clock that usually put us to sleep at afternoon nap time suddenly sounded like a bomb waiting to explode (1)]. Silence dominates the familial ambience and announces the narrative of separations throughout the novel.

In *Vi*, chapters are structured by places, where characters leave or separate from each other. The first narrative space, which is Viet Nam itself, is divided in two: "En 1954, le dix-septième parallèle fendait le Vietnam en deux. En 1975, le 30 avril traçait une ligne marquant la frontière entre l'avant et l'après, entre la fin d'une guerre et sa suite, entre le pouvoir et la peur" (*Vi*, 33) [In 1954, the seventeenth parallel cut Vietnam in two. In 1975, April 30 drew a line dividing before from after, between the end of a war and what followed, between power and fear (26)]. The middle of these two parts of the country installs a huge gap of silence, because this division forces family members to separate, as in the case of Hà, a family friend. The silence of Hà's parents announces the renunciation of a familial link when she decides to marry a general from the North. Furthermore, the Communist government applies a rule of silence to create a break between the new and old regimes: "Elle montait les marches comme une ombre, pour bien s'insérer dans le silence qui recouvrait le pays entier" (*Vi*, 34) [She climbed the steps like a shadow, to blend in properly with the silence that prevailed all across the country (27)]. In this new regime, words are used only for political orders or to denounce a violation of rules, while silence prevents all distractions that allow people to enjoy life. Many years later, silence still separates the adult protagonist and her mother when she renounces her engagement that had been agreed upon by both families. Then, her return to Communist Viet Nam moves her further away from her mother – all the more so when her mother's entourage blames Vi for being "une traître à la mémoire des soldats du Sud" (*Vi*, 115) [a traitor to the memory of the Southern soldiers (107)]. About forty years later, the rupture between two parts of a country, between two parts of a people, is still present, and the invisible silence still exerts its power of separation.

In Kim Thúy's novels, the lack of communication might give readers the impression of being introduced to emptiness. Though, according to Huai-nan Tzu, "The Great Beginning produced emptiness, and emptiness produced the universe."[8] Emptiness may lead to fullness, permitting the attainment of plenitude, in the same way that emptying the lungs completely enables one to take an even deeper breath. In the back-and-forth movement of breath, fullness comes from emptiness and emptiness continues to cycle into fullness. In a similar way, the silence in Kim Thúy's works is filled with meanings. And the absence of dialogue to the point of muteness allows her characters to exhaust other abilities and possibilities, especially their sensitivity and their sensuality. Inaudible communication is even conceived by *Vi*'s narrator as belonging to Vietnamese identity, as she explains: "À l'opposé de la culture occidentale, qui encourage l'expression des sentiments et des opinions, les Vietnamiens les gardent jalousement pour eux et ne les verbalisent qu'avec beaucoup de retenue parce que cet espace intérieur constitue le seul endroit qui soit inaccessible aux autres" (*Vi*, 57) [Unlike in Western culture, which encourages expressions of feelings and opinions, the Vietnamese keep them jealously to themselves, and speak of them with great reluctance, because this inner space is the only one inaccessible to others (50)].

In this sentence, the narrator's voice merges with the author's voice. The author suspends narrative time and intervenes in the narrative to express her own opinion about a Vietnamese cultural characteristic. By noting that the Vietnamese have a tendency to preserve their interior space, Kim Thúy highlights discretion as a common element of Vietnamese culture. It is such discretion that prevents Mãn from exteriorizing her feelings to her best friend: "J'ai parfois tenté de verbaliser toute ma reconnaissance envers Julie, mais je n'ai jamais vraiment réussi" (*Mãn*, 72) [I sometimes tried to put into words my gratitude towards Julie, but I was never really successful (66)]. Language is only allowed to allude to things and is not used to designate directly, especially when it comes to loving emotions or affectionate acts. For example, a simple word, "*gần*" (to be close), is enough to indicate that there had been sexual relations (*Mãn*, 102).

But if fewer words are required, the more feelings will be perceived in their purity, as Thúy suggests in *Ru*: "Je me demande encore aujourd'hui si les mots n'auraient pas entaché ces moments de grâce. Et si, parfois, les sentiments ne sont pas mieux compris dans le silence" (*Ru*, 44) [To this day I still wonder whether words might have tainted those moments of grace. And whether feelings are sometimes understood better in silence (21)]. By contrast with the first cultural shock encountered by the narrator of *Ru*, her family settles in Granby, Quebec, and immediately receives a warm and friendly welcome from their sponsors and from the citizens of the town. Even if they cannot understand each other because of the different languages they speak, that does not prevent them from exchanging acts of generosity and gratitude. Granby's citizens go to great lengths to feed Vietnamese families with rice even though rice is not their traditional food. They also teach their language and their customs to Vietnamese refugees to help them become familiar with the host society. In the same way, Mãn is very impressed by the loving expressions of her friend Julie and demonstrates her sincere affection to her friend through daily gestures, by paying attention to Julie's desires (*Mãn*, 73).

The love story between Mãn and Luc is particularly marked by this special nonverbal communication. Sometimes Luc talks to her, just enough to provoke in Mãn a huge range of emotions. The heroine, by remaining completely silent, develops internally a sense of the sensuality of every tiny gesture. Physical touch by Luc awakens in her more subtle feelings of love. For example, when Luc holds her hand for the first time, for one "seconde de trop" (*Mãn*, 86) [second-too-long (80)], it arouses thoughts of the subtle contact between her fingerprints and his. This furtive second even prompts her to imagine his enveloping hand, endowed with a pianist's fingers, which are associated with a reassuring male character. During Mãn's entire trip from Paris to Montreal, her memories of his touching her eyes is so sharp that she can materialize the sensation through the verb "rapporter" as if it were a physical memory: "La seule trace de Luc que j'ai pu rapporter à Montréal était celle de ses mains sur mes yeux" (*Mãn*, 104) [The only trace of Luc that I could bring back to Montreal was that of his hands on my eyes (99)]. In particular, without a word, Luc's look is filled with affection. All it takes for Mãn to feel fulfilled is for him to look at her: "Quand le regard de Luc se posait sur moi, j'avais cette même impression d'exclusion, où les choses alentour disparaissent et où l'espace entre nous contenait ma vie entière" (*Mãn*, 110) [When Luc's gaze was on me, I had that same impression of exclusion, where the things around me disappeared and the space between us contained my whole life (107)]. Her love for him is demonstrated in the way that she observes and admires his body, then his face, and also his manner of cooking and serving dinners (*Mãn*, 125, 129). Then, love is faithfully transmitted in the dishes that Mãn cooks.

It is worth noting that food is particularly associated with Vietnamese culture; it is distinctly present in literature of the Vietnamese diaspora. In Kim Thúy's writing, the flavour of foods is a stimulus for intense emotions and silenced memories. In the absence of words, food is the language of love. For a Vietnamese woman, the best way to take care of someone she loves is assuring that he experiences pleasure in eating the food she cooks. Knowing how to cook a good meal is a form of secret seduction exercised by Vietnamese women: "Les mères enseignaient à leurs filles à cuisiner à voix basse, en chuchotant, afin d'éviter le vol des recettes par les voisines, qui pourraient séduire leur maris avec les mêmes plats" (*Mãn*, 12) [When mothers taught their daughters how to cook, they spoke in hushed tones, whispering so that neighbours couldn't steal recipes and possibly seduce their husbands with the same dishes (4)]. As such, the amorous Mãn is happy to see Luc's pleasure when he tastes the Vietnamese crepe she made for him. The love story of Vi and Vincent is also marked by cooking scenes, when Vi devotes herself to preparing a Vietnamese hot pot with all kinds of local vegetables (*Vi*, 126–7).

If cooking can take the place of a thousand words to express love, keeping silent is also a way to express resignation; it is one of the main lessons that a Vietnamese woman has to absorb. Through the lessons of Mãn's mother, Kim Thúy emphasizes the education in resignation of Vietnamese women: "Maman m'avait enseigné très tôt à éviter les conflits, à respirer sans exister, à me fondre dans le décor" (*Mãn*, 102) [Maman had taught me very early to avoid conflicts, to breathe without existing, to melt into the landscape (97)]. Mãn has actually learned to become self-effacing, even invisible. In order not to be noticed, she becomes able to anticipate the needs of others, especially those of her husband, and to be quietly useful. She also maintains her daily activities in the kitchen without ever questioning or speaking out because she was never taught to call into question anything that happens: "Je ne trouverai jamais de réponses à mes questions et c'est peut-être pour cette raison que je n'en ai jamais posé" (*Mãn*, 37) [I will never find answers to my questions, and that may be why I've never asked one (30)]. In the same way, the women characters throughout Kim Thúy's narratives appear quietly and discreetly, like Hoa, the wife of Vi's brother who "supportait tous les excès de [sa belle-]mère en silence" (*Vi*, 55) [endured in silence all my mother[-in-law]'s demands (49)], or the prostitutes who bend down to pick up dollar bills that their male customers have fun throwing at them in *Ru*. The silence of these women contains in reality all their pain of being oppressed but also contains their voluntary sacrifice to men, husbands, children, or male strangers. In fact, while masculine figures furtively appear in Kim Thúy's novels, feminine figures are strongly present, described like heroes overcoming ordeals and struggling constantly for a better life without claims or complaints. Kim Thúy makes this clear in *Ru*:

> On oublie souvent l'existence de toutes les femmes qui ont porté le Vietnam sur leur dos pendant que leur mari et leurs fils portaient les armes sur le leur. On les oublie parce que, sous leur chapeau conique, elles ne regardaient pas le ciel. Elles attendaient seulement que le soleil tombe sur elles pour pouvoir s'évanouir plutôt que s'endormir … Quand les hommes sont sortis de la jungle et ont recommencé à marcher sur les digues de terre autour de leurs rizières, les femmes ont continué à porter le poids de l'histoire inaudible du Vietnam sur leur dos. Très souvent, elles se sont éteintes ainsi sous cette lourdeur, dans le silence. (*Ru*, 72)

> [We often forget about the existence of all those women who carried Vietnam on their backs while their husbands and sons carried weapons on theirs. We forget them because under their cone-shaped hats they did not look up at the sky. They waited only for the sun to set on them so they could faint instead of falling asleep … When the men emerged from the jungle and started to walk again along the earthen dikes around their rice fields, the women continued to bear the weight of Vietnam's inaudible history on their backs. Very often they passed away under that weight, in silence. (38–9)]

The hunched back of an old woman in the Mekong delta makes Kim Thúy question not only the living conditions of the woman but the courage and the sacrifice of Vietnamese women for their country. The image that Vietnamese women carry the weight of a people alludes to the mother goddess Nüwa, who mends the Heavens to save humans, in Chinese mythology. The myth is introduced very early in Vietnamese folk literature and becomes the myth *Nữ Oa vá trời*. As such, Kim Thúy attributes to Vietnamese women a primordial role in Vietnamese history. They are too often forgotten because of their invisible existence, but the survival of the Vietnamese people would be impossible without the inaudible sacrifice of women.

POETICS OF SILENCE: READING BEYOND THE WORDS

According to Taoist ideas, speech is devalued in favour of silence, because words and concepts can reveal only a part of reality. Words are limited by their character of fixity and reification. However, they can be used as clues to represent the world in a picturesque way or by figures of speech, to stimulate the imagination to question the unspeakable and what is beyond representation. When Jullien interrogates cultural alterity between Eastern and Western literature, he argues that Chinese literary criticism is based on questioning the deeper realities beyond the letter of the text, whereas Western criticism values conceptual clarity, which is associated with the democratic mentality.[9] The ancient Chinese locution 意在言外 (in Vietnamese: *Ý tại ngôn ngoại*) signifies "meanings inside language outside." Thus, words in literary expression possess an allusive and evocative function. The meaning is implied between the lines, beyond the words; the poem means more than meets the eye. As such, poetic words must be very consciously chosen to ensure that the text will be rich in figurative meanings and will leave readers totally free to interpret using their own subjectivity. Words bring into play their sharpness and profundity once they are used and chosen with care. Without explicitly mentioning these philosophies, Kim Thúy's most recent novel, *Em*, suggests a similar method of teaching beyond words: "Dans ce livre, la vérité est morcelée, incomplète, inachevée, dans le temps et dans l'espace. Alors, est-elle encore la vérité? Je vous laisse répondre d'une manière qui fera écho à votre propre histoire, à votre vérité. Entre-temps, je vous promets dans les mots qui suivent un certain ordre dans les émotions et un désordre inévitable dans les sentiments" [In this book, truth is fragmented, incomplete, unfinished, in both time and space. Then is it still the truth? I'll let you reply in a way that relates to your own story, your own truth. Meanwhile, I promise you in the words that follow a certain ordering of the emotions, along with feelings whose disarray cannot be denied].[10]

While reading *Ru*, *Mãn*, and *Vi* for the first time, readers might be disconcerted by the structure of these texts: all three present fragmented writing with very short chapters of one or two pages; each novel is no longer than two hundred pages. We recognize in the art of Kim Thúy's writing a hybridity between the Vietnamese traditional poetry based on philosophic reflection about silence and Western poetics in the narrative form. Her text intentionally has an evocative function; each chapter is a signpost to recall an experience, latent in her children's minds through stories she told them when they were younger, and more widely through the historical knowledge of her readers, as she admits: "En effet, dans un premier temps, c'était comme si j'écrivais à mes enfants, à la manière qu'on loge des informations sur un *post it*, chaque chapitre est un *post it* … Selon moi, c'est en réduisant l'information, en synthétisant de la sorte qu'ils allaient pouvoir trouver après ma mort l'information qu'ils cherchaient, ces petits paragraphes allaient les aider à se remémorer toutes les histoires que je leur avais racontées" [As a matter of fact, at first, it was as if I was writing to my children, like how you use a post it to jot down information, each chapter is a post it ... To me, it's by boiling down the material, by synthesizing in this way that they would, after my death, be able to find the information they were seeking, these short paragraphs were going to help them remember all the stories I had told them].[11] The fragmentary nature of Kim Thúy's works seems very similar to some of Marguerite Duras's writing and her idea of "épurer le français" [refining the French].[12] Duras tends also to use fewer words to explain many things, as Olivier Ammour-Mayeur points out about the novel *L'Amour*: "Les êtres, en tant que *phénomène* (au sens philosophique du terme), ont un sens, dans la mesure qu'on accepte que cela soit un sens *de surface*. Images du monde données dans leur indécision, imprécises, mutables et transformables à merci. C'est par la tranche de ces effets qu'opère le texte *L'Amour*. C'est-à-dire que le texte affiche dans le cours de son écriture ce par quoi il traverse et provoque le changement" [Beings, as a phenomenon (in the philosophical sense of the word), have meaning, inasmuch as one accepts that it is a surface meaning. Images of the world offered in their undecidability, imprecise, mutable and transformable at will. It's by the grouping of these effects that the text of *L'Amour* works. In other words, the text displays in the process of its writing what it is navigating through and how it provokes change].[13]

As such, most of the chapters in *Ru* start with an ordinary object or a banal daily event that subsequently triggers an impressive story. For example, the image of spruce tree branches gathered in the woods recalls values that the narrator has inherited from her parent's education. These values are linked to a family past and not to any material heritage, as she suggests: "Mes parents nous rappellent souvent, à mes frères et moi, qu'ils n'auront pas d'argent à nous laisser en héritage, mais je crois qu'ils nous ont déjà légué la richesse de leur mémoire, qui nous permet de saisir la beauté d'une grappe de glycine, la fragilité d'un mot, la force de l'émerveillement" (*Ru*, 75) [My parents often remind my brothers and me that they won't have any money for us to inherit, but I think they've already passed on to us the wealth of their memories, allowing us to grasp the beauty of a flowering wisteria, the delicacy of a word, the power of wonder (41)]. This education is clearly influenced by the concept of impermanence in Buddhist doctrine: all material things are ephemeral. Material heritage, being temporary, has no importance; only a sound soul helps humans to go on. The traumatic experience of the narrator's family as they faced danger and risked dying during their sea voyage illustrates this principle. To be alive after such an ordeal is much more important than the survival of any luggage or material things. Kim Thúy thus uses short sentences and words to create the evocative images above, which call us to interpret all their underlying meanings.

This idea of luggage then sends the narrator straight to another memory about things that "boat people" carry on board. Attacks by pirates and fishermen are still an obsession for many Vietnamese survivors today. Thai pirates represent for them all the most atrocious crimes: robbery, torture, rape, and murder. Some refugees survived physically but lost their soul forever after being raped or tortured by pirates; others were murdered, and their loved ones who witnessed the scene survived, often to descend into madness. The trauma caused by the pirates' attacks is still a rich and disturbing inspiration behind the literature of the Vietnamese diaspora. For example, Viet Thanh Nguyen addressed this question in some of the stories in his 2017 collection titled *The Refugees*. For fear that carried things could be stolen by pirates, some hid money or diamonds in their body – as Kim Thúy reminds us in *Ru*, "des diamants encastrés dans les molaires, de l'or sur les dents et des dollars américains enroulés dans l'anus" (77) [diamonds embedded in his molars, gold on his teeth and American dollars stuffed in his anus (42)] – and ended up by being mutilated by pirates. Nevertheless, losing teeth does not appear terrible at all from a child's point of view: "Elle brandissait chaque fois devant nous la dent arrachée sous le soleil brûlant de la Malaisie. Ces dents maculées de sang étaient fièrement exhibées, avec en toile de fond une plage au sable fin et une clôture de fils barbelés" (*Ru*, 78) [She waved each extracted tooth in front of us under the blazing Malaysian sun. Those blood-stained teeth were proudly displayed against the backdrop of a fine sandy beach and a barbed-wire fence (42)]. Tooth extraction reveals for the young girl a normal childhood memory but in a singular context. Such a beautiful picture composed of baby teeth, sunshine, and a fine sandy beach is placed in contrast with the atrocious reality of pirates' crimes, from which the mother wanted to protect her children: "Elle savait aussi que si notre bateau avait été intercepté par des pirates thaïlandais, les dents en or et les molaires diamantées auraient été arrachées" (*Ru*, 78) [She also knew that if our boat had been intercepted by Thai pirates, the gold teeth and those that were filled with diamonds would have been pulled out (43)]. This antithesis highlights the cruelty of the refugees' destiny and also reveals a positive posture that Kim Thúy has taken to relate her past.

The fragmentary nature of the texts with their blank spaces, as in the works of Duras, is silence full of meaning. This writing is further influenced by Vietnamese poetry. Vietnamese classical poetry suggests many meanings in its brevity and in what remains unsaid, that is, silent. Similarly, the brief chapters of Kim Thúy provoke stifled emotions because of the series of images described by words delicately chosen and integrated in figures of speech, especially in the figure of antithesis. In this way, her writing releases multiple stories of exiled life that many "boat people" like her experienced.

Otherwise, the influence of Western narration is expressed through the structure of the narrative. The way that memories are triggered by concrete things is similar to Proust's madeleine experience. Kim Thúy seems to follow the chain of involuntary memories to expose a flow of stories of refugee camps and of the time on the boat but also stories of love and happiness. Chapters connect to each other through repetition, in which a word or image appears both at the end of one chapter and at the beginning of the next, containing still other reminiscences. This technique is inspired by a Western poetic figure of speech called anadiplosis.[14] Kim Thúy solicits not only a material form of words and their musicality but also their semiotic side and sociological connotations. In the example mentioned above (*Ru*, 75), the chapter comes to a close with the topic of travel, associated with the abstract meaning that is travel in time. The same signifier, "voyager" [to travel], appears at the beginning of the following chapter but this time involves its concrete meaning, travel on a boat. Then boat people's memories are pervasive throughout the chapter and spill over into the next about Vietnamese-Chinese refugees. Another chapter will take off with the Chinese narrator's great-grandfather and his story, and so on.

In Kim Thúy's second novel, words continue to exercise their evocative function. A single word alludes to a story, including at the same time numerous ineffable and unexpected connotations. In *Mãn*, each chapter's title is a Vietnamese noun: *dừa* (coconut), *chồng* (husband), and *văn hoá* (culture), to mention a few examples. The first chapter of *Mãn* is named *mẹ*, meaning "mother." It is worth noting that the Vietnamese language does not distinguish plural or singular nouns by derivation as in English or French. The Vietnamese noun *mẹ* can signify one mother or several mothers. However, the French translation removes this textual polyvalence. The chapter, contained in a single page, appears like a prose poem, full of meanings. The sentence opening the fiction – "Maman et moi, nous ne nous ressemblons pas" (*Mãn*, 9) [Maman and I don't look like one another (1)] – announces a rupture between the autodiegetic narrator and her *maman* (mom). This rupture is clarified and accentuated by three successive antitheses: "Elle est petite, et moi je suis grande"; "Elle a le teint foncé, et moi j'ai la peau des poupées françaises"; "Elle a un trou dans le mollet, et moi j'ai un trou dans le cœur" (*Mãn*, 9) [She is short, I am tall. Her complexion is dark, my skin is like a French doll's. She has a hole in her calf and I have a hole in my heart (1)]. The poetic form is identified not only by the symmetry of opposing terms (petite/grande, teint foncé/la peau des poupées françaises) but also by the syntactic parallelism of juxtaposed propositions in each sentence. The second antithesis illustrates a physical rupture between the narrator protagonist and her adoptive mother. Like a tree torn from its original soil to be planted in new soil, this rupture provokes emptiness in her heart. But it is the third adoptive mother whom she calls "Maman" (Mom) – an affective word that is used to name a cherished mother. Just as this third mother brought up Mãn, from her first attempted steps to when she became an adult, Mãn benefits from her mother's cultural heritage, which develops her personality. Then, the third antithesis is constituted by the opposition between a concrete image and a figurative one, "un trou dans le mollet" / "un trou dans le cœur." "Trou," a hole, represents emptiness, something that has broken – or it alludes abstractly to silence. Connecting to the problematic of silence, another antithesis emerges: the "hole" symbolizing emptiness is the opposite of the meaning of the heroine's name, Mãn: "fullness." Again, the absurd signification of her name emphasizes the gaps in her inaudible existence.

Does this individual story imply or refer to the collective story of Vietnamese people? The rupture expressed by these antitheses seems to reference to the exile's experience. When Vietnamese refugees have to leave their homeland to settle in another land, sometimes at the ends of the earth, differences between climates and cultures – specifically, those of Viet Nam and Quebec – might cause them culture shock, perceived as "a hole in the heart." Otherwise, stories about the three mothers of the autodiegetic narrator constitute a metaphor referring concretely to the journey that Kim Thúy's family had to go through, from Viet Nam to Malaysia and then to Canada. Mãn's biological mother symbolizes Viet Nam, a premature nation unable to take care of its people, like an adolescent mother who cannot raise her child. Her first adoptive mother "[l]'a cueillie" (*Mãn*, 9) [plucked her (1)], scooping her up and temporarily taking care of her, as Malaysia hosted Vietnamese boat people for a short time and with minimal comfort. Then, Canada welcomes them with generosity and friendship, and so this country of adoption becomes their "mom" who gives them "une seconde naissance" (*Mãn*, 9) [a second birth (1)]. Because of the way that language forges our manner of thinking, the metaphor is clearly evident in the Vietnamese mind: the equivalent term of "homeland" in Vietnamese is "đất mẹ," which literally means "land-mother." Another Franco-Vietnamese writer, Pham Van Ky, translated "đất mẹ" as the neologism "matrie" in his 1964 novel *Des Femmes assises çà et là*. Having experienced exile and "double culture" between Viet Nam and France himself, Pham Van Ky confers a singular importance to the homeland's and the host land's place in reflections about his education and his acculturation. But unlike Kim Thúy, Pham Van Ky distinguishes host country from homeland by calling France "patrie,"[15] as the word exists in the French language, and Viet Nam "matrie" – "đất mẹ." Homeland summons memories of his childhood in the way that his mother summons him by telegram, and the host land conditions his maturity like a father and mother: "Car, dans cette patrie-ci de ma maturité, à l'ombre large de Paris, ou dans cette matrie-là de mon enfance, l'obligation m'est également et périodiquement signifiée de me soumettre à la cérémonie d'expulsion, pour arracher, emmurer, reléguer dans une retraite provisoire tous acquêts ou résidus acquêts" [Yet, in this homeland of my maturity, in the broad shadow of Paris, or in that motherland of my childhood, I find myself periodically and equally obliged to submit myself to the ritual of expulsion, to tear away, wall up, relegate to provisional removal all acquests or residual property].[16] Thus, readers can observe in these two authors' works the Eastern poetics, especially Tang poetry, in the way they use words and in the evocative function of words. Rich hidden meanings are compacted in the single word "*mẹ*" (mother) in Kim Thúy's work. Pham Van Ky went further when he created a neologism "matrie" to talk about his homeland. Like the image of an iceberg, the visible part is presented by separate words, *mẹ* and *matrie*; the invisible part under the speech's surface is included in the silence that contains many more meanings than the visible part.

In her third novel, *Vi*, Kim Thúy develops a topographical narration: names of places, linked to events or characters, expand into chapters. The narrator's life is thus related by fragments, from her ancestors' stories and her family's exile to her romantic trips with her lover on her ancestors' soil. The novel is presented like a travel diary, chronicling the narrator's displacements through time and through space. This topographical question, especially associated with the quest for identity, occupies a singular place in the literature of exile, as well as in Kim Thúy's novels. The interrogation of identity is omnipresent: through childhood memories in *Ru*, through tasty flavours in *Mãn*, and more intensely through significant places in *Vi*, creating a continuity across her first three novels. Her third novel appears clearly as an extension of her first two as it further develops the topographical question, already raised in *Ru* and *Mãn*.

The first thirty chapters expose the family story of the autodiegetic narrator Vi, from Cochinchina, with the Mekong River and diverse corners of Saigon, to the capital of Hanoi, and then the seventeenth parallel separating the two parts of Viet Nam according to the Geneva Agreements of 1954. From the narrator's point of view, Cochinchina before the war was a peaceful and rich land, where people lived in harmony with nature: "De loin, la couleur du bois se mêlant au brun de l'eau argileuse donne l'impression que les melons, les ananas, les pomélos, les choux, les courges flottent par eux-mêmes jusqu'aux hommes qui les attendant dès l'aube sur le quai pour les attraper au vol" (*Vi*, 12) [From far away the colour of the wood, mingled with the muddy brown of the water, gives the impression that the melons, pineapples, pomelos, cabbages, gourds are floating independently of the men who have been waiting on the wharf since dawn to snap them up at the first opportunity (5)]. Saigon was animated and as modern as a Western city, which the narrator's father appreciated: "[Mon père] préférait le centre-ville de Saigon avec ses cafés français et ses bars américains. Il aimait surtout prendre sa bière sur la terrasse de l'hôtel Continental, où les journalistes étrangers passaient leurs journées à analyser le mouvement des troupes et les plus récentes chansons à la mode" (*Vi*, 24) [He preferred downtown Saigon with its French cafés and American bars. Above all, he liked to drink beer on the Hôtel Continental terrace, where the foreign journalists spent their days analyzing troop movements and the latest popular songs (16–17)].

It is on Cochinchinese soil that the genealogy of the narrator's family was drawn: her grandparents' origins and activities, her parents' marriage, residence, and so on. Genealogy is a significant preoccupation of many Vietnamese, both exiles and residents. Genealogy symbolizes a family's memories and the identity of a people. The identity question is strongly associated with the question of heredity in Kim Thúy's writing in particular and in contemporary Vietnamese francophone literature in general. It is linked to the singular context of the country that was divided in two for two decades (1954–75) and where the wounds of war have never healed. National identity as well as family identity are repetitively crushed, then reconstructed, through the tribulations of wars and different political regimes. Vietnamese family members were dispersed and even sometimes became enemies because of opposing political opinions. People in South Viet Nam had to leave their ancestors' land, abandon their original identity, and adopt the culture of a host country. Residents in the North lost their relatives who died during the war. Nowadays, they are still seeking to identify soldiers who died in the war. But while war imposes many silences or gaps in history, we know that family, places, and love may well serve to create continuity in a time of rupture and lost memories.

Therefore, Kim Thúy herself seeks reconciliation and to heal breaches left by conflict and exile by creating love stories in her works. A love story between two young Vietnamese students in Nha Trang, one whose father is a soldier from the South and one whose father is a soldier from the North, is revealing. Their mothers forbid them from being together because they consider the relationship "une union entre ennemis" (*Vi*, 59) [a union between enemies (52)]. Realizing that they cannot get married in life, the two lovers choose death to be together. Love is more powerful than everything, and even family pressure or the weight of war cannot prevent love, as Kim Thúy describes it: "Même si la jeune étudiante n'avait jamais eu le droit de lire *Roméo et Juliette* ni de voir le film *Love Story* ou d'entendre parler de *Tristan et Yseult*, même si ses connaissances littéraires se résumaient à la biographie de Hô Chi Minh et des héros de guerre, même si les décorations épinglées sur l'uniforme de son père lui auraient assuré un avenir privilégié, elle avait choisi de rejoindre son amour. Elle s'était libérée de la lourde histoire laissée en héritage par une guerre qu'elle n'avait pas connue en marchant vers la beauté de la mer paradisiaque de Nha Trang" (*Vi*, 61) [Even if the young student had never been allowed to read *Romeo and Juliet*, or to see the film *Love Story*, or hear of *Tristan and Isolde*, even though her literary knowledge was restricted to the biography of Ho Chi Minh and some war heroes, even if the decorations pinned to her father's uniform guaranteed her a privileged future, she had chosen to join her love. She had freed herself from the burdensome history that was the legacy of a war she had not known, by walking towards the beauty of Nha Trang's sublime sea (54)].

With such anecdotes Kim Thúy suggests that people should overcome the destructive heritage of the war, that love should be a way to reach true reconciliation. This intention is clarified by the narrator's story afterward, when she decides to return to Viet Nam for a professional mission. The narrator's reconciliation approach is initially processed by her rediscovery of her native country and her reappropriation of its language and culture: "Pour ma part, je continuais la nuit mes recherches dans les dictionnaires anglais-français / français-anglais / anglais-vietnamien / vietnamien-anglais / français-vietnamien / vietnamien-français ... La langue vietnamienne que je connaissais était marquée par l'exil et figée dans une ancienne réalité, celle d'avant la présence des Soviétiques et des liens étroits avec Cuba, la Bulgarie, la Tchécoslovaquie, la Roumaine" (*Vi*, 98–9) [As for me, I spent a good part of the night searching through dictionaries of English-French / French-English / English-Vietnamese / Vietnamese-English / French-Vietnamese / Vietnamese-French ... The Vietnamese language I knew was marked by exile and trapped in an antiquated reality, one that preceded the Soviet presence and the strong ties with Cuba, Bulgaria, Czechoslovakia, Romania (90)]. By conceiving Viet Nam in the past as "une ancienne réalité" [an antiquated reality], the narrator, who seems to represent the author's point of view, rejects her mother's opinion – "A ma dernière visite, [ma mère] tremblait chaque fois que je prononçais les mots vietnamiens nouvellement appris dans le Nord, avec l'accent du Nord" (*Vi*, 115) [On my last visit, she died a little whenever I pronounced Vietnamese words newly acquired in the North, with a Northern accent (106)] – in order to adopt a neutral posture from which to look at Viet Nam today. As such, the word "Viet Nam" evokes complex emotions and the affection of the narrator with respect to her mother. Her feeling is again hidden in silence as she expresses, "Si je devais être frappée par l'éclair, je voulais qu'elle sache que j'avais rencontré des mères qui n'avaient pas choisi d'envoyer leurs fils au front, qui n'avais pas choisi d'allégeance politique, qui avaient seulement espéré que leurs enfants leur survivraient, tout comme elle. Mais je ne l'ai pas appelée. Car je l'aurais inquiétée avec ma peur au milieu du déluge" (*Vi*, 115–16) [If I were to be struck by lightning, I wanted her to know that I had met mothers who had not chosen to send their sons to the front, who had not chosen their political allegiance, who had only hoped that their children would survive them, just like her. But I did not call her. Because I would have worried her with my fear in the middle of the storm (107)]. By her silence, she hopes to protect her mother from worry.

If pronounced by a native speaker, these two syllables alone, "Viet Nam," also recall from the inaudible the collective memory of the complicated reality linked to the Viet Nam war. And in spite of the exile forced upon her by the Communists, the narrator perceives her first return to Viet Nam not with anxiety or hatred but with enthusiasm, as she expresses, "J'ai tenté de rattraper quelques bribes des vingt ans passés par le Vietnam derrière le rideau de fer en traînant autour des tables-restaurants" (*Vi*, 100) [I tried to seek out some fragments of Vietnam's twenty years behind the Iron Curtain by hanging around restaurant tables (92)]. Then, with Vincent, her lover she meets at the French Embassy, she really rediscovers the landscapes and the people of Viet Nam, from a far remote region to various areas of the capital. Readers can recognize a similar narrative from the last century when the young girl in *The Lover* (1984) by Marguerite Duras falls in love with the Chinese man and follows him through the Mekong Delta. Kim Thúy admits this herself: "C'est grâce à Marguerite Duras, en 1984, que j'ai vu le Vietnam autrement, c'est-à-dire autrement que par le regard de mes parents" [Thanks to Marguerite Duras in 1984, I saw Viet Nam otherwise, that is, other than through my parents' eyes].[17] The silence under the word "Viet Nam" contains the narrator's intense impression of an open and friendly country despite the poverty in its countryside. In addition, used as the context for a beautiful and sensual love story, Viet Nam becomes a romantic place, a land of love. It is such a new identity, separated from the cruel war of the past, that Kim Thúy would like to attribute to her homeland.

Kim Thúy's novels thus reveal the sensitivity and sensuality of the author through both the absence of speech and thoughtfully chosen words. Silence marks the narration and opens up space for nonverbal communication. Without words, Kim Thúy aspires to replace extreme feelings, such as fear, with love and compassion. The fragmentary nature of Kim Thúy's writing is in fact an expression of the losses, gaps, and silences; the fragments make clear what is missing, in a sense, or the lack of continuity, even as efforts are made to connect those fragments through images and words. Moreover, powerful images are created by the words so delicately chosen by Kim Thúy to portray the experiences of boat people and immigrants in Canada. The frequent tension between beautiful and atrocious images leaves readers deeply moved. Terror emerges in accounts of such experiences by most boat people. Kim Thúy describes the boat people's ordeal philosophically, as a chance to have had this experience and to acquire the ability to see silver linings. In this way, Kim Thúy invites her readers to travel with her in time and in space, through the history of Viet Nam and the different cultures of the West and the Far East.

NOTES

1 Boué, *L'Éloquence du silence*, 9.
2 Laozi, *Tao Te Ching*, 56.
3 Ching, *Chinese Religions*, 88.
4 Jullien, *La Valeur allusive*, 226–7. Translation by Miléna Santoro.
5 Kim Thúy, *Ru* (Paris: Liana Levi, 2010), 20; Thúy, *Ru*, trans. Sheila Fischman (Toronto: Random House Canada, 2012), 7. Quotations from this novel refer to these editions. The original French will be cited in the text with title and page numbers. English translations will appear in square brackets with page numbers in parentheses after the quotation.
6 Kim Thúy, *Mãn* (Paris: Liana Levi, 2013), 34–5; Thúy, *Mãn*, trans. Sheila Fischman (Toronto: Random House Canada, 2014), 27–8. Subsequent references to this novel are from these editions and are cited within the text (see note 5).
7 Kim Thúy, *Vi* (Paris: Liana Levi, 2016), 7; Thúy, *Vi*, trans. Sheila Fischman (Toronto: Vintage Canada, 2019), 1. Subsequent quotations refer to these editions of the novel and are cited in the text (see note 5).
8 Huai-nan Tzu quotation cited in *Encyclopedia of Science and Religion*, ed. J. Wentzel Van Huyssteen (New York: Macmillan Reference, 2003), s.v. "Chinese Religions, History of Science and Religion in China."
9 Jullien, *La Valeur allusive*.
10 Kim Thúy, *Em* (Montreal: Libre Expression, 2020), 11; Thúy, *Em* (New York: Seven Stories Press, 2021), 3. All references to *Em* will be to these editions of this novel. The original French quotations are cited in the text with title and page numbers. The English translations follow in square brackets, with page numbers in parentheses.

11 Plamondon, "En remontant les rus de l'enfance," 154. Translation by Miléna Santoro.
12 Ammour-Mayeur, "Écrire l'amour," 142–3. Translation by Miléna Santoro.
13 Ibid., 143. Translation by Miléna Santoro.
14 For example, to quote Shakespeare, "As thou being *mine*, *mine* is thy good." *Shakespeare's Sonnets: An Original-Spelling Text*, 181.
15 Pham Van Ky, *Des Femmes assises çà et là*, 87.
16 Ibid., 90. Translation by Miléna Santoro.
17 Thúy, "Habiller le vécu de mots et d'images," 171. Translation by Jack A. Yeager.

4

Epistolarity, Exchange, and Transdiasporic Identities

Writing À toi

Juliette M. Rogers

After the international success of her first novel, *Ru* (2009), Kim Thúy's second publication, *À toi* (2011), surprised many readers. Thúy herself explained in an interview in *La Presse* that her editor had been worried: "Ma maison d'édition était inquiète. Mon éditeur avait les cheveux dressés sur la tête parce que je ne respectais pas les délais pour la suite de *Ru* en me lançant dans ce projet pour lequel je voulais aller jusqu'au bout" [My publishing house was worried. My editor was going crazy because I was not respecting the deadlines for the sequel to *Ru* by throwing myself into this project that I wanted to see through to the end].[1] Instead of a follow-up to *Ru*, her second book was a co-authored text, written with Swiss-Slovak author Pascal Janovjak and structured as a series of emails that the two exchanged for three months, following a chance encounter in Monaco at the prize ceremony for a literary competition.

À toi does not have a plot-driven narrative but rather is a series of reflections and short anecdotes, similar in some ways to the brief "chapters" in *Ru*. *À toi* also contains continued references to exile, migration, and adaptation, themes that are also found in *Ru* and other works by Thúy.[2] However, both the structure of *À toi* and its impact on the reader are quite different from those of *Ru*, *Mãn*, *Vi*, and *Em*, making it a unique text in Thúy's oeuvre. The volume contains a total of 112 email messages (61 written by Pascal, 51 written by Kim),[3] each beginning a new page with the author's first name, then the date and time, starting with "Pascal 3 octobre 08:11" and ending with "Kim 26 décembre 08:36."[4] The epistolary exchange begins with more than 80 emails in October, sometimes several composed in the same day, and sometimes with one author writing two or three emails in a row before receiving a reply from the other. The exchange begins to slow down in November (twenty-one emails) and then trickles to only 9 messages in December. The length of the emails varies considerably throughout the book, ranging from one or two sentences (4 October, 9 October, 16 October, 3 November), to over two pages long (13 October, 31 October, 26 December), with the majority falling in the one-page range. This chapter will examine how Thúy and Janovjak's innovative use of the epistolary genre both reinforces and dismantles recent theories on transnational and transcultural identity formation, thus creating a new voice for transdiasporic literature in *À toi*.[5]

As historians and theorists have long argued, immigrants' letter-writing practices have often served not only to maintain familial or intimate relationships across distances but to allow for the development of transnational and transcultural roots. For immigration historians Bruce S. Elliott, David A. Gerber, and Suzanne M. Sinke, letters have allowed immigrants to maintain a "transnationalized rootedness," establishing identities in both the new and the old cultures where they lived.[6] Yves Frenette, in his 2006 essay in the volume *Envoyer et recevoir: lettres et correspondances dans les diasporas francophones*, describes letters as an entryway: "une porte d'entrée dans l'univers mental des francophones des diasporas et de leurs correspondants" [an entryway into the mental universe of francophones of the diaspora and their correspondents].[7] The emails in *À toi* perform both of these functions, yet they go further, as they transform and construct new identities for both Pascal Janovjak and Kim Thúy. As Patrice Proulx explains, "letter writing, then, implies a negotiation between the self and the other, and also shows the construction of self to be an ongoing process. The characteristics of the letter also reinforce the notion of textual *métissage*."[8] The following pages will explore the importance of these new identities that Thúy and Janovjak create through their email exchanges and the ways in which they resist the traditional definitions of "littérature migrante." But first, an examination of the ways in which Thúy and Janovjak's epistolary back-and-forth confirms some of the established roles for letter-writing between immigrants, even as the two authors experiment and invent new literary paths.

LETTERS, MIGRATION, AND TRANSNATIONAL ROOTS

Elliott, Gerber, and Sinke explain the importance of the personal letter for immigrants throughout the nineteenth and twentieth centuries: "For many international migrants, transnationalized rootedness could be maintained by keeping in contact with family and friends in the homeland … The personal letter sent throughout interlinked national postal systems was the most widespread instrument of migrant communication throughout the nineteenth and most of the twentieth century."[9] Historian Sonia Cancian, in her discussion of Italian immigrants to Canada, confirms "the interconnections between personal correspondence and migration" and "illustrates the links, continuities, conflicts and negotiating efforts shared between kin and lovers in transnational households living apart."[10] Both Elliott et al. and Cancian focus on the thousands of immigrants who moved to North America, where the letter-writers were corresponding with parents, spouses, friends, and other acquaintances who were now at a great distance from them and whom they might never see again in person. The main purpose of these letters included announcing news and explaining different events and transformations in their lives.

But these were not the only effects that their letters had: correspondence also allowed the recipients in America to retain a link to their home cultures, even as they experienced new ways of life on a daily basis, including influences from other cultures and different patterns of work, leisure, and education. The letters thus permitted immigrants to create a "transnational" identity. Further, these letters also allowed those who remained in the home country to begin to understand their kin, as well as themselves, in a new light – that is, as a hybrid of both their traditional customs and identities and their new transnational or transcultural identities.[11]

The twenty-first century has seen a major shift from postal letters to various forms of electronic communication, including email, texts, and applications such as FaceTime, WhatsApp, and other social media, leading to stronger "virtual communities" for transnationalized rootedness among immigrants.[12] Thus, even though this chapter examines *À toi* through the lens of epistolary traditions dating back two centuries in immigration history, it acknowledges that the authors' use of email does distinguish their correspondence from the past in several ways that are discussed below. Pascal and Kim are definitely members of this new generation of "virtual" correspondents, since their letter exchange is done not through the post but electronically.

It is also important to note that Pascal and Kim are, of course, not family members who have known each other for years or who grew up together in the same culture; in fact, they only met once, at the literary prize ceremony in Monaco. Therefore, one of the initial purposes of their email exchange is to become more familiar with each other's pasts; instead of "maintaining" their transcultural rootedness, we find that these emails often serve to "explain" their transcultural roots and origins to each other, through a series of anecdotes and recollections of their past experiences. For example, Pascal explains that because his parents had different cultural backgrounds, his childhood in Switzerland was a multilingual one: "Je parle en slovaque avec lui [mon père], en français avec ma mère, entre eux ils parlent en allemand ... Ainsi mes frères et moi avons-nous baigné dans un monde étrange où, à table, le sel devenait *sol'*, ou *Salz*, selon la personne devant laquelle il était posé" (*À toi*, 89) [I speak in Slovak with him (my father), in French with my mother, while they speak German to each other ... Thus my brothers and I were immersed in a strange world at the dinner table where the salt became *sol'*, or *Salz*, depending on the person in front of whom it was placed]. In one of Kim's anecdotes about growing up in Viet Nam, she offers a childhood memory of seeing Vietnamese women dancing for the first time, when she was only three or four years old: "Dès que j'ai pu m'asseoir dans une chaise haute, j'ai accompagné mes parents aussi bien aux dîners de fonction qu'aux amicales tables de poker ... Un soir, nous étions invités dans un club appelé Maxime où il y avait un spectacle de danse ... Or, sur cette scène, des femmes se départaient de leur costume, un morceau à la fois" (*À toi*, 13–14) [As soon as I could sit up in a high chair, I accompanied my parents at official dinners as well as at friendly poker tables ... One evening, we were invited to a club called Maxime where there was a dance show ... On the stage, women were divesting themselves of their costumes, one piece at a time]. Kim adds that, after watching these striptease dancers, she decided to imitate them after her evening bath – throwing off her towel and shaking her tiny hips. These amusing anecdotes give us a glimpse into the very different cultural backgrounds of Kim's and Pascal's childhoods.

As their correspondence continues, we also discover one of the major distinctions between their two childhoods. Kim describes how, at age ten, she directly experienced her parents' decision to flee their home in Viet Nam, surviving a refugee camp in Malaysia and then moving and adapting to a new culture in Quebec. For Pascal, however, it was his father who, as a political dissident, fled Bratislava in 1968, several years before Janovjak was born. Therefore, as the *child* of a refugee, Pascal grew up hearing stories about his father's escape, such as his recurring nightmare about being trapped on the tram while trying to leave Bratislava (*À toi*, 60). But Pascal's knowledge about the struggles of a refugee is only secondhand. Kim, in contrast, recalls in several emails the details of her family's flight on a makeshift boat and their landing in a refugee camp in Malaysia four days later. She also gives details of her experiences living in the refugee camp. In one email, for example, she remembers that she had been deathly allergic to fish and seafood before she left Viet Nam, but when she arrived at the camp in Malaysia, where the only food available was the canned sardines that the Red Cross distributed, her body suddenly accepted fish with no allergic reaction whatsoever (*À toi*, 83). The letters thus serve not to maintain transcultural ties but to *explain* the two writers' contrasting childhoods and their distinctly different cultural backgrounds. Given the great divergences between their lived experiences and their written memories of them, readers might begin to wonder why Kim Thúy was so obsessed ("voulait aller jusqu'au bout"[13] [wanted to go all the way]) with this project, even postponing her second novel after *Ru* to complete *À toi*.

The email exchange, however, does not merely provide a space for the two authors to describe their cultural roots to each other; the messages also serve the traditional purpose found in immigrant letter-writing: that of relaying recent news and events that are changing or transforming their lives. Pascal uses the emails in this traditional function, as a way to inform Kim (and us readers) about the news in his life. For example, he recounts several very recent incidents relating to his first child, who will be born in just a few months. These events often underline Pascal's trepidations about becoming a father, and about losing his current way of life with his wife, Francesca, even though some of the emails are more optimistic.[14] Kim also writes to tell Pascal news about her child, but from a very different perspective: Kim writes to say that her eight-year-old autistic son roused her from a nap that day when he spoke his very first words: "Je n'avais pas compris ce mot tout simple ['chat'] parce qu'il était étranger dans sa bouche ... Ce n'était pas tant sa capacité à prononcer ce mot que son désir de communiquer avec moi, de partager avec moi, de m'inclure dans sa bulle qui m'a surprise. Pourquoi maintenant, après huit ans de vie ensemble, de sommeils aléatoires, de silences imposés? Je n'aurai jamais la réponse" (*À toi*, 46) [I had not understood that very simple word "cat" because it was foreign in his mouth … It wasn't so much his ability to pronounce the word as his desire to communicate with me, to share with me, to include me in his bubble, that surprised me. Why now, after eight years together, after unpredictable somnolences, after imposed silences? I will never have the answer].

Here, Kim does not focus on the word that her son spoke but on his wish to communicate with his mother, to bring her into his "bubble." We can extend this message on the importance of reaching out to others, both in her email exchange with Pascal and with readers more generally, as an example of Thúy's efforts to communicate with us and to include us in her past experiences. She is not only telling us what happened but also allowing us to become a part of her own "bubble." Yet she does not always let us in, and there are potential barriers to understanding Thúy, as we shall see later, that are similar to the open-ended unknowability that she experiences concerning her son's first words ("je n'aurai jamais la réponse").

Both authors thus offer news and announcements from their current lives as well as explanations about their past lives, providing the base for what Elliott, Gerber, and Sinke define as "transnationalized rootedness."

These more traditional epistolary exchanges between immigrants are supplemented by many email messages that function as "une porte d'entrée" [an entryway], as Yves Frenette labels them, that is, as an entryway into the minds of the letter-writers.[15] Pascal, for example, describes his feeling of somehow always living "apart," as though in a series of different bubbles: "Bien après le cocon de l'enfance, j'ai souvent eu l'impression de vivre dans des bulles. Celles de la différence: être slovaque en Suisse, suisse en France, français ailleurs, expatrié en Asie, riche parmi les pauvres. Habitant à Ramallah, dont on dit souvent que c'est une bulle … On pourrait y voir une série d'aventures quand il n'y a là que poupées russes, à l'infini" (*À toi*, 59–60) [Long after the cocoon of childhood, I often had the impression of living in bubbles. The bubbles of difference: being Slovak in Switzerland, being Swiss in France, French elsewhere, expatriate in Asia, rich among the poor. Living in Ramallah, which is often called a bubble. We could see a series of adventures when really there's only Russian dolls, to infinity]. Pascal creates here an image of infinite unknowability, mirroring the unknowability that Thúy alludes to in her email message, cited above. At the same time, Pascal opens up for Kim, and for us readers, a window into his world, so that we may understand not only his nomadic pattern of living in many different expat communities but also the fact that he has never felt as though he was truly a part of any of them.[16] Pascal continues this idea of always being on the outside, never fitting in, through an anecdote about the cafeteria in a factory where he worked when he was younger. "À la cantine, chaque fois que j'essayais de poser mon plateau quelque part, on me rejetait. 'Non, ça c'est la table des électriciens, mon gars.' 'Non, pas là, do sicher nüüt, ici c'est seulement pour les Suisses. Mets-toi avec les Alsaciens.' 'Non, ici c'est la place de Jean-Marie. Va avec les Arabes, là-bas.' Je finissais au fond de la salle, avec les autres intérimaires, et c'était effectivement la place qui me convenait" (*À toi*, 77) [In the cafeteria, each time that I put my tray down, I was rejected. "No, that's the electricians' table, my son." "No, not there, *do sicher nüut*, here is only for the Swiss. Go over there with the Alsatians." "No, this is Jean-Marie's spot. Go over there with the Arabs." I ended up at the back of the room, with the other interim employees, and it was effectively the place that suited me]. This memory comes from one of Pascal's first jobs as a teenager, while still living in his home country of Switzerland, yet he explains that even there, he had the impression of always finding himself in a temporary position ("intérimaire"), never truly rooted. Pascal continues that, even though he has never had a sense of belonging, he seeks more stability now, especially with a child coming: "Ma vie me semble soudain d'une extrême fragilité, une vie menée au gré des vents, sous des cieux incléments. Alors je rêve d'un ancrage, d'un golfe calme, de quelque chose de tiède, et d'immobile. C'est la peur qui murmure, dans ces moments-là" (*À toi*, 66) [My life suddenly seems extremely fragile, a life led by the whims of the wind, under inclement skies. So I dream of an anchor, of a calm gulf, of something warm and immobile. It's fear that whispers, in those moments]. It is interesting to note that Janovjak was living in Ramallah at the time that he co-wrote this book, in late 2010, but by the time his child was born in 2011, he and his wife had moved to Italy, her home country, and they have lived in Rome ever since.

Even though Kim has also led a nomadic life, in her replies to Pascal she claims that unlike him, rather than being "in a bubble" or an "outsider," she has the sense that she fits in anywhere and everywhere: "Contrairement à toi, je me sens à ma place partout. Je suis comme l'eau: j'épouse la forme du contenant, sans savoir comment résister" (*À toi*, 78) [Contrary to you, I feel at home everywhere. I am like water: I hug the form of the container, without knowing how to resist]. Thus, Kim's mental universe appears quite different from Pascal's. Yet despite her perception of being able to adapt and adjust to almost any environment, Kim does note that the instability of her childhood as a refugee also makes her seek an anchor ("un ancrage"), similar to Pascal: "Tout m'échappe, tout le temps. Souvent, quand je reviens tard, au milieu de la nuit, pendant que rêvent mes enfants, je m'assois au salon durant de longues minutes pour me convaincre que ce lieu est ma demeure, mon point d'ancrage, mon adresse sur terre" (*À toi*, 67) [Everything escapes me, all the time. Often, when I return home late, in the middle of the night, while my children are dreaming, I sit in my living room for several long minutes to convince myself that this place is my abode, my anchor point, my address on earth]. Even though Kim describes living and working in various parts of Southeast Asia as a young adult, including in Viet Nam and Thailand, she is thankful to have found a safe and secure harbour: her home in Montreal, Quebec.

LETTER-WRITING, TEXTUAL *MÉTISSAGE*, AND TRANSDIASPORIC IDENTITY CONSTRUCTION

We have seen how both writers use letter-writing in traditional ways: as an entryway into the immigrant's state of mind and as a way to exchange news and to create and maintain transnational identities. In those roles, the emails mainly point to the *differences* in their experiences and the *distinctions* between the two writers' cultural and emotional states. However, when we explore the ways in which their emails open up discussions that lead to a hybrid or transdiasporic identity – where identity formation, as Patrice Proulx labels it, is "an ongoing process"[17] – then we begin to see numerous parallels between Janovjak and Thúy. We may understand better the priority that Thúy gave to this epistolary work after she published *Ru* and the reasons why a co-authored work might have seemed preferable to a sole-authored text at the time.

The two authors whom Proulx discusses in her article, Nancy Huston and Leïla Sebbar, both left their home countries of Canada and Algeria, respectively, and settled in their new home in the city of Paris. In contrast, as mentioned above, both of the correspondents in

À toi, Thúy and Janovjak, are nomads of the world: they have moved to new countries multiple times and have experienced feelings of exile and abandonment frequently; Kim Thúy was even labelled a "refugee author" by some critics and members of the press. However, I assert that both authors should be considered "transdiasporic" writers. It is through an examination of their transdiasporic identities that we begin to appreciate the deep connections between them.

With this term I am following the lead of Alexandra Kurmann, who, in her 2018 article on *Ru*, notes that "the word 'migrant' is problematic when discussing the work of Kim Thúy, a former refugee."[18] Kurmann uses instead the term "transdiasporic" to explain Thúy's position and characterizes this kind of subject as "less connected to the notion of home as a real or imaginary place of genesis than to the fluidity of contemporary diasporic spaces; one who freely traverses the transnational borders."[19] Like Kurmann, I also focus on the fluidity or mobility of individuals and expand the use of the term "diasporic" to include those individuals, like Thúy and Janovjak, who are nomadic. In addition to the fluidity and mobility, I will also examine the disjunctures and "broken" elements of their narratives and the parallels both in their responses to experiences of trauma and in their discussions of the centrality of letters and epistolarity to their thought. All of these together lead to stronger connections between the two and display more fully their transdiasporic identities.

One of the major themes that runs throughout the work centres on the perceived fluidity or mobility that has engaged both authors during their lifetimes. Many of their messages discuss their international travels, not only during their past lives, when they were living and working in different countries, but also in the present, as they are often found writing their correspondence "in transit," with messages being read, composed, and sent from airport lounges, hotel lobbies, or hotel rooms. For example, "Je t'écris de l'aéroport, en attendant l'embarquement" (*À toi*, 153) [I am writing to you from the airport, waiting for boarding]; "Je ne sais pas comment me brancher depuis ma chambre. Alors je t'écris du lobby de l'hôtel, où un ordinateur est mis à la disposition des clients" (*À toi*, 161) [I don't know how to connect to the wi-fi from my room. So I'm writing to you from the hotel lobby where a computer is made available to clients]; "La fenêtre de ma chambre 209 donne sur un parking à perte de vue. Et pourtant, mon hôtel s'appelle Ocean Breeze" (*À toi*, 103) [The window of Room 209 looks out on an endless parking lot. And yet the hotel is called Ocean Breeze]. As they crisscross both the European and North American continents, we even find emails showing that during their three months of correspondence, they sometimes visited the same cities but missed running in to each other by a few days or weeks.[20] Pascal even stops by Kim's home in Montreal but only meets her husband there, because Kim is away on another book tour (*À toi*, 133). It becomes very apparent to the reader through these constant references to travel and movement coming from both sides of the correspondence that, even though they have had very different life experiences as well as different cultural origins, their international mobility contributes to a shared transdiasporic identity for both authors.

Pascal furthers this notion when describing his "métissage," as it connects his identity to his desire to travel: "En fait, notre étrangeté est exponentielle. C'est mon métissage qui m'a donné le goût du voyage, lequel provoque d'autres métissages" (*À toi*, 43) [In fact, our strangeness is exponential. It's my mixed cultural background that gives me a taste for travel, which provokes more mixing of cultures]. The perpetual circle that is created through mixing cultures, travel, and then further mixed cultures all lend to the development of Pascal's transdiasporic identity. We return again to the central notion of infinity and open-endedness that is interwoven throughout the email exchange. Kim, as well, discusses the influence that her background has had not only on her interest in travel but also on the creation of her hybrid identity.

The geographical and emotional mobility and fluidity that both authors demonstrate in the text is juxtaposed with a certain disjointed or fragmentary nature in their discursive practices. Both authors thus use techniques of fragmentation, or what Jenny M. James describes as "self-reflexive polyphony" and "broken narrative discourse."[21] James explains that these disjunct narratives "formally echo the unavoidable moments of interruption, juxtaposition, and translation that constitute living in diaspora."[22] While James is focused on Thúy's novel *Ru*, we find a similar style of interruptions, delayed responses, and "broken" narratives in the epistolary exchanges of *À toi*.[23]

The text is made up of many short messages, and while they sometimes provide a direct response to the previous message, or might echo the other author's thoughts or stories, just as often, the emails that Kim and Pascal send to each other are not immediate replies to the message that they just received. Instead, we frequently find that the response might refer to a concept or an incident described several emails earlier, or might even bring up an entirely new topic. This style is due in part to the effect of electronic communication and differs somewhat from crossed letters that we find in eighteenth-century epistolary novels. However, it is because *À toi* is structured as an epistolary work, with letters written back and forth between Kim and Pascal, that these narrative breaks are more noticeable and perhaps even more striking to the reader than they are in *Ru*. For example, in his email from 10 October, Pascal describes a woman who sat next to him at the prize ceremony in Monaco and explains that she was so ridiculously artificial that she made him cry from hysterical laughter. While Pascal cracks up at her behaviour, he also draws a lesson from the moment, writing that "on n'a jamais que la beauté que l'on mérite – celle du regard que l'on porte sur les choses" (*À toi*, 57) [we always only have the beauty that we deserve – the beauty of the gaze that we focus on things]. In Kim's response to this particular email, written on 11 October, she launches into a description of a trip she took that summer with her husband and sons to see whale sharks in Mexico. At first, there seems to be no connection at all between her story and the one in Pascal's email about the woman at the Monaco prize ceremony. However, Kim ends her message with an oblique comparison between her focus on the krill (rather than the whale sharks) at the seaside resort and an earlier email that Pascal had sent describing his father's attempts to teach him to jump into the water and swim when he was a little boy. Her phrase "le petit garçon et la plume blanche" (*À toi*, 59) refers to the white feather that Pascal described as the lure that finally persuaded him to plunge into the water. This is but one instance of the delicate threads that both authors weave between their emails, creating a lyrical whole out of many disparate anecdotes and helping us to make sense of their disrupted or broken transdiasporic identities through the practice of *métissage*.[24]

We also find more direct examples of interruption or disconnection in emails where the authors focus on dealing with trauma, both physical and mental. Pascal, for example, remembers an extremely threatening encounter during a routine border closure between Ramallah and Jerusalem. As he is trying to bring his parents to the airport, he ends up in a long line of traffic and walks up to the parked Israeli military jeep at the front of the line to ask how long the border will be closed, hoping to find out if it would be better to take an alternate route to the airport or just wait there. The reaction he receives is shocking: "il y eut un hurlement, et surgi de nulle part un soldat avait planté son arme dans mon ventre, l'avait amorcée; j'avais le canon de son arme dans le ventre et le visage du soldat était défiguré par ses cris" (*À toi*, 84) [there was a scream, and appearing out of nowhere, a soldier had planted his weapon in my stomach, had cocked the trigger; I had the barrel of his gun in my stomach and the face of the soldier was disfigured by his shouts]. Although the young soldier is screaming with anger that Pascal "is an Arab" and trembling with fear and terror as he clutches his gun, Pascal is eventually able to hand him his papers (very slowly) and the soldier finally releases him. Pascal explains to Kim that he experienced some kind of traumatic disconnection during this event, resulting in a delayed reaction: it was only an hour later that his hand began to tremble. In a parallel story, written ten emails later, Kim describes a near-death incident that she witnessed while sitting in her car six months earlier, when her autistic son walked into the street and was almost hit by a large SUV: "un klaxon fort et insistant m'incite à me retourner, à regarder par la fenêtre fermée et à voir mon fils de sept ans au milieu de la rue, les deux doigts enfoncés dans les oreilles, le nez à dix centimètres du pare-chocs d'une voiture tout-terrain, les yeux dans son univers" (*À toi*, 98) [a loud and insistent horn spurred me to turn around, to look through the closed window and to see my seven-year-old son in the middle of the street, his two fingers dug into his ears, his nose just ten centimetres from the bumper of an all-terrain vehicle, eyes in his own universe]. Kim is surprised by her response, or rather her *lack* of response – she is frozen in place and cannot even make herself leave the car to talk with the other driver or to pick up her son; he opens the back door of the car himself and climbs in. Similar to Pascal, Kim experiences a fragmented or interrupted emotional response, stating that the shock only set in about an hour later, when her hands began to tremble. We see here that their shared depictions of traumatic events, while highlighting the disconnected or interrupted emotional response, serve to create a common bond between them.

ON THE IMPORTANCE OF CORRESPONDENCE

The final point of comparison between the two writers will focus on their continual references to the importance of letters and correspondence. Both Kim and Pascal write about postal letters that they have written, received, saved, read, and reread, and both agree that reading (and saving) old-fashioned postal letters has an immense emotional importance for them. They also write on what it means to correspond via email in their contemporary lives.[25]

Pascal first narrates his discovery at a Parisian market of a large box that looks on the outside like a collection of Maupassant books; he explains that he used that large box for years to store postal letters (*À toi*, 114). Kim recounts the story of a friend in Munich with whom she has exchanged postal letters for twenty-seven years; she is amazed to visit him and find that he has saved her letters in a shoebox in his closet (*À toi*, 115). And they both wonder about the effects that technology will have on the correspondence of future generations. Pascal remembers passing a note to a girl in his class in middle school, wondering what her reaction would be when the paper finally reached her and she read it. How will students do that now, he wonders, when everything is digital and nothing is permanent, the way that paper letters were? "Dans les collèges les plus sages, les adolescents mettent leur téléphone en mode silencieux, et c'est d'un regard sous la table qu'ils déchiffrent, sur l'écran lumineux, les mots qui les feront vibrer ... Sans doute les mots sont-ils les mêmes, tout comme les émotions. Mais comment feront-ils, eux, les soirs de mélancolie? Pourront-ils renverser une rangée de faux livres, ouvrir une boîte en fer, un tiroir oublié?" (*À toi*, 114) [In the most well-behaved middle schools, teenagers put their phones in "silent mode" and with a sneak peek under the table they decode, on the lit-up screen, the words that will make them tremble ... No doubt the words are the same, just like the emotions. But what will they do on those melancholy nights? Will they be able to empty a set of fake books, open a metal box, a forgotten drawer?]. At times their nostalgia for paper letters would even seem to offer a critique of the entire project behind *À toi*, where emails, rather than postal letters, are the source of communication that makes up their epistolary volume. However, we need only to reflect on the fact that Thúy's ultimate goal was to see these electronic missives become a book in print, available on paper.

We also see the two correspondents reflecting on the complex process involved in composing an email at a keyboard. Pascal states, "Ce que j'aime dans notre correspondance, c'est cet étrange silence des messages, qui ressemble au faux silence des déserts. En ce moment précis un magnétophone posé dans la chambre ne capterait rien d'autre que mes doigts sur les touches, un léger cliquétis, quand dans nos têtes résonnent les voix d'une conversation ininterrompue, les nuances et les modulations de nos gorges et le claquement des langues contre le palais, les exclamations et les rires, et les interrogations muettes" (*À toi*, 101) [What I like in our correspondence is that strange silence of messages that resembles the false silence of deserts. At this precise moment, a recorder set up in the room would capture nothing more than my fingers on the keys, a light clicking, when in our heads resonates the voices of an uninterrupted conversation, the nuances and modulations of our throats and the clacking of our tongues against the palate, exclamations and laughter, and silent interrogations]. His reflection on the cacophony inside the email writers' heads indicates that perhaps it does not matter what the medium is, be it traditional postal letters or fleeting electronic messages. What counts is the important exchange of ideas that is transpiring – cultural, emotional, and personal – and the development of transdiasporic identities that go beyond the external appearances of a person sitting alone in a room in front of a computer screen.

CONCLUSION

The book concludes with two emails about Christmas and family: first, Pascal describes the ways that the quotidian takes over at his wife's family celebrations in Rome. The focus in their conversation is on shopping, meal preparation, and children's games and they eliminate any possibility of discussing philosophical topics or existential anxiety, although Pascal does bring the narrative back to his recurring reflections on his upcoming new fatherhood and how that new role will change him. In her email reply, the last entry of the book, Kim also focuses on the "everyday" activities of her family gathering in New York for the holidays, explaining what each member is doing, from sleeping on the couch to preparing a dessert in the kitchen to playing video games. Her final sentence for the book therefore surprises the reader, because she does not ask a question about "everyday" activities but rather one that sends us off into a metaphorical or existential dimension: "N'est-ce pas un moment parfait pour mourir?" (*À toi*, 169) [Isn't this a perfect moment to die?]. The question could of course be interpreted as a veiled reference to Kim's elderly grandmother, whom Kim has described as having "retired" from her traditional spot at the centre of all the family activities to lie in a daybed tucked in the corner, where she has peacefully fallen asleep. But Kim's question may also indicate a possible critique of the everyday and of stability: as we have seen in this analysis, both Kim and

Pascal highlight the importance of mobility, adaptation, and the unknown as key elements of their transdiasporic identities.

No response is offered to the question. Such an open ending serves as a "perfect" conclusion to this epistolary text, because it forces us readers to decide on our own how to answer the provocative question. Thus, even though the text *À toi* may fall outside the more well-known Kim Thúy corpus of *Ru*, *Man*, *Vi*, and *Em*, the unique epistolary form offers readers an important meditation on the multiple links between writing, exchange, and transdiasporic identity formation.

NOTES

1 Quoted in Guy, "Kim Thúy et Pascal Janovjak," n.p. All English translations in this chapter are my own unless otherwise noted.

2 Indeed, Thúy's most recent novel, *Em* (2020), continues in this vein, with a focus on the experiences of exile and adaptation.

3 I have chosen to use the authors' first names (Kim and Pascal) when referring to their characters as letter-writers in *À toi*. I will use their last names (Thúy and Janovjak) when referring to their activities as authors.

4 Thúy and Janovjak, *À toi* (Montreal: Éditions Alain Stanké, collection 10/10, 2015), 9, 167. All subsequent references are to this edition and will be cited in the text with the title and page number in parentheses.

5 In the context of francophone Vietnamese writers who chose an epistolary form for their literary works, we note Linda Lê's *Lettre morte* (1999), which has no implicit reader, as her father has died. Linda Lê's literary production and style are quite different from Kim Thúy's; however, they have similar backgrounds and trajectories: both authors were born in the 1960s in South Viet Nam (Lê in 1963, Thúy in 1968), both left their home country in the late 1970s (Lê in 1977, Thúy in 1978), and both settled in a French-speaking country (Lê in France, Thúy in Quebec). A major difference, of course, is that Linda Lê began writing at a young age, publishing her first novel in the mid-1980s, while Kim Thúy came to writing only three decades after she arrived in Quebec, at the age of forty. For more on the epistolary form and letters more generally in Lê's works, see Courville, "Melancholic Epistolarity," esp. chap. 2 ("*Lettre morte*"). See also Bacholle-Bošković's book, *Linda Lê, l'écriture du manque*, esp. 125–37.

6 Elliott, Gerber, and Sinke, "Introduction," 2.

7 Frenette, "Introduction," 10.

8 Proulx, "Writing Home," 81.

9 Elliott, Gerber, and Sinke, "Introduction," 2.

10 Cancian, *Families, Lovers, and Their Letters*, 6.

11 An excellent example of this kind of transnational identity created through letter-writing can be found in the twentieth-century epistolary novel *Les lettres chinoises* by Ying Chen. Although Pamela Sing's 2013 article does not specifically address the text *Les lettres chinoises*, she does examine the links between these two Asian francophone writers: both Thúy and Chen moved to Quebec and published their first works there. See Sing, "Migrance, sensorium et translocalité."

12 Elliott, Gerber, and Sinke also mention fax machines, international long-distance telephone calling, jet travel, and internet cafés as modern factors that assist in "migrants' quest for maintaining personal networks" ("Introduction," 2). More recently, however, we find that even those technologies have been replaced by more ephemeral, but at the same time more immediate, communication methods, to further supplant traditional letter-writing on paper. See, for example, Jordan, "On Migrant Journeys with WhatsApp and Google Translate," or Kerstetter, "WhatsApp Is Embraced by World's Immigrants."

13 Quoted in Guy, "Kim Thúy et Pascal Janovjak."

14 See, for example, Pascal's emails from 3 octobre 8:11 (*À toi,* 10), 3 octobre 15:56 (*À toi,* 12), and 4 octobre 13:56 (*À toi,* 25).

15 Frenette, "Introduction," 10.

16 Janovjak grew up in Switzerland, moving to France for university studies and then to Bangladesh, Jordan, Lebanon, Palestine, and, finally, Italy. It was while living in Ramallah that he wrote his emails to Thúy for *À toi*. See "Pascal Janovjak, biographie," *Viceversa Littérature*, n.d., accessed 18 October 2022, https://www.viceversalitterature.ch/author/3535.

17 Proulx, "Writing Home," 81.

18 Kurmann, "*Aller-retour-détour*," 65.

19 Ibid., 69.

20 For example, Pascal writes, "J'arrive à Rimouski, au Tropical Beach Hotel, on m'annonce que tu viens de repartir" (*À toi*, 132) [I arrive in Rimouski, at the Tropical Beach Hotel, and they tell me that you just left] and "Je serai à Rome dans deux semaines, et tu n'y seras plus" (*À toi*, 160) [I will be in Rome in two weeks, and you will no longer be there].

21 James, "Frayed Ends," 43.

22 Ibid.

23 Thúy's recent text *Em* (2020) also contains a fragmented narrative, even though it is not in the form of an epistolary exchange, like *À toi*. The

short chapters in *Em* frequently jump between different time periods, locations, and characters; they include topics as wide ranging as Cold War political history, southern American culture, women-owned nail salons, and the harsh life of street children during the war in Viet Nam. The fragmentation is simultaneously disorienting and engaging for readers and creates a powerful bond between reader and author.

24 Thúy continues with this weaving together of disconnected threads in her recent work *Em*, where the two protagonists, Louis and Emma-Jade, live a series of disruptions and detours. After Viet Nam, they are separated for many years but find points of intersection and finally rediscover each other in North America. One major difference between *À toi* and *Em* is the focus on children in *Em*; we find detailed portraits of the childhoods of Louis and Emma-Jade, both in war-torn Viet Nam and growing up in North America. *À toi*, in contrast, focuses mainly on the adult lives of Kim and Pascal, with some scattered references to their childhood memories.

25 In one of the few literary references in the book, Pascal discusses the letter that is famously "hidden in plain sight" in Edgar Allen Poe's *The Purloined Letter*. He says that we are satisfied with this ending, "cette énigme résolue" [this solved mystery], but also comments that the author, Poe, has the last laugh because, despite the many questions and hypotheses and analyses made of this text, "de cette lettre, posée en évidence devant le nez du lecteur, on ne connaîtra jamais le moindre mot" (*À toi*, 108) [of this letter, placed clearly in front of the reader's nose, we will never know so much as one word]. Translations by Miléna Santoro.

5

Post-migratory Identities

Changing Masculinities in Kim Thúy's Vi

Ashwiny O. Kistnareddy

Je savais que les deux plus vieux devraient partir sur un champ de bataille le jour de leurs dix-huit ans. Qu'ils soient envoyés au Cambodge à combattre Pol Pot ou à la frontière avec la Chine, les deux destinations leur réservaient le même sort, la même mort.

[I knew that the two older boys would have to leave for the battlefield on the day they turned eighteen. Whether they were sent to Cambodia to fight Pol Pot or to the frontier with China, both destinations reserved for them the same fate, the same death.]

Kim Thúy, *Vi*

Kim Thúy's novel *Vi* (2016) is the first-person narrative of Vi,[1] whose family flees Viet Nam when she is eight years old due to the newly established Communist regime and the imminent threat of her three older brothers being sent to war. Through the eyes of the youngest child and only daughter, Thúy begins the narrative with the distress of the mother watching the calendar signal the impending death knell for her sons. The repetition of "même" [same] reinforces the fact that two of the boys are twins, thereby leading to the mother losing two sons simultaneously, compounded with the fact that the third would also get conscripted shortly after his brothers, since he is close in age. "Même" also places destiny on the same level as death, thus underlining the inevitability of the loss of life in war zones. From the beginning of the novel, the mother is portrayed as a pivotal figure, while the sons are crucial to the narration as the potential victims of war who must be saved. Being male here is thus seen as a liability, as it is men who are enlisted and who will die senseless deaths, and it is the women who will mourn their husbands, siblings, and sons.[2]

Thúy's *Vi* invites the reader to ponder gender and the stereotypes associated with gender. The text is recounted from Vi's point of view and spans decades and continents, between Viet Nam, Malaysia, where the family finds refuge for a short period before being given asylum in Canada, and Quebec, where they eventually settle, and where Vi grows up. This trajectory is similar to Thúy's own: she left Viet Nam with her parents and two brothers at the age of ten, arriving in Quebec after weeks spent in a Malaysian refugee camp. Thúy's first narrative, *Ru* (2009), which won the Governor General's prize in 2010, has garnered a great deal of interest owing to both her style and the way in which she depicts the experience of exile and the place given to family memories.[3] Shortlisted for the New Academy Prize in Literature, the "alternative Nobel prize" in 2018, Thúy has attained a level of popularity with her writings that attests to the sustained interest in the repercussions of war and displacement on Vietnamese refugees, as depicted through her fiction and nonfiction. *Vi* is Thúy's fourth text and the last one to foreground a main fictional character; her next novel, *Em* (2020), sees Thúy using a *je* who is not part of the narrative but a conduit through which silenced stories are threaded together, setting herself up as the teller of those stories. In *Vi*, Thúy accords importance to the family, and to relationships between men and women in particular, as migration from a traditional, familiar space in Viet Nam to the unfamiliar space of Quebec invites us to rethink gendered roles, especially masculinities.

Defining "masculinity" broadly, Michael Donaldson states that it is "a personal and collective project" that closely links breadwinning and manhood.[4] In *Men and Masculinities in Southeast Asia*, Michele Ford and Lenore Lyons claim that it is vital to underline that masculinities are plural and must also be contextualized according to the culture and values in play.[5] In a chapter dedicated to masculinities and Viet Nam in Ford and Lyons's edited volume, Huang Cam Thai argues that masculinity in Viet Nam is associated with men's social position and therefore their livelihood. For Thai, in the aftermath of obtaining asylum in North America because of the war, the notion of what it means to be masculine is interrogated since Asian men, as refugees, were given only low-wage employment, leading them to feel emasculated. In Thai's analysis, a considerable number of the immigrant Vietnamese men interviewed for the study "made strong links between making money and providing for their families, including their wives and parents, as significant to their identity as men."[6] In this chapter, I examine the different generations of men portrayed in *Vi* with a view to mapping the ways in which masculinities evolve according to the changes that operate around them: from colonial Viet Nam to postwar life in Quebec. In so doing, I demonstrate that migration permits a shift to individuation and personal ways of conceiving one's own notion of masculinity.

COMPARING MASCULINITIES IN *VI*'S FRENCH INDOCHINA

Vi offers two very different forms of masculinities prevalent in Viet Nam, as represented by the title character's grandfather and father. Thúy sets up her text in the context of a family saga that begins with her grandfather's youth in Saigon under French rule. Subtly linking upward social mobility to France while underlining the double standards in play at the time, Thúy portrays the grandfather as a highly successful man who takes advantage of the opportunities under colonial rule, such as a French education system. Yet he is also a secondary subject in his own country, as his law degree carries the stigmatized term "indigène": "Mon grand-père paternel était diplômé de la faculté de droit de l'Université de Hanoi à titre d''indigène.' La France s'occupait de l'instruction de ses sujets, mais n'attribuait pas la même valeur aux diplômes décernés dans ses colonies" [My paternal grandfather had graduated from the Faculty of Law at the Université de Hanoi, where he was identified as "indigenous." France took charge of educating its subjects but did not accord the same value to diplomas awarded in its colonies].[7] Moreover, the micro-aggressions that take place with the French teachers' inability to pronounce (and indeed, unwillingness to learn) Vietnamese names is glossed over quite quickly: "mon grand-père n'avait jamais protesté lorsque ses enseignants lui donnaient un nom français ... d'une année à l'autre, d'un professeur à l'autre, il portait un nom nouveau" (*Vi*, 10) [my grandfather had never protested when his teachers gave him a French name ... from year to year, from one professor to another, he would acquire a new name (2–3)]. Nonetheless, in the text, there is a sense that the absence of a French name is problematic, as the grandfather is given a different name and, essentially, a different identity every school year.[8] Such experiences can be traumatic for a child whose individuality and identity is constantly in flux and who must comply with decisions made by others regarding his identity.

Conversely, the choice to keep the name Antoine is seen as an act of recuperation and subjectivation insofar as this gesture allows him to gain agency and, eventually, take control over his legacy. The grandfather's French education and perseverance lead to his prominent position in society: "un empire et une réputation enviables en répétant son nom pour chacun de ses enfants" (*Vi*, 11) [an empire and an enviable reputation by giving his own name to each of his children (4)]. The act of reclaiming his name represents a way of fighting against the imposition of a name by the colonial powers that be. In addition, following Thai, this necessity to build an empire and a social position for himself is in keeping with Vietnamese traditions that associate social position with masculinity. Thus, in *Vi*, Thúy foregrounds the hybrid nature of life under colonial rule: the grandfather harnesses both the social and educational advantages that French rule affords while upholding the values of precolonial Vietnamese society. This focus on traditional values is particularly evidenced by, for example, his insistence on having a son. His wife bears six daughters before finally giving birth to Vi's father, whose arrival is celebrated: "mon père était le seul garçon de la famille qui comptait six filles ... un porte-étendard" (*Vi*, 11) [my father was the only boy in a family of six girls ... a standard-bearer (4)]. The use of the word "porte-étendard" is significant here since, as the only son, the father is the only offspring who can officially carry on the family's legacy and name, thereby strengthening Vi's grandfather's social position and guaranteeing a future for the family.

Importantly, the narrator underlines the fact that in Vietnamese society, it is not unusual to be polygamous in the absence of male offspring. For Vi's grandmother, it is her husband's preference for France's monogamous model of marriage that saves her from having to concede to his taking another wife: "heureusement pour elle son mari était de ceux qui avaient adopté le modèle monogame français" (*Vi*, 11) [Luckily for her, her husband was one of those who had adopted the French practice of monogamy (4)]. In the narrative, while Vietnamese society is under French rule, France does not impose its own laws of monogamy in Viet Nam and allows the Vietnamese to uphold their values. As the final child, Vi's father is perceived "Comme un miracle ... Son unique garçon" (*Vi*, 14) [Miraculously ... His only boy (7)], thereby leading to his overindulgence as a child by everyone in the household and his eventual lack of application at school. Later he eschews looking after the family business since his entire life he has been the object of others' attention. His father's estate would also have allowed him to spend his life outside of society's expectations for labour and earning, thereby placing him outside the paradigm of masculinity indicated by Thai, as discussed in the introduction above.

From this perspective, Vi's narrator recounts the societal changes as conducive to modifications in her father's way of living. Agricultural reforms change his life at twenty as workers become entitled to own the land they toiled on (*Vi*, 16). This leads to the father's acute awareness of his precarious position as a landowner who relies on this source of income: "malgré son air insouciant, mon père s'inquiétait de l'érosion de son confort" (*Vi*, 21) [Despite his carefree manner, my father was concerned about the erosion of his comfort (13)]. Indubitably, it is not the sociopolitical repercussions of such agricultural reforms that preoccupy him but his own fear of becoming a "beau prince sans royaume" (*Vi*, 21) [a handsome prince with no kingdom (13)]. As a direct consequence of this fear, he marries Vi's mother on her promise that, "Oui, je vais m'occuper de tout" (*Vi*, 21) ["Yes, I'll take care of everything" (13)]. She is an astute manager who takes over both the household and the business and makes them flourish, albeit from the shadows.[9] Thus, "il est devenu le maître de ce point de chute où marchands et acheteurs venaient passer leurs commandes auprès d'une équipe montée par ma mère et officiellement dirigée par mon père" (*Vi*, 22) [He became the master of this depot where merchants and buyers came to submit their orders to a staff hired by my mother and officially overseen by my father (15)]. Perceptions of masculinity in the society and gendered roles dictate that the husband must officially be the head of both the household and the business, even though in reality women have a significant role to play in both spheres. Thúy thus highlights the hypocrisy of the society and the double standard that prevails.

In contrast with Vi's mother, her father is seen as lacking interest in business and effectively not earning money for the family. From this point of view, he defies the expectations of masculinity in his society, as outlined by Thai, and of traditional masculinity as delineated by Donaldson. If masculinity is associated with breadwinning and social status, then Vi's mother is more masculine than her father. Conversely, rather than running the prospering business, "Il préférait le centre-ville de Saigon avec ses cafés français et ses bars américains" (*Vi*, 25) [He preferred downtown Saigon with its French cafés and American bars (16)]. Vi's father provides a sharp contrast to the model of masculinity that his own father represents. Indeed, Vi's grandfather had bought houses in Hai Bà Trưng road in Saigon in order to "rappeler à mes tantes d'être indépendantes d'esprit et surtout combatives" (*Vi*, 26) [remind my aunts that they should be independent of mind and above all combative (18)]. These houses were used by the girls and women of the family during their studies. The grandfather is thus set up as a very progressive figure who aids women in pursuing their independence and, especially, encourages his daughters to get the education needed to free themselves from the fetters of patriarchal society. By contrast, his son, Vi's father, transforms these houses into venues for sexual encounters with women and games with other dilettante young men like himself. He continues this lifestyle, one considered the norm among young men at the time, despite his marriage – "à l'instar de beaucoup d'hommes de son entourage" (*Vi*, 27) [as did many of the men in his circle (18)]. At a time when social status and stability are associated with the husband, as depicted in the narrative, Vi's mother is aware of her husband's many dalliances and concedes to sending food to the house for her husband's and his friends' consumption. This portrayal of high-class Vietnamese masculinity is stark, and yet there is no judgmental critique from the narrator, who maintains a purely descriptive style here, leading us to wonder whether she is as accepting of her father's foibles as her mother was, or perhaps is simply recounting the facts. However, the opposition between the grandfather and the father is reinforced in these passages. Where the grandfather respects women and their intelligence, the father reduces women to chattel and service, giving little to no respect to his wife beyond the fact that she runs the business that permits him to maintain such a lifestyle.

Using "if" clauses, the narrator deplores the fact that Vi's father's upbringing has led him to retreat from social problems, thereby blaming her grandparents but also, ultimately, Vietnamese society's valuing of sons for the rift in her own family. Since he was born "avec un destin de prince" (*Vi*, 30) [with the destiny of princes (22)], the father spends only two months in the reeducation camps after the Communist takeover of Saigon, and as soon as he is released "il s'est retiré dans le cocon de sa garçonnière, isolé des vagues de la vie" (*Vi*, 30) [he withdrew into the cocoon of his bachelor apartment, isolated from the uncertainties of life (23)]. According to the narrator, if her father had seen the other men who were called by the guards and never returned from the camps, he would have sought to flee Viet Nam with his family. The father's indolence, his inability to face real life and the terrible consequences of war, leads to the family breaking up; the mother takes charge and brings the children to safety by buying their way to refugee camps in Malaysia and subsequently to Quebec.

Nonetheless, Vi does not fully condemn her father, as he had a valuable impact on her during her early years. Her memories of him are associated with food, as his gourmet choices resulted in her consuming foie gras from Brussels (*Vi*, 42), the family's ability to have a yule cake for Christmas, and her having a three-tiered cake to mark her third birthday – all Western delights not afforded to most Vietnamese people. Her father's absence from her life as an adult is also experienced through food as she travels to Brussels later in life and eats waffles, hearing his voice as she remembers that he had bought his wife fabric on a trip there.[10] She recalls when one of his many mistresses visited their house with his illegitimate son, Trí, of whose existence he remains blissfully unaware (*Vi*, 44). Vi's memories of her father are ambivalent as every delightful morsel is marred by an equally prominent manifestation of his lack of restraint and, ultimately, his disrespect of the family values that underpin Vietnamese society. Even as his wife and children surreptitiously leave Saigon for his sons' survival, he remains asleep (*Vi*, 37). This apathy toward the war, toward the world as it rends around him, and especially toward his family who are fleeing testifies to a type of masculinity that is evanescent and discombobulated, at odds with the fortitude needed to escape from the Communist dictatorship at the time.[11]

MIGRATION AND THE CHANGING NARRATIVE OF MASCULINITIES

Conversely, the families who leave, including Vi's, experience a profound change in their attitude toward life and survival. The perilous voyage from Viet Nam to Malaysia, life in the derelict camps, and the subsequent move to Canada take a toll on those who survive. According to Kwok Bun Chan and Louis Jacques Dorais, "Most *Viet Kieu* now living in Montreal and in the rest of the province of Quebec originally arrived there as refugees."[12] Chan and Dorais argue that the family remains an important anchor for transnational Vietnamese families, or *Việt Kiều*,[13] who seek to reestablish themselves in the new society while maintaining ties with their traditions through links with the wider community. For Chan and Dorais, "within allowable limits, Vietnamese refugees strived to move across continents and oceans as families and rarely as individuals other than as pioneers" and maintained their culture, a fact the authors attribute to the Confucian traditions of family as continuity.[14] For Vi's older brothers, escaping conscription in Viet Nam, and leaving the family wealth behind to become refugees in a Malaysian camp and eventually in Quebec, represents a complete transformation in the way that they conceive of masculinity. Indeed, they have lost any social status they had, thereby disrupting the notion of masculinity as outlined by Thai. Yet this does not mean that they do not bring their values with them. Thus, another aspect of masculinity is foregrounded as the family settles in Quebec: that of primogeniture and the burden placed on the eldest son.

In this section I examine the evolution of Vi's brothers, particularly Long's, in the text through the lens of narrative, or, more precisely, the narrative of masculinities as developed by Stefan Horlacher. For Horlacher, masculinities take on different guises and are intersectional.[15] It is important to think of the performativity of masculinity as a narrative or script. Drawing on Walter Erhart's concept, Horlacher states that for Erhart, men "acquire masculinity 'by performatively acting out a narrative script' … according to which masculine gender identity 'predominantly works via imitation, performance and enactment.'"[16] For Horlacher, this narrative script "thus brings into play imaginary role models – examples, images, narrations, which circulate among individual 'men' and official images of 'masculinity,'" and this "implies that it can successfully combine literary, social, and historical sciences."[17] However, Horlacher asserts that while it is important for many individuals to construct what Winfried Fluck calls a "self narrative,"[18] which is contingent upon culture and the social framework in which they operate, it is important to create one's own reference points, one's own narrative. As Fluck argues, cultural narratives "may provide cultural frames of interpretation and furnish genre and plot structures for self-narration but we still have to turn these into the scripts of our own life."[19] For Horlacher, literature and real life become inseparable in the study of masculinities, as the former shapes our view of reality. While this particular point is not the focus of this analysis, it is important to note that the premise that the individual should create his own version of masculinity that is commensurate with his own experiences is crucial in my discussion of Vi's brothers.

It is my contention that Long and his brothers redefine their own sense of self and masculinity on their own terms, much as Fluck and Horlacher advocate, rather than defining their masculinity according to the model to which they were exposed in Viet Nam, as provided chiefly by their father. Significantly, beyond Vi revealing the fact they were about to turn eighteen and were facing compulsory conscription, the brothers have no presence in the text until they arrive in Canada. The first words uttered by a man in this novel are Long's exclamation "nous sommes arrivés au paradis!" (*Vi*, 48) [We've landed in paradise! (39)]. In her interview with Miléna Santoro in this volume, Thúy admits that she does not write in direct speech and therefore her characters do not usually speak.[20] Thus, on the rare occasions when one does, as is the case here with Long, what they say and how they speak becomes even more crucial to our understanding of their position. In this case, Long sees the light at the end of the tunnel of war, displacement, and the refugee experiences that have led to the family's arrival in Quebec. For those who are bereft, arriving in a land that is at peace feels like paradise.

Yet, for Long, his responsibilities commence as soon as they land. He registers his siblings at school and looks after them while their mother washes dishes at a nearby restaurant. He also builds networks in the neighbourhood, creating links in order to ensure new roots are being planted, so much so that "en quelques semaines, tout le voisinage connaissait son nom" (*Vi*, 51) [Within a few weeks, the whole neighbourhood knew his name (42)]. Aware of his new responsibilities as the man of the house, due to being the first born, Long finds employment in a Japanese restaurant, capitalizing on the Québécois's lack of differentiation between the Vietnamese and the Japanese to accomplish his dreams. While this idea is problematic because of the conflation of all Asians, Long takes advantage of it and secures employment, since survival is more important than claiming his ethnic identity. Combining "le charisme de [s]on père et l'audace de [s]a mère" (*Vi*, 54) [the charisma of [his] father and the daring of [his] mother (45)], Long draws on the positive attributes of both of his parents to forge a new life for the family. While his father was not a traditional role model, his ability to charm people becomes a tool that Long harnesses to achieve success both for himself and the family.

In their study of stressful experiences of masculinity in both US-born and migrant Asian American men, Alexander Wu and Joel Wong state that "participants viewed themselves as workers and emphasized success."[21] Participants also underlined the importance of work and the stress stemming from pressures to achieve in their career, whether they had such ambitions or not. In Thúy's novel, Long is focused not solely his own career but also on the success and progress of his siblings. As the head of the family, Long becomes the person who creates opportunities for his siblings, but he also begins to have his own ambitions for them, as if they were his own offspring. As with previous generations of Vietnamese migrants in Canada, Long would like his brothers to become engineers. However, the brothers acquire their own independence as they settle in their host country. Following their own desires and ambitions, one brother becomes an oncology biologist and the other a computer programmer. Long himself eventually chooses to study management, which enables him to open new branches of the restaurant where he had initially worked as a waiter. In this case, Long, as a father figure, is flexible. He does not impose his choices on the other boys, nor does he follow the beaten path himself. While previous generations would follow the choices imposed on them by parents, here the fact that Long becomes the head of the family allows for a more accommodating, less hegemonic, form of masculinity, following Raewyn Connell's concept,[22] one that is understanding and egalitarian, even as he takes on the responsibilities assigned to him. In this way, I contend that Long creates his own narrative of masculinity, as Horlacher and Fluck recommend.

Equally interesting in this respect is the contrast between Long and his father in this text. While the father took advantage of the fact that his features, his confidence, and his charm attracted women, Long is depicted as having only Hoa, his girlfriend, and later wife, in his life from the moment they meet, establishing him as more like his grandfather than his father in that respect. Long is as sociable as his father and has inherited from his father "une beauté qui attirait autant les hommes que les femmes" (*Vi*, 56) [a beauty that attracted as many men as women (47)]. While the homoerotic is foregrounded in this statement, it is not commented upon further. Rather, his father's attractiveness is exposed as a charm that affects both sexes without calling into question his sexuality or raising questions about his friendships. Vi's father's dalliances with women are perhaps enough to emphasize his unquestionable heterosexual masculinity, while the homoerotic aspect serves to explain the group of male friends who are always ready to surround him. Similarly, Long's male friendships are not seen as anything more than testifying to his popularity as a friend and host. His relationship with Hoa cements his heterosexual masculinity in the text. As with Long's mother, Hoa chooses to take the traditional position of the woman who remains "dans l'ombre de Long sans l'encombrer" (*Vi*, 57) [staying close to Long without getting in his way (47)]. Long does not perceive this positioning as problematic, as he has himself had to give in to his mother's every whim since his arrival in Quebec, although traditionally, and officially, he is the head of the family and she owes him obedience as per the three obediences in Confucian philosophy that dictate a woman should obey her father, her husband, and her son.[23] Long is portrayed as a son who understands his mother's suffering at having left her home, her business, and her life behind, at having been abandoned by their father, and "[est] toujours plié aux demandes de cette dernière même lorsqu'elles étaient déraisonnables, car il portait le poids de sa déchirure" (*Vi*, 57) [always acceded to her demands even when they were unreasonable, for he knew the magnitude of what she had lost (47)]. Contrary to his father, who took his mother for granted and to whose whims his mother had to cater, Long's masculinity is lenient, fluid, and permits an understanding of the suffering of women. In Viet Nam, Long would have had the final say in all decisions, while in Quebec, he deviates from the rules and adapts. Yet even as he concedes some power to his mother, Long – like his brothers, who are only tangentially mentioned in the novel through their education and their brief roles in certain episodes – does not always follow her instructions and wishes.

In this way, Long and the two other brothers do deviate from the set path of their culture as promulgated by their mother in specific circumstances, where their own subjectivities come into play. This divergence is seen in their reaction to Vi's relationship with with Tân, a Vietnamese man to whom she becomes engaged but subsequently breaks off the engagement because he mistreats her, which leads to a turning point in the novel. Vi's mother feels the breakup is a result of her having failed to educate her daughter properly; when she visits Vi, she communicates this in only two sentences. From this perspective, it is salient to discuss how education is perceived in Vietnamese Canadian society. For Chan and Dorais, discussing Vietnamese Canadian children who are raised in Canada, "educational achievement is a central element of Vietnamese self-definition. But better education begets questions about its purposes and consequences. A better-educated child invariably asks important questions about the balance-of-power among parents and children in a traditional Vietnamese family."[24] Vi and her brothers do not contest their mother's attitude, nor does Vi respond to her mother in the text. Yet, while the mother is adamant that she will not see her daughter again and leaves after chastising her in their brief interaction, Vi's brother, Lôc, leaves money in her postbox and a letter from all three brothers: "Reviens nous voir pendant la semaine des vacances si tu peux" (*Vi*, 90) [Come to see us during your reading week, if you can (81)]. The mother's short visit leaves Vi kneeling in pain, which is contrasted to the brothers' message of solidarity. The difference between the mother's attitude based on her extant values from her home country and the brothers' acceptance of Vi and their support is significant, as it testifies to their diverging values. It gestures to their rewriting of their own narrative of masculinity in a more flexible social and cultural space abroad. Their sister and her happiness become more important than traditions and values. In telling Vi that they want to see her, in not blaming her for her actions, they demonstrate a different, more open-minded attitude toward their beloved youngest sibling, thereby allowing for a new, understanding form of masculinity to emerge, which is at odds with their culture according to the text. Nonetheless, the narrative underlines the fact that they too are caught in between cultures, as they cannot condone her sending them souvenirs during one of her escapades with Tân. While they love their sister, constant reminders of her breaking the rules of their culture are not deemed acceptable.

Vi's different attitude and values stem from her being brought up in Quebec and following the lifestyle and choices of the society in which she lives rather than the values inculcated by her mother and their community. In turn, this has an impact on her relationship with men. According to Chan and Dorais, migration "released the Vietnamese woman from the former housework by virtue of her participation in the labour force. As a consequence of her newly found economic independence, she experiences an upward shift in her status in the family *relative to* her husband's downward shift because of his inability to find work in the host society that would enable him to recover his middle-class status he once enjoyed back in Vietnam."[25] In Vi's family, while her mother has maintained her position in the household, Vi was raised through the educational system in Canada from the age of eight until her postgraduate studies. Here, it is not a case of men finding themselves displaced in the traditional family structure because of women's access to employment but an actual gap between generations and cultures. It also reinforces Vi's ability to challenge the way a man treats her and to refuse to marry him. Thúy emphasizes the irony of being a man existing in between cultures when Vi describes Tân murmuring that "il avait su dès le début, dès que j'avais cédé à son premier baiser dans la voiture, que j'étais trop occidentale" (*Vi*, 96) [he'd known since the very start, as soon as I'd yielded to his first kiss in the automobile, that I was too Western (86)]. Tân begins the relationship with her and indulges in premarital sex, which suits him; however, Vi does not tolerate his abuse, thus proving to be uncontrollable, and he immediately blames her for being too easy and, therefore, too Westernized.

According to Homi Bhabha in *The Location of Culture*, the "in-between" is empowering as it allows for the individual to take advantage of two identities, two cultures.[26] For Bhabha, this is perhaps the best position to be in since one can harness the best of both worlds. In this case, though, it is also the worst of both cultures that is being foregrounded insofar as Tân's comment about Vi's Westernized behaviour demonstrates prejudice from their community against Western culture, which is here perceived as morally loose. Conversely, through her depiction of the bigotry of traditional cultures and their inability to accept change as a part of evolution, and especially post-migratory identities, Thúy highlights and subtly criticizes individuals who cling to erstwhile values and reject those who embrace the transformations brought about by mobility.

By contrast, Long and his brothers' decision to change with the times and according to the society in which they now live, in Quebec, is seen as empowering. For instance, as the head of the family, Long chooses to change their family name to simply "Lê" since their father had "perdu ce privilège le jour où il avait laissé sa femme et ses enfants se battre seuls" (*Vi*, 123) [forfeited this privilege the day he'd allowed his wife and children to struggle on alone (112–13)]. Nonetheless, the son remains heartbroken at his father's choice to abandon his family. He would have liked his father to witness his ascension and his flourishing business. The return to social status and business prosperity being important to Vietnamese men is significant here, but the narrator reinforces the fact that Long wishes for his father to regret the decision he made in staying behind and reveals his disappointment. Moreover, rather than follow in his father's footsteps in terms of the mistreatment of women, Long respects his wife and takes the time to treat her to dinners. From the father to the son, masculinity takes on different guises as the son learns from his father's mistakes. Long is still bound by the rules of his community's traditions and values, but he breaks from tradition by creating and sustaining a loving relationship with Hoa. Nonetheless, rather than a hybridized form of masculinity that takes on both Western and Eastern characteristics, following Bhabha's theory, which would be premised upon the existence of two monolithic types of masculinities that are being hybridized, I contend that it is the narrative of masculinities that Long adapts to his own circumstances. This narrative of masculinities is fluid and flexible and can be rewritten as and when the individual wishes it to, as per Fluck and Horlacher. In this way, Long is constantly rewriting the narrative of the masculinity that suits him from circumstance to circumstance and in his relationships with different members of his family, including his father.

In fact, both Long and his mother offer the father the chance to join them in Quebec, by volunteering to sponsor him – an offer that is rejected, as the father is a proud man. The father's inability to accept help from his wife and his son testifies to an erstwhile masculinity that is redundant and must adapt in order not to perish. The text also suggests that perhaps the lack of mobility entails stasis and the inability to move forward in the father. The ending of the novel leaves it open to the imagination of the reader as to whether Vi will go and see her father, whether she will convince him to accompany her to their new home in North America. According to Brian Bethune, Vi's abrupt ending "leaves thematic room for the writer's exploration of the other major gulf between refugee and immigrant experience – the return."[27] However, from the father's perspective, the question posed is whether those who stayed and survived the war can ever again be part of the family who left, whether reconciliation between fathers and sons, fathers and daughters, and husbands and wives can ever be fully possible when such a rupture has occurred.

CONCLUSION

From this perspective, Vi's narrative is a family saga that covers different periods of history and highlights the changing faces of masculinity, from the grandfather who made a name for himself to the father who took advantage of that name to live in comfort to the son who changes the name to create his own path in another country as a refugee. Intricately linked to the story of a man's name is the nature of work as a symbol of masculinity and a purveyor of social status. In *Vi*, as I have demonstrated, labour is undertaken by both men and women in order to provide for the family. Thúy's novel allows for a delineation of the ways in which masculinities, and especially the narrative of masculinities, can shift, change, and be constantly recreated to adapt to the demands not only of societal changes but also of personal choices. In her abrupt ending, Thúy also permits the reader to imagine the father's decision, and the eventual conclusion, allowing for the plurality of possibilities for changing masculinities.

NOTES

1 In her latest novel, *Em*, Thúy moves away from this model to situate the narrator as the teller of other people's stories rather than of the narrator's personal experiences. See Thúy, *Em* (Montreal: Libre Expression, 2020), 9–11.

2 See also Ly Thu Ho's trilogy of novels about thirty years of war in Viet Nam, especially the last, *Le Mirage de la paix* (1986), focusing on the loss of men in war and the women left behind.

3 See, for instance, Den Toonder, "Migrant Writing in Quebec." See also Lohka, "Senteurs de l'ailleurs."

4 Donaldson, "What Is Hegemonic Masculinity?," 645.

5 Ford and Lyons, "Introduction," 1–19. See also Demetriou, "Connell's Concept of Hegemonic Masculinity."

6 Thai, "Low-Wage Vietnamese Immigrants," 57.

7 Kim Thúy, *Vi* (Paris: Liana Levi, 2016), 9; Thúy, *Vi*, trans. Sheila Fischman (Toronto: Vintage Canada, 2019), 2. All subsequent references to this novel in the text are to these editions; the English translation appears in square brackets after the original French, with page numbers in parentheses.

8 See also Kim Lefèvre's own experiences of receiving different names, including the number 238, in *Métisse blanche*.

9 In "'Against the Flow': Exile and 'Willful Subjects' in Malika Mokeddem's *Mes Hommes* and Kim Thúy's *Vi*," I argue that Vi's mother demonstrates "willfulness" in the way that she establishes herself in both the domestic and the public space while remaining in the shadows.

10 The relationship between food and memory is a recurrent notion in Thúy's novels. I discuss the intertextuality with Proust's *A la recherche du temps perdu* in Kistnareddy, "Transnational Vietnamese Refugee Families."

11 Vi's father is also set up as a contrast to the men whom Thúy describes in *Ru*, her first novel, as I have discussed elsewhere (see Kistnareddy, *Migrant Masculinities in Women's Writing*, 214–25).
12 Chan and Dorais, "Family, Identity, and the Vietnamese Diaspora," 286.
13 The term is generally seen as derogatory, as Andrew X. Pham explains in *Catfish and Mandala*. Nonetheless, Clément Baloup has sought to recuperate it in his *Mémoires de Viet Kieu* graphic novel series.
14 Chan and Dorais, "Family, Identity, and the Vietnamese Diaspora," 293, 295.
15 Horlacher, "In Reality Every Reader Is, While He Is Reading, the Reader of His Own Self."
16 Erhart, "Das zweite Geschlecht," 203. All translations from German by Stefan Horlacher.
17 Ibid., 204.
18 Fluck, "Reading for Recognition," 51.
19 Ibid., 52.
20 See Kim Thúy's interview with Miléna Santoro, "Chasing Beauty," p. 153 in this volume.
21 Lu and Wong, "Stressful Experiences of Masculinity," 359.
22 Connell, *Masculinities*, 71–86.
23 Nguyen, "Confucianism 'Three Obediences and Four Virtues' Theory," 1.
24 Chan and Dorais, "Family, Identity, and the Vietnamese Diaspora," 303.
25 Ibid., 302.
26 Bhabha, *Location of Culture*, 56, 94.
27 Bethune, "Kim Thúy on How 'Refugee Literature' Differs from Immigrant Literature," n.p.

6

Kim Thúy's Many Mothers

Miléna Santoro

A striking feature of feminist novels in France and Quebec in the 1970s and 1980s is the centrality of the mother-daughter dyad, characterized by generational differences, conflictual relationships, or experiences of anger, loss, oppression, and rebellion, often inflected by a critique of Freudian and Lacanian interpretations of female subject development.[1] In Kim Thúy's novels, all published since 2009, this formative bond is markedly different from previous Québécois and French writers' treatments of the theme. Thúy's cultural context seems key to understanding the distinctiveness of her portrayals of maternal relations and mothering, a context that Thúy consistently mentions, both in her writings and in many of her interviews.

Signs of the importance of family, and specifically mothers, abound in Thúy's published work. Her best-selling 2017 cookbook, *Le Secret des Vietnamiennes*, opens with two photos. The first is of her grandparents, where two captions identify Lý Quí Phát as "le père de mes mères" [the father of my mothers] and Lê Kiêm Gương as "la mère de mes mères" [the mother of my mothers]. Thúy lost her grandmother, Lê Kiêm Gương, in 2016, as one learns at the end of the book. The second photo at the beginning of *Le Secret des Vietnamiennes* is of Thúy as a child with her own mother, Lý Kim Thủy. It is captioned "Avec maman et les ramboutans," a descriptor where the conjunction perhaps subtly suggests an equivalence between the mother and the intriguing, spiny fruits that are in fact soft to the touch and sweet on the inside. With its touching pictures of the author's female relatives (including her many aunts who are designated by numbers, according to birth order), and those telling opening captions that reference a plurality of "mothers,"[2] this visually seductive volume bears eloquent witness to how important mothering is to Thúy's identity and, indeed, to Vietnamese identity more broadly.

The reverence for mother figures is embodied, in Thúy's works as in her life, by multiple iterations of the mother figure, rather than expressed in a single biological relative. Interestingly, the Vietnamese word for mother is *mẹ* in the North, or *má* in the South, among other terms, depending on the dialect. Without context or a specific marker, such kinship words can be understood as singular or plural. In a sense, then, the idea of several individuals playing the role of the mother is supported by the Vietnamese language and its grammar, because the word itself can be used as a pronoun, variably singular or plural, and is not even exclusively reserved for one's own biological mother.

Several times in the course of my research on family dynamics and the place of the mother in a culture so different from my own, I encountered a Vietnamese folk poem that has been translated as follows: "Father's deeds are as great as Mount Thái Sơn, / Mother's compassion is like the water of an eternal spring, / One should revere mother and respect father wholeheartedly / To fulfill the filial piety of a child."[3] This poem, much like the nursery rhymes I grew up with, has been passed along from parents to children in Viet Nam[4] and offers a window into the attitudes that convention dictates should prevail between children and their parents, summed up in the translation by the words "filial piety." Piety, in particular, may strike readers as a strong word, and yet, as I discovered, it is a *mot juste*, a perfect term, in a culture where the religious tradition of ancestor worship is common, making the relationship of children to their living parents the first step on a journey toward veneration of ancestors who have passed on. Even more intriguing, however, is that the mountain referenced in this Vietnamese poem is not even in Viet Nam: "Taishan" mountain is in fact in China, more than a thousand miles from Viet Nam. This allusion points to another layer of complexity, given that Vietnamese culture owes much to its past colonizers and foreign cultural influences, including those of China and France, but of course the United States as well. This one example drawn from the annals of traditional wisdom says much about how complex and layered, or syncretic, Vietnamese culture is and, in particular, signals the enduring influence of a thousand years of Chinese rule and the socioreligious practices of Confucianism.

Recognizing the complexity of Viet Nam's multifaceted, multiethnic cultural history becomes all the more important when dealing with an author who left Viet Nam when still a child and whose acculturation in Quebec is an additional factor that shapes her writing. Mapping Thúy's work requires recognizing her position at the intersection of her formerly divided and war-torn country, its history of repeated colonization, her own refugee experience, and her choice to publish in French in Quebec. For a readership whose notions of Viet Nam may be vague, monolithic, or, worse still, afflicted by negative stereotypes that are a holdover from what we call the "Viet Nam War" and what is known in Viet Nam as the "American War," this conjunction of considerations requires attention and explanation, a fact of which Thúy herself seems acutely aware. When asked about her "pedagogical bent" in one interview, Thúy affirms, "J'ai cette chance d'avoir ces deux cultures, d'être capable d'expliquer la tradition vietnamienne aux lecteurs qui viennent d'ailleurs … Je ne crois pas que la culture vietnamienne soit meilleure que les autres, je veux simplement partager mes connaissances. J'aime offrir un moment de découverte" [I have the good fortune to possess these two cultures, to be able to explain Vietnamese tradition to readers who come from elsewhere … I don't think that Vietnamese culture is better than any other, I just want to share my knowledge. I like to offer an experience of discovery].[5] Running through the differences that Thúy references here and elsewhere as potential discoveries for an implicit readership she thus hopes to educate, the thread of family remains central. It is a principle of identity and coherence that unites communities, both those "back home" and those in exile, and thematically connects all four of Thúy's novels to date. Tracing the contours and multiple faces of "filial piety" in Thúy's writing, as expressions of reverence for mother figures but also of an attachment to and rootedness in what she preserves of her Vietnamese cultural heritage, is thus crucial to understanding how Thúy's authorial voice possesses such a distinctive appeal and resonance.

In the decade since the publication of her multiple-award-winning first novel, *Ru*,[6] Kim Thúy's works have been touted as exemplary of diasporic, migrant, post-migrant, post-memory, and transnational tendencies, depending on the agenda or theoretical framing of the critic. Thúy is not the first Vietnamese Canadian writer to write novels in French in Quebec, although she is the most successful and internationally renowned (see this volume's introduction).[7] In a time when anti-immigrant rhetoric has at times inflected Quebec's politics, Thúy is indisputably an "exemplary immigrant" in the sense that she has achieved true success, becoming a best-selling author and a media-savvy public figure who regularly appears on the radio and television, her humour and candour making her a sought-after guest speaker. Moreover, her works offer genuinely approachable and teachable-length stories that display a gratifying appreciation for her host society.[8] All of these facets of her persona and career aside, however, what is most intriguing is how effectively Thúy weaves together her Vietnamese cultural heritage and her socialization as an immigrant in Quebec. While others have focused on the trauma of the experiences of those who were once termed "boat people," and the strategic forgetting of the past by protagonists adapting to their new lives in North America,[9] I observe that familial bonds, and thus connections to past generations, remain central to her work – a thematization that I will argue is more indebted to and influenced by Vietnamese traditions than defined by the experience of immigration and assimilation.

In European and North American scholarship of the past few decades, feminist and, more recently, queer readings of mothers and their bonds with daughters have revitalized our understanding of female subject development. From Marianne Hirsch's *The Mother/Daughter Plot* (1989) to Gill Rye's *Narratives of Mothering: Women's Writing in Contemporary France* (2009), and, more specific to the Quebec context, including Lori Saint-Martin's *Le Nom de la mère: Mères, filles et écriture dans la littérature québécoise au féminin* (1999), my own *Mothers of Invention: Feminist Authors and Experimental Fiction in France and Quebec* (2002), and even Loïc Bourdeau's edited collection *Horrible Mothers: Representations across Francophone North America* (2019), studying the mother and the bond between mothers and children has been and continues to be a rich vein for reflection and theorization. However, there are gaps in our knowledge, particularly given our increasingly heterogeneous cultural landscape. Rye notes, for example, that among women-authored French novels in the decade prior to the end of the twentieth century, there are few narratives by immigrants and even fewer still where the immigrant mother speaks in her own voice.[10] In Quebec, by contrast, where the presence and institutional recognition of *littérature migrante* dates back to the 1980s and where, according to Daniel Chartier, immigrant authors constitute up to a fifth of all writers in the province in the period from 1800 to 1999,[11] there is a fairly robust tradition of works by immigrant women that portray mother figures. To cite but a few examples of such authors, we could include Marie Célie Agnant, the late Abla Farhoud, and Ying Chen, immigrant writers from Haiti, Lebanon, and China, respectively, who all began publishing in the 1990s in Quebec. However, while the mother may be a universal figure whose presence has been studied but whose relative lack of agency may engender feminist critiques, the treatment of her roles and her influence is often shaped in migrant texts by cultural specificities that may both disconcert and fascinate an audience potentially unfamiliar with such traditions and histories. In order to illuminate what distinguishes Kim Thúy's novelistic treatment of the mother figure, therefore, it is important to appreciate the role of her Vietnamese heritage, in addition to her place within Quebec's migrant literature, which gained status as a tradition not long after the time of her arrival in the province as a refugee in the late 1970s (see this volume's introduction for more on this literary context).

Phạm Quỳnh Phương and Chris Eipper's co-authored article, "Mothering and Fathering the Vietnamese: Religion, Gender, and National Identity," offers some helpful insights into the mother's place and role in Vietnamese culture. According to their research, the "enduring cultural pattern" of "venerating mothers and fathers" is, in the case of Viet Nam, coupled with "a cultural legacy that prides itself on respecting and honoring women" such that "to speak of the position of women in Vietnamese society is to speak of the position of women within the family – of women as wives and daughters, certainly, but most importantly of women as mothers."[12] Moreover, by contrast with "the imported Confucian attitude of valuing men above women ... in Vietnam the feminine element is deemed to be more emphatic than the masculine."[13] Without engaging the debates surrounding what are considered endogenous Vietnamese traditions by contrast with the enduring exogamous influence exerted by the Chinese, who were, historically, colonizers in Viet Nam from 111 BCE to 938 CE,[14] I find it persuasive that a number of recent scholars tend to concur that "the Vietnamese family and kinship system seem[s] much more complex and flexible than the Confucian model,"[15] which privileges male-line kinship. Indeed, Hirschman and Vu, in their 1996 article "Family and Household Structure in Vietnam," summarize ethnographic work in northern Viet Nam, long a stronghold of Chinese cultural influence, that indicates "neither a patrilineal model nor a bilateral model does full justice to the complexity of Vietnamese kinship patterns."[16] In other words, even during a time not long after Kim Thúy's family fled the south of Viet Nam following reunification in 1975, the traditions governing family structure and kinship practices were not exclusively oriented by the patriarchal and patrilineal traditions that characterize Confucian cultural influence. A robust respect for women as mothers and as central to the family structure was also present and points to an alternative, "bilateral" conception of kinship that, according to some, predates Chinese domination and persists to this day. Notably, this "feminine element" in Vietnamese culture is on display at the Vietnamese Women's Museum in Hanoi, where exhibits recall certain historical figures and traditions in order to support the Communist government's desire to align its nationalist program with contemporary Vietnamese feminism (and vice versa).[17] It is thus that legends, such as that of "the mother of the Vietnamese race, Âu Cơ," find a place next to a presentation of the historical resistance of the Trưng sisters to Chinese rule during the first century CE and to "a display that highlights female deities worshipped by the Vietnamese; further evidence of women's high status."[18]

Goddess worship is indeed one manifestation of the feminine emphasis noted by Pham and Eipper, and they, among others, have underscored the importance of goddesses to Vietnamese identity. Despite a period after the Communist takeover in Viet Nam when the state banned what it deemed the backward superstitions of such "matrifocal tendencies," more recently goddesses have been rehabilitated and reinterpreted, such that there are now seventy-five of them recognized as representative within Viet Nam's specific cultural practices and heritage.[19] Anthropologist Philip Taylor elaborates on the connection between the return of goddess worship and women's roles in society when he explains that

> Vietnam's goddesses are all designated as mothers *(mẹ)* and most commentators regard this practice as mother worship *đạo mẫu* ... be that a fertility cult, a celebration of human origins and nurturance, an expression of respect for the role of mothers in society ... or, in the case of those described as "mothers of the nation" ... the nurturers of its heroes and leaders ... *Readings of Vietnam's goddesses* [my emphasis] as symbols of the nation's origins, nurturance and renewal *draw inspiration from Vietnamese kinship roles, which accord mothers primacy as providers of life, nurturance and familial reproduction. Mothers are held to be authoritative arbiters over children, mediators between lineages and representatives of the household* [my emphasis].[20]

In other words, in the Vietnamese tradition, and despite a short-lived policy of suppression of goddess worship under the Communists, mothers hold singular importance and even power, obviously embodied by goddess myths, but more crucially and enduringly made manifest as part of the cult of female ancestor worship. This vital cultural practice is underscored by Kurmann and Do when they remind us that "most Vietnamese households today have an altar for honoring the spirits of family ancestors, where offerings are made to the ancestor's spirit ... [as] an expression of gratitude to the forebears, who provided for forthcoming descendants; in return, these spirits are seen to reciprocate by watching over the continuing family line."[21] Essentially, Vietnamese women are inspired by and revere both goddesses and women ancestors, because such figures personify, arguably in magnified form, the qualities that are valued by their culture.

Kim Thúy's knowledge of and adherence to such cultural traditions is made clear both in her novels and in interviews, where she has said things like "Le rôle des parents au Vietnam est très différent de celui d'ici. Les parents ne sont pas là pour être des amis ou pour jouer avec les enfants, ils sont là pour les élever, tout particulièrement la mère" [the role of parents in Vietnam is very different than the prevailing one here. Parents are not there to be friends or to play with the children, they are there to raise them, particularly the mother].[22] In another interview, Thúy affirms, "Les valeurs que je transmets à mes enfants restent très vietnamiennes: l'esprit de partage et le respect des aînés" [the values I transmit to my children remain very Vietnamese: the spirit of sharing and the respect of one's elders].[23] In this latter quotation in particular, we see clearly the filial piety underscored in the poem cited earlier, a poem that schoolchildren in Viet Nam have learned for generations and that many carried with them even when they emigrated, if the abundance of online family narratives that cite the poem is any evidence. In what follows, I elucidate how Thúy's traditional Vietnamese attitude of reverence and gratitude toward mother figures is expressed in her first three novels, *Ru* (2009), *Mãn* (2013), and *Vi* (2016), and also emerges in surprising ways in the orphan stories central to *Em* (2020).

The semi-autobiographical story of *Ru* follows the female narrator Nguyễn An Tịnh, from her relatively comfortable childhood in Viet Nam through the Communist takeover, the family's escape to Malaysia by boạt, and their ultimate resettlement in Quebec as refugees. Of the 113 short passages of the novel, which detail the vicissitudes of the narrator's nonlinear memories, fewer than ten actually begin with the word "mother,"[24] but the novel itself is presented from the beginning as being shaped by the mother's presence and influence. Born in 1968 on the day of Tết, the celebration of the Vietnamese new year when the eponymous military offensive was launched by the Northern forces, the narrator proclaims, "Ma naissance a eu pour mission de remplacer les vies perdues. Ma vie avait le devoir de continuer celle de ma mère" [The purpose of my birth was to replace lives that had been lost. My life's duty was to prolong that of my mother].[25] Not only a continuation of her mother, An Tịnh is given a name almost identical to her mother's, for "seul un point sous le *i* me différencie d'elle, me distingue d'elle, me dissocie d'elle. J'étais une extension d'elle, même dans le sens de mon nom ... Par ces noms presque interchangeables, ma mère confirmait que j'étais une suite d'elle, que je continuerais son histoire" (*Ru*, 12) [a single dot under the *i* differentiates, distinguishes, dissociates me from her. I was an extension of her, even in the meaning of my name ... With these almost interchangeable names, my mother confirmed that I was the sequel to her, that I would continue her story (2)]. The Viet Nam war, however, irrevocably compromises this continuity, as nothing in the South goes on as before once the North assumes control; within the novel's first two pages, we learn of the family's risky escape to the shores of Malaysia.

Once in Quebec, in a semi-autobiographical parallel of Thúy's own refugee journey, An Tịnh's family faces the many challenges of adapting to a culture where they do not know the cultural codes and customs, including the use of a toaster, the concept of seasonal clothing, and the dangers of bug-infested, secondhand mattresses. However, the narrator prefers to focus on the kind intentions, rather than the unintentional mistakes, that make of their host town of Granby "le ventre chaud qui nous a couvés durant notre première année au Canada" (*Ru*, 31) [the warm belly that sheltered us during our first year in Canada (21)]. By contrast with the motherly feeling of nurturance that this community's welcome creates, the narrator notes how harsh the expectations of her own mother seem to be. Because she places her daughter in "des situations de honte extrême" (*Ru*, 30) [situations of extreme shame (20)] where she loses face and feels publicly humiliated, such as going to the store alone to buy sugar when she can barely communicate, the narrator affirms that "pendant longtemps, j'ai cru que ma mère prenait un plaisir fou à me pousser constamment au bord du précipice ... J'ai ... compris plus tard que ma mère avait certainement des rêves pour moi, mais qu'elle m'a surtout donné des outils pour me permettre de recommencer à m'enraciner, à rêver" (*Ru*, 30) [For a long time, I thought my mother enjoyed constantly pushing me right to the edge ... I also understood later that my mother certainly had dreams for me, but above all she'd given me tools so that I could put down roots, so that I could dream (20)]. The past tense in passages such as these allows for the reader to perceive the distance between then and now, between the painful lessons of the past that it seemed the mother was inflicting on her daughter and the later realization that such strategies were necessary to the daughter's ability to survive and thrive. Indeed, these lessons in adaptation are actually a continuation of the harsh menial work that her mother had had the children perform in Viet Nam before things got so bad that they had to escape: "Elle nous préparait à la chute" (*Ru*, 23) [She was preparing us for the collapse (13)], as the narrator observes with the benefit of hindsight, because their refugee experience would indeed involve the humbling necessity of having to start from scratch in Quebec as custodians and harvest workers.

An Tịnh's mother's practicality and authoritative demeanour had developed when she was young, when she, as the eldest sister, had "approprié les fonctions d'homme de la maison, de ministre de l'Éducation, de mère supérieure, de PDG du clan" (*Ru*, 70) [taken on the duties of man of the house, Minister of Education, Mother Superior, chief executive of the clan (61)]. It is interesting to see the list of leadership roles in this description, because, clearly, the daughter-narrator is deliberately juxtaposing male-associated positions alongside that of the "Mother Superior" as familiar to an implied non-Vietnamese readership as to a Vietnamese one. If, recalling the earlier quotation from Taylor, "mothers are held to be authoritative arbiters over children, mediators between lineages and representatives of the household"[26] in Vietnamese culture, then we must recognize that An Tịnh's mother's behaviour is perhaps not as unusual as it may seem at first blush, particularly given the higher degree of respect accorded to those whose birth order makes them the eldest of either gender within families. Thus, what makes her mother unusual is in fact not necessarily a reversal of typical gender roles but rather the manifestation of the kind of authority that Vietnamese women can customarily exercise within the family. In *Ru*, the mother's force of character is later judged by her daughter to have been admirable, as is her decision, at age fifty-five, to "se laisser emporter, à se réinventer" (*Ru*, 72) [to let herself be carried away, to reinvent herself (63)] by learning the social dances she would have rejected as unseemly were she still in Viet Nam. She is a mother who is both capable and capable of change.

Although An Tịnh's biological mother is always with her during and after their refugee experience, the daughter finds that acculturation in Quebec creates distance from her heritage, such that her own maternity, later in life, does not echo the pattern of the past. As she puts it, "mes enfants n'ont jamais été des prolongements de moi, de mon histoire ... Pascal et Henri ... ne me ressemblent pas" (*Ru*, 13) [my children have never been extensions of me, of my history ... Pascal and Henri ... don't look like me (3)]. By contrast with her mother, a severe figure who, as we have seen, never treats her daughter as a "princess" (an enviable relationship that An Tịnh had witnessed between her cousin and her "Number Two"[27] uncle), An Tịnh eventually comes to love not only with her head, in the Vietnamese tradition, but also with her heart, in keeping with her newfound Québécois cultural models. As she explains, for the Vietnamese, "l'amour vient de la tête et non pas du coeur. De tout le corps, seule la tête importe. Il suffit de toucher la tête d'un Vietnamien pour l'insulter, non seulement lui mais tout son arbre généalogique" (*Ru*, 104) [love comes from the head and not the heart. Of the entire body, only the head matters. Merely touching the head of a Vietnamese person insults not just him but his entire family tree (96)]. However, An Tịnh's sons, one of whom is autistic and can hardly bear to be touched at all, help her discover and redefine the verb "*to love*" (*Ru*, 110, in English in the original), granting her that maternal magic that is "le pouvoir exclusif de souffler sur une plaie pour faire disparaître la douleur, de comprendre des mots non prononcés, de détenir la vérité universelle, d'être une fée. Une fée éprise de leurs odeurs" (*Ru*, 120) [the exclusive power to blow on a wound to make the pain disappear, to understand words unpronounced, to possess the universal truth, to be a fairy. A fairy smitten with the way they smell (113)]. Although she displays a different, more affectionate form of mothering than what she experienced herself, An Tịnh does respect and reconcile herself to the mother she has, realizing early on in the novel that "il n'est peut-être pas nécessaire que ma mère soit ma reine, c'est déjà beaucoup qu'elle soit uniquement ma mère, même si mes rares baisers sur ses joues sont moins majestueux" (*Ru*, 69) [perhaps my mother doesn't need to be my queen; simply being my mother is already a lot, even if the rare kisses I place on her cheeks aren't so majestic (60)].

One of the factors in An Tịnh's ultimate acceptance of and admiration for her mother is suggested by the positive experiences of mothering that she has after arriving in Quebec. Her description of her first Quebec-born teacher, Marie-France, as "une maman cane" who treats her immigrant pupils with "la délicatesse d'une mère envers son nouveau-né prématuré" (*Ru*, 19) [a mother duck [with] ... the sensitivity of a mother for her premature baby (9)] is but one of several examples of nurturing that the narrator witnesses and appreciates. Such experiences, rather than inciting rejection of her Vietnamese mother's stoicism, serve to make her more aware of the silent suffering and love of her compatriots, whom she is able to see with new eyes as heroines of Viet Nam's history. As she observes, "On oublie souvent l'existence de toutes ces femmes qui ont porté le Vietnam sur leur dos pendant que leurs maris et leurs fils portaient les armes sur le leur" (*Ru*, 47) [We often forget about the existence of all those women who carried Vietnam on their backs while their husbands and sons carried weapons on theirs (38)].[28]

This is in fact what Thúy herself experienced, as she explained in the interview cited earlier where she expresses gratitude for "cette chance d'avoir ces deux cultures, d'être capable d'expliquer la tradition vietnamienne aux lecteurs qui viennent d'ailleurs" [the good fortune to have these two cultures, to be able to explain Vietnamese tradition to readers who come from elsewhere], to which she adds "une grande gratitude envers elles ... [m]on désir premier était de les vénérer ... ces femmes au dos courbé" [an enormous gratitude ... my primary desire was to honor them ... those women with bowed backs].[29] In her writing for a readership she explicitly conceives of as non-Vietnamese, Thúy thus affirms she seeks to honour the generation of women whose existence is forgotten or invisible but whose sacrifice ensured her country's and her people's resilience. In this way, Thúy echoes the kind of reverence that Taylor highlights in his examination of women's status in Viet Nam, a respect imbricated with the ancestor veneration that *Ru* also clearly presents to its readers. It is this tradition of honouring one's forebears that Thúy successfully weaves into her story of new beginnings and cultural change, or what An Tịnh terms "l'indicible beauté du renouveau ... l'impalpable ravissement. Quant à moi, il en est ainsi ... jusqu'à ces feuilles blanches qui tolèrent mon sillage, ou plutôt le sillage de ceux qui ont marché devant moi, pour moi" (*Ru*, 144) [the unspeakable beauty of renewal ... intangible rapture. As for me, it is true all the way to ... the sheets of white paper that put up with my trail, or rather the trail of those who have walked before me, for me (140)]. This lovely closing image clearly frames *Ru* as an homage to the female forebears whose stories the novel emphasizes and whose formative influence the novel seeks to illuminate through the daughter-narrator's remembrances.

The influence of heritage and the optimism engendered by new opportunities are also at the heart of Thúy's second novel, *Mãn*, of which the title is the name of the main character and means "parfaitement comblée," or "perfectly fulfilled."[30] Whereas in *Ru* the biological mother is primary, and secondary characters merely take on motherly roles, in *Mãn* the first page presents a surprising list of the three mothers the narrator claims to have – and to only one of whom, and not the biological one, she accords the intimacy of using the word *Maman*. Abandoned by her birth mother, scooped up by a future religious woman, and finally adopted by a teacher and frozen banana vendor, Mãn – whose name can be seen if not heard within the word Ma*man* – is given "une seconde naissance" (*Mãn*, 9) [a second birth (1)] by three women with whom she claims to share an experience of being damaged. If her birth mother had "un trou dans la tête" (*Mãn*, 9) [a hole in her head (1)] because she got pregnant while unmarried, and if the future nun who found the infant had "un trou dans la foi" (*Mãn*, 9) [a hole in her faith (1)] because she was disillusioned, her adoptive mother, as Mãn says, "a un trou dans le mollet, et moi j'ai un trou dans le coeur" (*Mãn*, 9) [has a hole in her calf, and I have a hole in my heart (1)]. Her *Maman*'s bullet wound, incurred during her years as a bush fighter and spy during the Viet Nam war, is a scar that echoes the emotional pain that this woman had experienced at the hands of her stepmother, known in Vietnamese as a Mẹ Ghẻ, a "mère froide" or "galeuse" (*Mãn*, 23), literally, a "cold," "mangy" (Fischman translation, 16), or "black" mother, connoted negatively, as in the expression "black sheep." With the heritage of three damaged "mothers" who fill in for what they "lack" by finding ways to help Mãn survive, it is no wonder the daughter feels she is not truly whole, even if, ironically, the meaning of her name "[lui] impose [un] état de satisfaction et d'assouvissement" (*Mãn*, 34) [imposes … a state of satisfaction and satiety (28)].

Mãn's adoptive *Maman*, who assumed the name Nhẫn, meaning patience (*Mãn*, 25), when she was first captured by resistance fighters during the war, tells Mãn many stories that the latter relays in fragments throughout the novel. In one, Nhẫn relates how she memorized and used to recite for her father the eighteenth-century epic poem *Truyện Kiều*, about "la pureté et l'abnégation, deux couleurs essentielles à l'âme vietnamienne" [purity and selflessness, two shades essential to the Vietnamese soul], that are displayed by "une jeune fille qui s'est sacrifiée pour sauver sa famille. Certains disent que, aussi longtemps que ce poème de plus de 3000 vers continuera d'exister, aucune guerre ne pourra faire disparaître le Vietnam" (*Mãn*, 25) [a girl who sacrificed herself to save her family. Some say that as long as the poem, with its more than three thousand lines, still exists, no war can make Vietnam disappear (18)]. This specific reference to a classic text of Vietnamese literature, itself inspired by a Chinese source, is one way this novel evokes the worship of mythic figures, in this case Thúy Kiều, a heroine whose story begins with a trip to pay respect to the graves of her ancestors and whose subsequent misadventures result from a gesture of self-sacrifice motivated by filial devotion to her family. That Mãn's adoptive mother recalls this story shows how the principle of selflessness and service to the family, no matter what the cost, is deeply rooted and transmitted across generations of women, down to Mãn herself.

Although Mãn displays the traditional values of abnegation and submission in accepting an arranged marriage with a Vietnamese refugee restaurant owner who has settled in Quebec, we learn that mother and daughter nonetheless have different views on this opportunity to start a new life in Canada. Mãn believes that "nous sommes ce que nos ancêtres ont été … nos destins répondent aux gestes des vies qui nous ont précédés" (*Mãn*, 53) [we are what our ancestors have been … our destinies respond to what we have done in the lives that came before us (47)], while her mother, "contrairement aux autres mères vietnamiennes, qui misaient sur la loyauté et la gratitude de leurs enfants … voulait que j'oublie, que je l'oublie parce que j'avais une nouvelle chance de recommencer, de partir sans bagages, de me réinventer. Mais c'était impossible" (*Mãn*, 52) [unlike other Vietnamese mothers, who counted on the loyalty and gratitude of their children … wanted me to forget, to forget her because I now had a chance to start again, to go away with no baggage, to reinvent myself. But that was impossible (46)]. Although Nhẫn is thus not wholly a traditionalist, Mãn still maintains her sense of duty and cannot "forget" her bond with her mother even in the midst of making a new life in North America. In addition to writing to her mother regularly, Mãn preserves her heritage through her culinary skills, ultimately achieving international notoriety, and bringing Nhẫn over from Viet Nam to live with her family in Montreal in due course.

The centrality of the mother to this book is partly due to the fact that Mãn does not know who her father was, so he is absent, and partly due to how clearly the daughter carries her mother and her mother's teachings with her throughout her life. Of the novel's 104 passages, each titled with a word in Vietnamese followed by its French translation, "Maman" appears as the first word or within the first sentence in twenty of them and occurs a total of 105 times in all. The mother tongue and the mother herself are thus primary reference points of the narrator's story. Frequently, the narrator uses the Vietnamese phrases of passages' titles as an opportunity to elaborate on the cultural traditions she wants us to understand, even if she sees them dying out or even questions them herself. In discussing the rituals of marriage in the passage titled "saluer les ancêtres" (*Mãn*, 51, such chapter titles are lowercase in the original) [bowing to the ancestors (45)], for example, she notes that "la transmission des rituels d'une génération à une autre" [the transmission of rituals from one generation to the next (45)] is fundamental and that the first act of the newlyweds is to kneel before the altar to their forebears. In accepting the marriage arranged by Nhẫn for her, Mãn herself bows to her mother and to tradition, demonstrating the expected submission and filial piety. Indeed, early in her marriage, Mãn puts into practice the discretion that Nhẫn herself had learned as a rebel fighter: "Maman m'avait enseigné très tôt à éviter les conflits, à respirer sans exister, à me fondre dans le décor. Son enseignement était essentiel à ma survie" (*Mãn*, 103) [Maman had taught me very early to avoid conflicts, to breathe without existing, to melt into the landscape. Her teachings were essential for my survival (97)]. This self-effacing invisibility evolves once Mãn's career as a chef begins to take off.

As in *Ru*, there are other women who play an essential role in the narrator's acculturation and ultimate success in Quebec. In this novel, one of the restaurant's patrons, Julie, becomes both a surrogate mother and a big sister to Mãn: "Julie ... m'a adoptée comme elle a adopté sa fille, sans questionner notre passé. Elle était la grande soeur que je n'avais jamais eue, et moi j'étais la mère vietnamienne de sa fille" (*Mãn*, 54–5) [Julie ... adopted me as she'd adopted her daughter, without questioning our past ... She was the big sister I'd never had, and I was her daughter's Vietnamese mother (48–9)]. A "marchande de bonheur" (*Mãn*, 73) [merchant of happiness (67)], Julie "faisait

[s]on éducation en langues, en gestes, en émotions" (*Mãn*, 65) [educated [her] in languages, in gestures, in emotions (59)], helping the narrator open up to new experiences, give cooking classes, and then upgrade the restaurant, travel, and write a best-selling cookbook in which "chaque recette était portée par une histoire" (*Mãn*, 79) [each recipe was carried by a story],[31] recalling Vietnamese culture and history. Interestingly, this fictional milestone foreshadows Thúy's own later publication of *Le Secret des Vietnamiennes*, structured around the same principal of framing the recipes with stories of her family's cultural heritage. In *Mãn*, Julie's nurturing guidance and encouragement extends to Mãn's two children, for whom she becomes a second mother, or *Má Hai*, leading Mãn to quip, "Mes enfants avaient beaucoup de chance. Ils avaient à la fois une assurance-vie et une assurance-mère" (*Mãn*, 109) [My children were very lucky. They had life insurance and mother insurance (103)].

As much as Julie plays the role of "merchant of happiness" and maternal figure for the narrator, it is Mãn's "third" mother, the one who "taught school and sold iced bananas" (*Mãn*, 1) at the novel's opening, whose presence proves most enduring and comforting, particularly after Mãn's passionate but doomed love affair with Luc, a French chef whose family once lived in Viet Nam. When she was a child, sleeping with her mother on a train, Mãn remembers, "J'écartais tout, j'ignorais tout dès que j'étais couchée en cuillère avec Maman" [I dismissed everything, knew nothing as soon as I was lying spoon-fashion with Maman], because she could reduce "la vie, le monde entier en une seule bulle" (*Mãn*, 111) [life and the entire world to a single bubble (105)]. After her breakup with Luc, Mãn's grief is overwhelming, and the only thing that finally turns her around is when Nhẫn recounts her own first love, whom she found but did not reconnect with after the war because he had married another woman. Her adoptive mother's self-sacrifice, in honouring the choice of her lost lover to move on but not forget, helps Mãn to integrate and preserve Luc's legacy of demonstrative ways, by expressing her love for her children more and by keeping an open heart. Much as her mother had once offered her body as protection on the train, Nhẫn's empathetically told love story offers a kind of framework, or bubble, within which Mãn can recover her equilibrium and calm. If, in typical Vietnamese fashion, "le visage de Maman, comme celui de mon mari, ne laissait transparaître ni la peine ni la joie, et encore moins le plaisir" (*Mãn*, 67) [Maman's face, like my husband's, showed neither pain nor joy, to say nothing of pleasure (61)], then both Julie and Luc show the narrator more expressive ways of being and help her acquire a new voice in her profession and her personal life. After the breakup with Luc, it is ultimately the combined efforts of Nhẫn *and* Julie that help Mãn recover, by both reminding her of her heritage of self-sacrifice and guiding her onward. They are two mother figures who are related to Mãn not by blood but by equally strong bonds of affection, just differently expressed, and synthesized, in typical Vietnamese fashion, by the narrator as she recounts her path forward. The conclusion of the novel makes clear that, however different the narrator's identity and path are from those of the "mothers" she has known, in particular Nhẫn, she is indebted to each one and clearly appreciates how their legacy has contributed to who she becomes.

After the initially surprising multiplicity of mother figures in *Mãn*, Thúy returns in *Vi* to the story of a more traditional family, where the mother and children arrive as refugees in Quebec after leaving the father behind in Viet Nam in the aftermath of the war. In this novel, the family genealogy and history are traced back through both parents of the protagonist narrator, Bảo Vi, whose name means "Précieuse minuscule microscopique" [tiny precious microscopic][32] but whose stature makes her quite the opposite. Vi's narration – once again in the first person, as in Thúy's previous two novels – shares with *Mãn* a fragmentary structure, composed of fifty-eight short chapters, most of which are given place names for titles, with translations for some of the Vietnamese words, such as Grand Lac Hồ Xuân Hương, which means "lac au parfum printanier" (*Vi*, 23) [lake of the scent of spring (14)]. The emphasis on place is reinforced in the original Libre Expression edition by a two-page illustration at the end of the text that suggests a topographical map, with many of the novel's passages' place names – including Berlin, London, Malaysia, and Boston, as well as, humorously, "creux de la clavicule" (*Vi*, 141) [hollow of the collarbone] – superimposed in red on the pattern. This artistic yet impossible "mapping" is completely missing from the English translation, a loss that affects our ability to detect the conceit of these far-flung places as being connected and united by the pattern of Vi's life and loves.

The first third of this novel focuses primarily on the story of Vi's mother and father and their parents, two generations of ancestors whose cultural heritage predates the Viet Nam war. On the side of her father, Jean Lê Văn An, the family story of acquiring education and wealth under French colonial rule culminates with him, as the long-awaited and thus spoiled only boy in a family of six older girls. However, it is on her mother's side that Vi seems to find her true strength and strongest influence. Her description of her mother, Xuân, whose name means "printemps" (*Vi*, 18) [spring (9)], is telling: Xuân, who is not beautiful, having inherited "les gènes khmers de son père ... avait choisi de devenir une femme féroce, armée d'une volonté de fer et d'un vocabulaire dur, masculin" (*Vi*, 18) [her father's Khmer genes ... chose to become a woman who was fierce, armed with a will of iron and a hard, masculine vocabulary (9)]. An intelligent girl with a business acumen that leads her to contribute to the family's fortunes even though still an adolescent, Xuân manages her father's vacation rental properties in Đà Lạt, and meets and renders herself indispensable to Vi's father, whose family falls on hard times as a result of political reversals and ill health. Their improbable marriage is the complete opposite of the Confucian model, as Xuân, once she becomes Mrs Lê Văn An, is always in charge and keeps the family financially and socially stable despite the dissipation and indiscretions of Jean. As Vi will remark in discussing her efforts to live up to her name as a "microscopic girl, invisible" (Fischman translation, 22): "Si mon père avait été aussi invisible que moi à la fin de la guerre, il n'aurait pas été arrêté et envoyé dans un camp de rééducation" (*Vi*, 31) [If my father had been as invisible as me at the end of the war, he would not have been arrested and sent to a re-education camp (22)]. This wry observation highlights Vi's attitude toward her father, which contrasts greatly with her articulation of filial piety toward her mother.

Her maternal grandfather, she recounts, always reminded his daughters to emulate the legendary Trưng sisters, who appear in a chapter title, by becoming "indépendantes d'esprit et surtout combatives" (*Vi*, 27) [independent of mind and above all combative (18)]. In this way, we see that Vi understands and frames her mother's strength of character as a credit to her family and her country. Indeed, she will return to this point, stating, "Le succès d'un enfant appartient aux parents et à ses ancêtres. Chacun des membres de la famille est solidairement responsable de tous les autres" [The child's success belongs to his parents and ancestors. Every family member is responsible for all the others, out of solidarity] and must possess a "sens du devoir et ... la reconnaissance envers leur clan" (*Vi*, 60) [sense of duty and honouring of the clan (51)]. Once again, as in both *Ru* and *Mãn*, the daughter-narrator displays a stronger connection to her maternal influences and associates the mother's qualities with a reverence for literary or historical figures of women whose exemplary lives show resilience, strength of character, and filial or national devotion, where family and nation are understood to be virtually interchangeable facets of the same sense of duty. Of Thúy's first three novels, *Vi* shows most clearly the bilateral kinship model underscored by Hirschman and Vu in the article cited earlier: her maternal family ties and authority are shown to be present, operative, and respected, despite the prevailing Confucian model of patrilineal kinship on display in the male-obsessed attitudes of Vi's father's family.

Much as in *Mãn* and *Ru*, *Vi*'s protagonist also enjoys a mothering relationship with another woman, here a younger friend of Xuân's named Hà, who exerts a crucial influence on Vi's destiny and character, perhaps more important even than that of her biological mother. A former Miss Viet Nam beauty contestant initially presented as "la femme moderne à l'américaine" (*Vi*, 33) [the perfect modern woman in the American style (24)], Hà leaves Viet Nam and an abusive marriage with a Communist general at the same time as Vi's family, but on a different boat. She ends up in Denmark, where she becomes a massage therapist and meets Louis, who falls in love with her and with whom she moves to Canada. Reunited with Xuân and Vi after many years, Hà welcomes Vi for visits to Ottawa, also taking her to New York after Vi's mother "lui a donné la permission de s'occuper de [Vi] comme si j'étais sa fille" (*Vi*, 68) [gave her permission to look after [Vi] as if I were her daughter (59)], and, when Louis is posted to China, even inviting her to visit for summer vacation. In Shanghai, Louis and Hà's cook, A Yi, takes Vi "sous son aile parce que j'ai tendu mes deux mains pour recevoir sa tasse de thé avec l'humilité d'une enfant envers une aînée" (*Vi*, 71) [under her wing because I held [both][33] my hands out to her to receive a cup of tea with the humility of a child relating to an elder (62)]. Here again, we see one of Thúy's protagonists encountering multiple mother figures who guide her in her life and to whom she shows respect and gratitude.

However, Hà's influence, and in particular her admonition never to have regrets, leads Vi to do what no previous protagonist in Thúy's work does: "aller à l'encontre de la volonté de ma mère et de mes frères" (*Vi*, 85) [challeng[e] the authority of my mother and brothers (74)] by moving to Montreal to be with her older lover, Tân, and to study translation instead of pursuing a career in medicine. Although Vi's brothers continue to give her financial assistance, her pursuit of this relationship leads to condemnation from all quarters. Tân's parents, who are also Vietnamese immigrants, "m'ont convoquée pour passer en revue les us et coutumes vietnamiens en concluant avec un conseil paternel: 'Pense à la gratitude que tu dois à ta mère avant de continuer à l'humilier ainsi'" (*Vi*, 90) [summoned me for a lecture on Vietnamese customs and values, concluding with some parental advice: "Think of the gratitude you owe your mother before you keep humiliating her like this" (80)]. Xuân scolds her as well, saying, "J'ai raté ton éducation" (*Vi*, 90) [I failed in your education (80)]. When Vi goes to Berlin with Tân to celebrate the fall of the Wall, Vi knows that the "escapade ... constituait un manque d'égards envers mes ancêtres, ma culture et tous les efforts et les sacrifices de ma mère" (*Vi*, 93) [escapade ... represented a lack of respect for my ancestors, my culture, and all the struggles and sacrifices of my mother (83)]. When Vi finally breaks off her engagement, following Hà's advice not to get married too early, she admits she has both broken with tradition and broken hearts because she has become "trop occidentale" [too Western], adding, "Mon comportement avait détruit la réputation de deux familles parfaitement respectables ... J'ai brisé ma relation avec ma mère. J'ai brisé ma mère. Comme mon père l'avait brisée" (*Vi*, 96) [My behaviour had ruined the reputation of two perfectly respectable families ... I broke away from my mother. I broke my mother. As my father had broken her (86)]. This is a key moment in the story, a moment that represents a breakdown, perhaps in parallel to that of the Berlin Wall, as Vi hereby recognizes there is a price to pay for contravening cultural tradition. We see that she has in fact internalized the expectations placed on Vietnamese women, and, as a result of her failure to conform, she comes to see herself as betraying her mother just as her father had done by his weakness and lack of respect for Xuân.

Despite her failed engagement, Vi attains a law degree with support from her friend and classmate Jacinthe and lands a job in Viet Nam, where she meets her true love, Vincent, a French-born ecologist-ornithologist based in Hanoi. Vincent helps her appreciate the nuances of life in her birth country, which is no longer at all familiar to her and where even her ability to speak her mother tongue is put into question, given that the "langue vietnamienne que je connaissais était marquée par l'exil et figée dans une ancienne réalité, celle d'avant la présence des Soviétiques" (*Vi*, 100) [Vietnamese language I knew was marked by exile and trapped in an antiquated reality, one that preceded the Soviet presence (90)]. It is easy to see here the traces of

Thúy's own experience of returning to Viet Nam as a lawyer, earlier in her life. More important, though, is that Vi's relationship with Vincent gives her a new perspective on her relationship with Xuân and what her mother sacrificed to ensure the independence of her daughter. Xuân

> me répétait que, dans l'art de la guerre, la première leçon consistait à maîtriser sa disparition … j'avais toujours cru que ma mère préférait ses garçons par habitude, par amour pour mon père. L'écho de ma voix dans l'enceinte des bras de Vincent m'a finalement amenée à comprendre le désir de ma mère de me faire grandir autrement, de me lancer ailleurs, de me donner un destin différent du sien. Il m'a fallu deux continents et un océan pour saisir qu'elle avait dû forcer sa nature en acceptant de confier l'éducation de sa propre fille à Hà, une autre femme, loin d'elle, à l'opposé d'elle." (*Vi*, 118–19)

> [insisted that in the art of war, the first lesson consisted of mastering one's disappearance … I had always thought that my mother preferred her boys out of habit, out of love for my father. My voice echoing in the circle of Vincent's arms finally led me to understand my mother's desire to have me grow up differently, to launch myself elsewhere, to offer myself a fate different from her own. It took me two continents and an ocean to grasp that she had had to go against her nature to entrust the education of her own daughter to Hà, another woman, far away from her, and her exact opposite. (108–9)]

In this moment, the shame Vi has experienced at disappointing her mother and her brothers transforms into acceptance of her destiny and appreciation for what she now sees as a deliberate abnegation rather than a failure of nurturance on Xuân's part, in allowing her daughter to be influenced by a second mother, one who encourages a life with no regrets, including those that come of bucking the tradition of submission and respect for one's parents.

In the end, Vi's story of exile from country and from family is one of successive losses. Even her return to Viet Nam as a legal professional happens under the sign of loss: loss of language and culture, loss of traditions, and ultimately the loss of Vincent, because he does not return to Hanoi after being recalled to France by his grandmother's failing health. As Vi observes, "j'avais perdu mes quatre grands-parents et … je n'avais pas cherché à revoir mon père depuis mon retour au Vietnam. Mon histoire avait été coupée, réinventée. Aucun objet chez ma mère ou chez moi ne portait la trace des générations, contrairement à l'autel des ancêtres qui était témoin de tous les mariages, des anniversaires des morts, de la cérémonie du premier jour de l'an depuis au moins cent ans" (*Vi*, 131) [I had lost my four grandparents, and had not tried to see my father again since my return to Vietnam. My story had been cut short, reinvented. No object of my mother's or mine spoke of the generations, unlike the altar of the ancestors that bore witness to all marriages, anniversaries of deaths, of New Year's ceremonies going back at least a hundred years (121–2)]. When Vincent disappears, Vi also knows her mother "serait détruite d'apprendre que sa fille vivait le même destin, la même histoire, le même abandon qu'elle" (*Vi*, 135) [would be shattered to learn that her daughter was living the same fate, the same story, the same abandonment, as herself (126)]. In the end, then, Vi chooses to spare her mother the pain of this knowledge, swearing her friends to secrecy, and in so doing, she returns to the model of self-sacrifice and silence that so many of Viet Nam's mythic women exemplify. When the sacred tortoise "apportant de bonnes nouvelles, selon les croyances" (*Vi*, 139) [bringing good tidings, according to belief (130)] reappears in the "Lake of the Restored Sword" as Vi meets her friends to say goodbye at a café on the shore,[34] the reader understands that what is "restored," in part, is Vi's own relationship to her cultural traditions and respect for family. It seems telling that the word "croyances," a belief to which Vi herself longs to return, is the final word in the novel. Her loves and her losses have helped her understand and recover her respect for her mother enough not to increase Xuân's disappointments and suffering. While the novel does not reveal what Vi will do after leaving Viet Nam, it does underscore that Vi's period of abandonment of her mother and her teachings is also ending; even as she "hésite à [s]'enfuir du Vietnam une seconde fois" (*Vi*, 138) [hesitate[s] to escape Vietnam a second time (129)], she clearly feels a renewed attachment to and respect for both her parents. She has forgiven both of them for their mistakes and their failures of one another and herself, and she has recognized in that their full, and shared, humanity.

Although Vi is the only protagonist who openly flaunts the filial piety expected of her, the fact that the novel itself makes much of that expectation does reinscribe its importance to Vietnamese family culture, as in *Ru* and *Mãn*. Moreover, Vi's realization of her mother's sacrifice, in encouraging Hà's influence on her daughter, leads to the same appreciation for mother figures that emerges in Thúy's first two novels. In all three books, it does not matter if these figures are biological mothers, adoptive mothers, or merely women whose nurturing ways help the narrators build new lives, even as they recall and respect their histories and Vietnamese values. While there are no goddesses here per se, for mothers can often be cold, mistaken, or misunderstood, there is a strong sense in Thúy's novels that she is trying to educate her implied non-Vietnamese readers about Vietnamese respect for ancestors, and particularly for the sacrifices of the women who have gone before, who are shown a reverence that echoes goddess worship but that also leaves room for understanding the courage and intent inherent in their failures. Her vision is not one of critiquing a patriarchal mother, or a feminist paean to the pioneers who broke with tradition, but rather a portrayal of mother-daughter relationships that allows for imperfect mothering, disagreements, and a gradually developing understanding of the mother and her cultural and experiential legacy by the daughter.

Unlike her first three novels, the first-person narrator of Thúy's *Em* is not the protagonist but rather a self-identified writer who frames the task of telling the multiple stories of war orphans that are woven into the novel's narrative by identifying the writing challenge most clearly at the book's opening, in the chapter "Un début de vérité" (*Em*, 9) ["A Genesis of Truth" (1)], and near its conclusion, in "Des vérités sans fin" (*Em*, 127) ["Truths without End" (127)]. Tâm is the first of these orphans, "l'enfant du maître et de son ouvrière, de deux ennemis" (*Em*, 24) [child of the master and his labourer, two enemies (16)] who are both killed in an insurgent attack on the colonizer's rubber plantation. She is rescued and raised by her nanny, "devenue *de facto* sa mère" (*Em*, 26) [her de facto mother (18)], and then rescued again by an American soldier after the nanny's entire village is slaughtered in the My Lai massacre during the Viet Nam war. Louis is the second orphan, raised in the street where he learns to "différencier l'odeur de ses mères d'un jour" (*Em*, 64) [differentiate the perfumes of his mothers-for-a-day (61)], another situation of multiple non-biological caregivers, enumerated in a chapter titled "Les mères de Louis" (*Em*, 64) ["Louis's Mothers" (61)]. He in turn becomes the caregiver to an abandoned baby he calls em Hồng, where *em* means a younger sibling, as the explanation at the novel's opening tells us. One day while Louis is absent, em Hồng is discovered by Naomi, an aid worker, and she in turn ensures that the baby is evacuated as part of Operation Babylift before the North's takeover. Em Hồng is then renamed Emma-Jade by her American adoptive parents, while Louis gets adopted as a refugee in Guam by Tâm and her Montreal historian husband, Isaac. It is not until the end of the novel that we discover em Hồng/Emma-Jade is in fact Tâm's biological daughter and that Louis and Emma-Jade end up meeting again by chance and revisiting their childhood haunts in Viet Nam as a couple. Of these strangely crossed destinies and stories of mothering that defy biology, nationality, and gender, the writer-narrator affirms, "J'ai cherché à tisser les fils, mais ils se sont échappés pour rester sans ancrage, impermanents et libres. Ils se réarrangent par eux-mêmes selon la vitesse du vent, selon les nouvelles qui défilent, selon les inquiétudes et les sourires de mes fils" (*Em*, 128) [I tried to interweave the threads, but they escaped, and remain unanchored, impermanent and free. They rearranged themselves on their own, given the speed of the wind, the news streaming by, the worries and smiles of my sons (129)]. In this way, *Em*'s narrator reveals she is a mother too in a play on the French word "fils," which can mean thread or son (but is pronounced differently for each usage); the threads and offspring of her story, while connected, are somehow also disconnected, or rootless, due to their experiences of being orphaned, which, in the end, draw them into unpredictable familial configurations. In this way, *Em* takes the theme of many mothers into uncharted territory but still reinforces the importance of playing that role from one generation to the next.

Kurmann and Do see in what they call "1.5 generation narrators" imagined by Vietnamese expatriate writers an effort to "suture a tear in the fabric of their familial memory."[35] This is certainly true for Thúy's narrators: An Tịnh, Mãn, and Vi all grow to appreciate what their mothers have given them, their similarities to them and their differences from them, in a non-dichotomous process of identity formation that allows room for both mothers and daughters to cultivate their own style of mothering and to respect one another's life choices. The daughters who narrate this process, however, all show a need to recall and recover the memories that shed light on what their various mothers, *mẹ* or *má hai*, have sacrificed or given them. They are "suturing the tear" in their families' stories that war and migration have produced, by stitching together the pieces of their families' histories and trajectories that their fragmented narratives clearly represent. The wandering threads that emerge from the box in Louis Boudreault's artwork that graces the Libre Expression edition's cover of *Em* are an eloquent figuration of how Thúy's narratives flow variously from their Vietnamese source, be that the familiar structure of the traditional family or the dark secrets of an orphan's origins and the mysterious lifelines that ensure such a child's survival.

In her pioneering 1989 book on what she calls the "mother/daughter plot," Marianne Hirsch suggests "that if we start our study of the subject with *mothers* rather than with *children* a different conception of subjectivity might emerge."[36] This is, in a sense, what I have shown Thúy does, in my analysis of her many fictional mothers and their daughters, who, as culturally hybrid women in Quebec, learn to move forward, in the words of An Tịnh, "dans la trace de leurs pas comme dans un rêve éveillé où le parfum d'une pivoine éclose n'est plus une odeur, mais un épanouissement … où un pays n'est plus un lieu, mais une berceuse" (*Ru*, 144) [in the trace of their footsteps as in a waking dream where the scent of a newly blown poppy[37] is no longer a perfume but a blossoming … where a country is no longer a place but a lullaby (140)]. Both mothers and the mother country are precisely what is evoked in the traditional poem I quoted at the beginning of this chapter, and, indeed, this poem has been set to music and is familiar as a lullaby to many Vietnamese.[38] I return to this poem because the soothing presence of the "eternal spring" of women's compassion, worthy of a filial piety and respect that exactly parallels or echoes the feelings of appreciation for one's traditional culture, is what ultimately emerges from Thúy's novels. Even when the daughter moves on and accepts her difference and distance from that model, Thúy shows she does this, in the end, even while preserving an enduring veneration for the many mothers who give her the capacity to become who she is destined to be and survive the many losses that are inevitable in life. Like the sweet taste of the rambutans in the photo of Thúy and her mother in *Le Secret des Vietnamiennes*, Thúy's fictions first seduce us with their foreign allure and then engage us with their complex female characters whose formative relationships with their many mothers both touch us and teach us about their specific cultural identity and their universal humanity. Whether we are born with them or acquire them as we move through life, Thúy's writing reminds us how much the many "mothers" we come to know contribute to the flavour and texture of our lives.

NOTES

1 Santoro, *Mothers of Invention.*

2 The translation of the cookbook's title picks up on this plurality of mothers in its subtitle: *Secrets from My Vietnamese Kitchen: Simple Recipes from My Many Mothers.*

3 Quoted in Phạm and Eipper, "Mothering and Fathering the Vietnamese," 75, 49 (the original Vietnamese text of the traditional folk poem and its translation, respectively). For an analysis of this text, its interpretation, and its translation, see Nguyên Van Ky, "Rethinking the Status of Vietnamese Women."

4 According to the United Nations and to the government of Viet Nam's official website, the name for the country is two words: Viet Nam. This volume respects this practice except when quoting sources that show it as one word, such as Sheila Fischman's translations of Thúy's novels.

5 Thúy, "Habiller le vécu de mots et d'images," 171. All translations are mine unless otherwise indicated.

6 *Ru* won the Grand prix littéraire Archambault, the Prix Premio Mondello per la Multiculturalità, the Grand Prix RTL-Lire, and the Governor General's Literary Award for the best novel in French in 2010.

7 Indeed, in 2018, she achieved the distinction of being one of the five finalists for the New Academy Prize in Literature in Sweden. The Nobel Prize in Literature was not awarded in 2018 due to controversy over the conduct of one of the committee members. The New Academy Prize, established to compensate for the missing Nobel, was ultimately awarded to Maryse Condé. It should be noted that this "replacement" prize invited popular voting on a list of authors suggested by Swedish librarians, so it was decidedly more democratic and transparent than the Nobel prize process and can therefore be seen as a mark of an author's international popularity.

8 For a discussion on how gratitude expressed to the host society affects a novel's and author's success, see Vinh Nguyen, "Refugee Gratitude."

9 Ibid., 27.

10 Rye, *Narratives of Mothering*, 17–18.

11 Chartier, *Dictionnaire des écrivains émigrés au Québec*, 7.

12 Phạm and Eipper, "Mothering and Fathering the Vietnamese," 50, 55.

13 Ibid., 53.

14 According to historian K.W. Taylor, Ngo Quyen trapped the Southern Han fleet in the Bach Dang River estuary late in 938 and went on to claim royal status in the wake of the vacuum left by the Han dynasty's defeat (*A History of the Vietnamese*, 44–7).

15 Chihiro, "Rethinking Vietnamese Women's Property Rights," 59. See also Chan, *Vietnamese American 1.5 Generation*, 6.
16 Hirschman and Vu, "Family and Household Structure in Vietnam," 232.
17 See Soucy, "Vietnamese Warriors, Vietnamese Mothers."
18 Ibid., 123.
19 Taylor, "The Goddess, the Ethnologist, the Folklorist and the Cadre," 388, 386.
20 Ibid., 392.
21 Kurmann and Do, "Children on the Boat," 225.
22 Thúy, "Habiller le vécu de mots et d'images," 174.
23 Chaudey, "Kim Thuy raconte sa renaissance," n.p.
24 See Kim Thúy, *Ru* (Montreal: Libre Expression, 2009), 23, 29, 30, 60, 62, 63, 70, 71.
25 Kim Thúy, *Ru* (Montreal: Libre Expression, 2009), 11; Thúy, *Ru*, trans. Sheila Fischman (Toronto: Random House Canada, 2012), 1. All subsequent citations from *Ru* refer to these editions. The original French is given in quotation marks, followed by page number(s) in parentheses, and the English translation appears in square brackets after the French original, with only the page number in parentheses.
26 Taylor, "The Goddess, the Ethnologist, the Folklorist and the Cadre," 392.
27 Vietnamese offspring are given numbers dependent on their birth order, with Number Two being the oldest child of each gender. Hence, in this novel, we read of Uncle Two and Auntie Seven, for example, both siblings of the narrator's mother.
28 Women who were left behind and had to persist after the war are portrayed in the novel *Le Mirage de la paix* by Ly Thu Ho.
29 Thúy, "Habiller le vécu de mots et d'images," 171.
30 Kim Thúy, *Mãn* (Montreal: Libre Expression, 2013), 34; Thúy, *Mãn*, trans. Sheila Fischman (Toronto: Random House Canada, 2014), 27. All subsequent quotations from *Mãn* are from these editions. Following the original French, passages from the Fischman translation appear in square brackets, with page numbers in parentheses.
31 This sentence does not appear in the English version of the novel. The translation is mine.
32 Kim Thúy, *Vi* (Montreal: Libre Expression, 2016), 30; Thúy, *Mãn*, trans. Sheila Fischman (Toronto: Vintage Canada, 2019), 21. All future references to *Vi* are from these editions. Quotations from the English translation by Fischman are placed in square brackets, with page numbers in parentheses, after the original French.

33 The published translation does not include the word "both," but since this is key to the humility and courtesy of the gesture, I have added it here.
34 The establishment referenced here is likely the Thủy Tạ café in Hanoi, located on the northern edge of the lake.
35 Kurmann and Do, "Children on the Boat," 219.
36 Hirsch, *Mother/Daughter Plot*, 197.
37 It should be noted that the original French speaks of a peony, not a poppy. Given that peonies have an extraordinarily seductive scent, one wonders if the translator's choice of poppy is motivated more by its association with dreams than by its perfume. To my mind, this seems dangerously close to evoking stereotypes of opium addiction, which is not something Thúy is suggesting here.
38 See Phạm and Eipper, "Mothering and Fathering the Vietnamese."

7

Chasing Beauty

An Interview with Kim Thúy

Miléna Santoro

What follows is an edited version of interviews recorded by Miléna Santoro with Kim Thúy in June of 2019, March of 2020, and April of 2020, with transcription assistance by Jack A. Yeager and Ashwiny O. Kistnareddy. The translation of the April 2020 interview in French was completed by Jack A. Yeager. Some words are not translated because they were in French in our English conversations. In such cases, the translations will be in brackets or will be furnished by the context.

Miléna Santoro (MS): Why it is that some of your novels, when they are first published, have titles with all lowercase letters, like *ru*, but in later editions they [the publishers] capitalize the first letter? Is there a reason why they changed the typography of the title or should it be all lowercase for all three of your novels?

Kim Thúy (KT): I want lowercase for everything. But I think it was the decision of the graphic designer. I did ask for lowercase in Quebec, but once it's out there, each publisher has their own way. I don't want to have a say in it, because they know their market better and it has to fit with their catalogue. Some of them kept the lower case, but, for example, in Germany they changed it completely. The title is *Der Klang der Fremde.*[1] The only publisher I have control over is the one in Montreal, because they are close to me and they don't know how to say no to me anymore. But all the other ones I would say that I just leave everything to them because they know what they're doing.

I love the fact that the book could be interpreted in so many different ways. It's the same book inside, but each country, each culture, reads it from a different angle and I would say according to their cultural references. I will show you the different covers and you will see that from Bulgaria, it's pink, pink, pink, and then in Sweden, it's so quiet. But it's the same book. For the translation published in Ukraine, it has a really very busy cover, which is almost contrary to the text. It works for the aesthetics of the country though, because as soon as you arrive in the city you recognize the combination of colours. Sweden or Finland would choose colours in a very different way. That's why we have the colours of IKEA: as soon as you look at it, you know it's IKEA because of the combination of the colours. And you know, for cuisine it's the same thing, we basically use the same ingredients, like pork, shrimp, chicken, whatever. But the Asians would combine pork and shrimp at the same time, in the same pan, whereas here we have surf and turf. They are served separately. We don't cook them together, whereas in Asia, we mix those things together and it does give a different taste to it. The ingredients are the same, it's just how we mix it. And that's why I love the fact that each country would give their translation a different colour, as it fits with where *ru* got adopted.

MS: You said in an interview with Plamondon that you had written *ru* for your sons,[2] and I wondered if you could talk more about what that motivation was, what motivates you to write, and if there are specific incidents or triggers that inspired you to write.

KT: I think I did intellectualize everything afterwards, you know. Journalists would give me answers and I would steal these answers from them and give them to the next journalist. You become more and more intelligent over time because they analyze you, they understand you better. But the truth of the matter was that I just enjoyed writing. It was for nobody. It was just a hobby I would say. It's like knitting. To me it's exactly the same thing: baking a cake or writing; it's the same kind of pleasure. But I'm not good at baking cakes because I cannot follow a recipe! I love writing in the same way that I love any hobby.

MS: When you came to Georgetown you said that you had started writing *ru* when you were driving, and that you would write at stoplights, waiting for the light to change, right?

KT: Yes! It was really just to stay awake.[3] There was no intention behind *ru*. Even now, all the other books, they have no intention.

MS: So how are the ideas born? Where do they come from?

KT: It's just like that. When you walked in, I had a zillion stories to tell you.[4] Because I find them so beautiful, I have to share them with somebody. I cannot keep them just for me. It's not that I feel selfish for keeping them for me, but they are so beautiful, so we should all celebrate, like clapping at the end of a play. You just want to clap because it's so beautiful. Or tears roll down on your cheeks, just because it's beautiful. And so writing to me is that. I have no other intentions other than to share that beauty. I think I have this disease of being amazed all the time, or fascinated.

MS: I think it's not a disease, it's a rare gift, that of perceiving beauty and being able to share it. Do you think you have this kind of hypersensitivity for a specific reason? Do you think it's born out of adversity?

KT: No. I really think that everybody sees the same way that I do. That's why I cannot write any dialogue. Because I don't know how the other person could think differently. I instinctively think everybody sees the same thing as me. The same beauty. That they would be fascinated by the same people, by the same facts, and yet I realize that it's not always true. My husband is not at all fascinated by the stories I have to tell him. As I grow, I kind of understand now that not everybody sees the same way that I do.

MS: But I think a lot of people do and that's why they respond to your books; they are brought to see the beauty that you see, by the language that you put it in, that gives it shape, and they somehow are brought to see the world through your eyes.

KT: Probably. Maybe they don't have time to see it, and I just go, "Look! Look!" You know, I would drive to go look at one tree. One in particular, because it's just perfect. It's the most perfect magnolia tree I have ever seen. Every season we would walk to it, and just stand and look at the tree. Friends have been living in this neighbourhood for a long time, but never noticed that one tree. But when you stop and look at it, you get amazed as well. That's the problem we have today. We have distanced ourselves, so much, from beauty.

I saw a news story about this man who founded a company that has become huge. He is retired, and so he hired a new CEO. The new CEO wanted to change the structure, cut jobs, and so on. The founder said, "OK, you can do all this, on one condition: you will have to be the one who fires the first ten people yourself." This guy, after firing the ten people, he went back to the founder and he said, "You were right, I am sorry, we have to change our plans. I cannot cut all the jobs." Why? Because when we sit down and we take time to look at a human being, we find the human beautiful. We find the beauty in that person, right? And that hurts you, to kill beauty. I am sure if we say to the president of Brazil right now, "You want to cut down all the trees, but the first ten trees, you have to do it yourself," and if you find yourself in that beauty, that grandeur of those trees, and also experience the struggle for you to cut down those trees, because it's not easy to cut down a tree, especially big trees – you have to sweat a lot! – and to spend time in that forest – I think he would change his mind. And that's the thing: if we see beauty, we cannot remain indifferent. Impossible. So that's what we need to do. To expose people to beauty all the time.

That's our problem nowadays. It's easy to make a mean comment on social media because you don't see the person. But I am sure if you see the person, you feel their fragility, you feel that there's something about that person that would speak to you. There's nobody that has nothing to say to you. You can relate to any other human.

MS: I want to talk about this question of beauty, which feeds into a question about your novels, because they often start with the narrator as a child living through traumatic or difficult experiences, and yet the writing does not focus on the trauma. It focuses on moments of beauty that happen within this experience of trauma, within a difficult time. So, why write from the perspective of a child who speaks about these experiences? And does the fact that it's a child affect the choice not to dwell on the negative? Or is it in fact your impulse to always seek beauty that dominates?

KT: You know, I am fifty years old, and somehow in my mind I am still a child. I think because in Vietnamese – I speak Vietnamese mostly with my parents – we don't have personal pronouns. When I speak to them, I am always "child" speaking, father-child-mother. The word "child" is used every day a thousand times at least, in every sentence. So, I am always "child" to my parents and to my aunts. I speak in French to my children, so I would use a pronoun. In French, I never call myself "mother" speaking to "child." But I am always "child" in Vietnamese and so I think when I write about these moments in Viet Nam and when we arrived here, I am still always "child."

MS: That's fascinating. It seems your language shapes how you come to writing.

KT: Absolutely, and there's research now that proves that language totally influences how you think. Like in Russian you have many, many nuances for "blue" while in Viet Nam you have only one word for both "blue" and "green." And if you want to specify you have to [also] say *sắc* "sky" or *xanh* "leaf." But it's the same word. And so, I tested this on a Vietnamese friend who speaks English, and I said, "Can you tell me if it's blue or green?" It took her a while, because her mind was not shaped to say it, whereas the research has shown that if you show the blue to a Russian, they would see the nuances very quickly. We would go only "blue," while they would have indigo blue, turquoise blue. They see the nuances because they have the words for them. For sure language does shape the way you think.

We have talked about this before: Vietnamese doesn't have tenses. We're always in the infinitive and so it helps us to be in the present all the time. Because you don't have a *passé simple*, a *plus-que-parfait*, a *passé composé*, I don't know on a timeline where the *passé simple* is or the *passé composé*, with respect to the *imparfait*.

MS: So that must have been very hard when you had to learn French.

KT: It's still hard today. And there are theses about this, about people who come from languages without tenses, like Vietnamese or Chinese, because we cannot grasp that idea of tenses. Of course we can learn, but it doesn't come naturally. And so for French to have *futur antérieur*: How can you be in the front and in the back at the same time? At the same time, the French language illustrates the capacity of our brain to be that sophisticated. That's so beautiful.

MS: It's interesting, as I think Vietnamese expresses its beauty and its nuance and its sophistication by the tonal differences.

KT: Exactly, we have a vertical language. French and English are horizontal languages. You just add more sounds and you have a new word, whereas we would change the tone to have a new word.

MS: At different moments in your books you use *mẹ* and also *má* to speak of Mom, of mothers. Why do you use one or the other of the Vietnamese words to designate mother?

KT: In Vietnamese you can use both. As for example, I call my mother *mẹ* while my mother calls her mother *má*. I believe it's the choice of the mother. My mother calls herself *mẹ* and since then it's been *mẹ*, whereas for me, I chose "Mom."

MS: Would aunts who play a bit of the role of mother also call themselves *mẹ*?

KT: No, my cousins call my mother *má ba*, so "Mom 3." And there are others in the family that call the other aunts "*má* …" with a number attached. But for myself, I don't call any of them *má*, probably because I'm the daughter of the eldest [of the sisters] whereas the children of my aunts younger than my mother call my mother "Mom 3," but the children of my Uncle 2, who is older, call her "Aunt 3." Used according to the birth order, it's the children of the younger ones who call the elder ones *má*.

MS: Is it the same for the papas?

KT: No! And it's because of that that I don't call my uncle "Papa 2." It's really the mothers and it's in explaining this to you that I've just understood it. My mother, she has the right [of seniority] over all my cousins. And the second is going to be the matriarch of the younger ones, and the third, of the ones younger than she.

MS: Do questions of language influence why you choose titles for your books that come from Vietnamese, and while they may sometimes have a resonance in French, the Vietnamese word for you has a strong specificity?

KT: Yes, it has a meaning. It has an image. To me, when I look at "vi," I see *small*. The Vietnamese language was [written in] Chinese [characters], so it was created according to images and ideas.

MS: And that's why there's a passage in the book when you are talking about Chinese ideograms, to remind us that there is an image behind the word.

KT: Yes, whereas in the English and French languages you do not have images, only sounds. The problem with Vietnamese today is that the French, who "alphabetized" the Vietnamese language, also took away all the images.[5] So we changed it to the alphabet: in a, b, c, there's no image. There are no ideas in the shape of an a. It's very abstract. It's like a mathematical sign of some sort. Whereas the origins of the Vietnamese language were based on the images and ideas. And so the Vietnamese language is totally crooked. Damaged. Distorted. The language that was supposed to be in images is now expressed in symbols.[6] It is still a monosyllabic language. We cannot add syllables to make new words. So you see, the problem of identity is right there. In the language.

MS: And then of course, as you talk about quite often in your novels, the words used in the North and the South are quite different, so that when the country was reunified under the Northern Vietnamese, then there was a whole set of vocabulary that came with their life experience that didn't really apply to your life experience.

KT: Exactly. Language evolves. The word for computer didn't exist forty years ago or even thirty years ago. It was not used by people, normal citizens, in daily life. "Computer" is totally a new word, "environment" is a new word that didn't exist before the seventies, before we left Viet Nam. So that word was created after we left the country. You have to continue to create new words for the new reality. Today, because we can identify all these nuances of being, we can describe reality with more precision, for which we have to create new words. The beauty of language is that ... we keep on giving precision to reality. To the different realities that we live.

Here's the best example. If you live in Canada, the person who talks about the weather, they have so many words to describe different types of snow, and competition skiers have even more words to describe if it is icy, or whatever. But in Vietnamese you have one word. We know snow exists somewhere, but we only have one word. But that's it! We've never touched it, never seen it, so it's just snow. A language describes so much the geography of a place, if you look at it. And now, if I write a book in French or in Vietnamese, I would have many words for snow, because I have lived somewhere else. I have seen it. So I will talk about *les bancs de neige* [snowdrifts] or *le gel* [freezing temperatures] and so you can enrich the language by exporting an idea or an experience.

MS: I am interested in having you speak to the sense of present and past in Vietnamese culture.

KT: I think that because of the tenses, in Vietnamese culture we don't have a "past" in that sense. To me – but I don't know if it is true for all Vietnamese – I think that if you still remember, if you still are carrying something today, it's because it is in the present. And when I write, it's not about going into my past. It's about what is still here. What is in the present. If I talk about Estonia, while there were many people I met, there is one person who really touched me, who I want to talk about. So, if I sit down to write about her, I see her again. I can smell her, I can feel her, I can see how she moves her hands. So she's not in the past, she's in the present ... we always associate memory as something in the past, but no, memory is what you have *now*. So, our ancestors are not from the past, they are in us, they are with us, every single step of the way. And we carry them just above our heads. And that's why we cannot touch the head of a Vietnamese person because *they* are still *there* [gestures with a hand just above her head]. Without them we don't have the life that we have today. And so they are part of this life, they are present. That's why it's very difficult to separate the past from the present. It's one block.

MS: So tell me the story about the fellow who asked you if writing was like meditation for you.

KT: It was in Calgary. He is Vietnamese, and he says to me that he had read my book and he thought the book was so silent. And then he met me on stage and he couldn't put the two of us together. There was such a contradiction between me in person and me in writing. So he said, "Is it because writing is a form of meditation for you?" And frankly, I don't know what meditation is. I don't have time for it. Why would I want to chase away my thoughts? If I have a thought, it's a gift! I want to keep it! I want to celebrate it! My question to him was, "Where do you go when you meditate?" And, in the room, k.d. lang[7] was there, and I didn't know it. So she answered, and she said, "Meditation is about stopping your thoughts." And so I said, "Then no, writing to me is not about stopping my thoughts, it's about chasing my thoughts." You know, it's like when you wake up from a dream, and you try to remember, and that's what I do, when I write. I try to remember as many details as I can, so that you can live the same moment that I have lived, that I want to share. So, it's about chasing my thoughts, and like I said, I don't have many thoughts, so when I have one, I am just happy to own one! For sure, I want to keep it, and register it, and, if that thought would lead to another thought ... it's true that in order to do that, you need to be alone and not talking, to write. But I would say that my thoughts come to me much more when I talk about them to someone else. Somehow, by talking, one idea leads to the next. There's nothing I don't want to remember. I want to remember everything. As much as I can. But, you know, my head is limited. And my memory is fading. So, I try to remember as much as I can about everything, about conversations, about an earring, about whatever.

MS: To that point, I wanted to ask you what role silence plays for you – what is silenced and what is allowed to come through when you write. Isn't there also a cultural impetus toward discretion? In your novels, you talk about how love is not spoken, it might be shown, but not spoken. So, there are some things that don't get put into words. There are silences that are expressive.

KT: That's where we misunderstand Asia, or Asian culture. We think that, oh, they're so quiet. They don't express themselves, you know the cliché. No, actually: I think whatever idea we have, or that we want to make happen, we will find ways to make it happen, or to talk about things without ever naming them. We will never say "orgasm," for example. But there are a thousand other ways to talk about orgasm. That's why poetry plays a great part in Vietnamese culture. Because people will talk with images, that are not the exact words; we don't name the thing but that doesn't mean we don't get there. Or that we don't want it.

MS: Have you read a lot of Vietnamese poetry? There are revered Vietnamese poetic epics, like the *Tale of Kiều*. Are these part of your influences?

KT: I haven't read a lot, in my life, altogether. But the few that I have listened to or read, I love. For example, in a poem there's this guy who was waiting for his love, but he knows that she doesn't want him, so the poem is about him walking in a garden with the flowers falling to the ground, and he asks for an appointment or rendezvous, saying "I know you won't come." It's a passive-aggressive way of doing things, but that's the Asian way. You will find a way to make the other person understand what you need without you saying it.

MS: In *Vi*, at the end of the story, we understand that Vincent is not going to come back, and there's that point in the final chapters where the protagonist goes to the orphanage and it's while she's at the orphanage that she starts to think about the future without Vincent. But none of that is said explicitly. It's never said that she thinks "I know he's gone forever."

KT: No. Whereas in a normal book, someone will say or the author will write: he is not coming back. Or the protagonist will say, "I think he is not going to come back." Or, "I don't understand why he has disappeared." Whereas in *Vi*, nobody says it, but everybody understands. And it's the same thing with the father, the idea that Vi should see the father again: nobody says anything. But the father has done everything to make her come back. All those pictures, and then to have his friend talk about it, without pushing her, but at the same time, they are making the path so narrow that you have to go back. And so that's a Vietnamese way. The subtext is *so* important. So I think that's why you hear so many silences.

MS: So the silences leave space for understanding.

KT: Yes, absolutely. And that's what you need to read. I will give you one story and you will see how vicious we are! I don't know if it's the right word … but my parents have guests very often. They have taken care of the children since they were little. And there will never be enough ways to say thank you to them, the gratitude that I owe them. And so, it is normal that I would go and help out. But as soon as Justin was a little bit older, and could do it, I said, you have to go. I can go, and that would make my parents quite proud, that I take care of them in front of their friends. But if I send Justin, that's one more generation down, and still taking care of them. That means a great education on our part, in the caring and all that comes with it. So Justin would go and would pick up a couple of bowls, whatever, nothing really. And I still remember that first time he came back, and I asked him, "How did it go?" And of course, nobody let him do anything. But he just showed up, right? But he said that my parents didn't even react. They did not even stop, acknowledging him in front of their friends, or saying, "Oh, you don't have to do it, we'll take care of it." But my parents didn't react at all, so he came back, very disappointed. And I said, "No, it is not the way for Vietnamese to say thank you. That's not how we do it." But I didn't have the exact explanation. Later, after the evening, my mom came, and she said, "Huh, you know, they were all jealous of me, for how my grandson came." And she said she didn't react at all, because if she reacted, it would indicate it was something new, or unusual. But she made as if it was normal: "my grandson does this all the time." So, it's in the silences, which can be very precise!

And it still persists today, in the sense that Asians don't begin to express their emotions openly [making large gestures in the air], there is no saying "I love you." So how do you express it? We do it through food. That's why food has truly become a kind of instrument for expressing emotions. I'm speaking of Asian culture, but it's obvious that I believe it also exists in other cultures. And I believe that your parents are still happy to cook something for you. And when you eat something homemade, it's so much better than going out. Why do we call a stew "comfort food"? Why are there dishes that are called "comfort foods"? I really believe that is because those dishes take time to cook. When you eat, you eat time. You eat the attention that person paid, reserved to make that dish for you. And it's because of that, that fast food fills us up, but we are never satisfied. We never feel like saying "ahhh, satisfying." It's filling, even stuffs us, it's fast, and why? Because with fast food, we know subliminally that it took no time. There was no attention, no "caring" about the dish. And that's why food will always succeed in expressing [our emotions] well. When we are sick, why does soup, chicken soup, do us a lot of good? Because it takes a lot of time to make chicken soup. For Asians, it's not chicken soup, it's congee. Rice congee. Once again, why? Because it takes a lot of time to make congee. An Asian mom is going to say, if you are sick, you must eat congee. And a Canadian or Western mom is going to say chicken broth. Even though neither one has cured anyone! But it's the "comfort" or the fact that you eat the attention the person gave you. So food is very important is that sense.

MS: I want to come back to your definition of writing as a form of chasing after beauty.

KT: Writing for me is just telling a beautiful story. Writing is just about beauty. That's it. Beauty of the words, beauty of that thing that I live again. We think that in violence there is no beauty, but actually, there is. In the sense that we have to bring out the beauty that we lose in violence. We have to bring out the beauty that we lose in war. Because very often we don't pay attention to beauty until we lose it. Our face, we don't pay attention to it until we get burned. Then, all of a sudden, you're going to pay attention to that blue eye, that one blue eye that is left. Or that ear that is still unburned, whereas usually we don't even pay attention to the shape of our ear. So, I think writing is about that. It's about bringing out the beauty that we've lost, and the beauty that remains, because of what's gone.

I learned that from Tim O'Brien. Do you know that author? He wrote a book called *The Things They Carried*. If you don't have the time to read the whole book, read at least the chapter called "How to Tell a True War Story." It's magnificent. I've reread it about fifty times in my life. He described an image, how the soldiers, when they were on patrol, would always walk single file, one in back of the other, to avoid bombs and mines. So he described a moment when he was walking and a soldier, one of his buddies, stepped on a mine. Everyone knew very well what was going to happen a second later. That is, that the body was going to be torn apart with blood spurting all over. But he says that in spite of that knowledge in the brain, your eyes can't help but see an instant of beauty when the soldier raises his foot and the pressure of the mine [exploding] projects him into the air and the body of the soldier is suspended like an angel. For a fraction of a second. A split second. Even if you know the horror to come, your eyes can't help but see the beauty.

I wrote the image of that little boy who got killed in that rice field during the war, and yet the wind continues to blow those rice shoots, the grass still moves to the rhythm of the wind. But the beauty we have lost is right there. And what remains is that life continues. If I didn't describe the grass, and I only described the boy being killed, I don't think it would touch you as much. Because we are touched by beauty first. We have never been killed. We have never had our sons or daughters killed in front of our eyes. We cannot relate. You will not feel related to horror if you don't have any references. So you need something that you know. And I know that beauty is something all of us have known. That's the common denominator of humans.

If, in life, you don't allow yourself to see that beauty, you will not manage to find beauty or to create beauty. There are two pictures that have marked me. During the Viet Nam war there were many, many, many pictures. There may be more pictures of that war than of any other at the time. But of all those pictures, there is one that has marked everyone's imaginary. It's the one of the little girl running in the middle of the highway, after being burned by napalm.[8] And that photo, when you know the context, yes, it's horrible. But I believe that picture struck everyone's imaginary because first, it is above all beautiful. The framing is perfect, the little girl with her arms outstretched like this: the image in itself is beautiful, objectively. It catches our eye and once it has done that, it's too late. We fall into the trap, we are obligated to understand what the photo represented. And so horror may arrive thanks to beauty, through beauty's door.

The second picture, more contemporary, would be the one with the crisis of the Syrians who arrived in Europe; you remember the little boy in a red T-shirt on the beach?[9] There have been so many photos of migrants, but why did that one change our point of view on the migration of Syrians? It's because first the photo in itself is beautiful above all. The little boy doesn't look like he's suffering. He looks like he's sleeping. So that could have been our nephew, a child who is a cousin, any baby. And the framing was perfect so that image was striking to us. The next day there were many photos from a greater distance where you could see life jackets, members of the coast guard, all sorts of boats, but no one remembers those, because they are not beautiful. The first photo was beautiful. But the second photo, when you see the larger context, is no longer striking to us.

I believe that it matters little what subject you want to broach. I still believe that beauty is the best vehicle to talk about everything: whether it be a tragedy, or a drama, or horror. That's what is striking, that life is a paradox. There are so many pictures of the Viet Nam war, justifiably, where you see helicopters arriving in the rice fields and it's extremely beautiful! With the downdraft turning [in a spiral] and the young rice shoots, it's like an undulating carpet [she makes the gesture of waves moving to and fro] of green. It's magnificent! And when you see the soldiers who are crossing the rice paddies, it's so beautiful, but there's a paradox, and it's the atrocity that's going to take place at the same time as this beauty. I believe that life always has these two sides.

It's up to us to choose. What do we want? Do we want the beauty to last or do we maintain ugliness? And it's up to each one of us to decide. We have the power to do it. Even if it's only a gesture for you, today, to stay home, to remain confined, it's [a manifestation of] beauty. And it's difficult to convince people to stay home because, the gesture is invisible. And the result is invisible. The success one creates is that people don't die.[10] And how do you measure that? The result is invisible, but so is the beauty, quite often. What can we do to reveal the beauty, to underline beauty always?

But empathy is a thing that humans cannot do. I don't think so. I don't think we can be in anybody's shoes. I have been a refugee, and if you asked me, I don't know what that camp for Syrian refugees is like today in Turkey. It's not the same, it's not the same shape. Even for me, who has been a refugee, I cannot imagine what they are living today, literally … so empathy is basically impossible in my mind. And so when we speak about this, we should not use empathy to demonize those who cannot understand. We cannot say, "Oh, you're scared of refugees? You're a racist, you're a xenophobe." Because that will push the other person even further away. Whereas what they are saying is very normal. They cannot relate to that kind of situation. So if you want them to feel *interpellés* [engaged], you have to give them something that they can understand.

I told you the story of Tareq [Hadhad] who arrived [in Canada] a few years ago, after being sponsored by a town of five thousand people, Antigonish [NS].[11] In two years' time, they [Tareq and his family] now have a factory making chocolate, with fifty employees. Then, all of a sudden, you want to meet Tareq and you even forget that he is Syrian, you forget that he was a refugee, you forget that he was stuck in a room with sixty of his relatives and friends, in a basement where it was so tight that the person sitting next to the wall didn't even touch the floor. They were held up against the wall by the number of people around them for fifteen days. And they left that room just because they knew they were going to die anyway. And they ran, and they were the lucky ones who arrived in a refugee camp in Lebanon. So … you have to touch people, with a story. Chocolate? We all know what chocolate is. When you start with a chocolate story, it's more interesting. Oh my God, in two years' time, you created this company. How did it work? "Well, what happened was my father was in Geneva, but one day he was at a wedding and he saw the people around a chocolate table, they were all happy and he said, he wanted that, he wanted to give happiness to people and so he started a company making chocolate." It's no longer about being a refugee or being Syrians or being anything. It's a story of one human person, that's it, and that's how we have to create conversations. By conversations I mean, what? In the newspaper. If every day they published one story of one immigrant, good or bad, you know, very successful or still struggling, or whatever – one story. Just give a face, a name and a story – that would change the narratives altogether.

I looked at myself when I was ten years old in that refugee camp, and I could not see any potential in me. I would not choose myself ... even though I know what I have become today, and I would not choose any of the thirteen people who were there, and I know what they have become today and still when I go back and look at them ... But they had nothing left, they were refugees; we were refugees. You know, when you've been ejected out of the timeline, you don't have a past, you don't have a future, you don't have a present. Why? Because the present is empty, empty, it's meaningless, so what can you see in your eyes? You cannot see anything, or yourself. A refugee is like a dead tree, it's like a tree in the winter.

MS: A dormant tree ...

KT: A dormant tree. But like I said, if you put it back into a fertile soil, it will grow. Why? Because those who did not survive have already died. There's already a natural selection, of the lucky ones or the strongest ones; the weaker ones are already dead. So, you basically have the butter of the human race ... in a refugee camp. Those trees for sure will grow, because they have survived hell, right? And I'm the example of this, to be born weak and to become unkillable today, yes? And that's why we have to talk about that. It's OK for you not to feel that that person could become anything. It's a bet. But your bet is at 99.9 per cent, you know, a guarantee. But it's a bet, and we agree with you that it's a bet. So *le discours*, the speech ...

MS: the prevailing discourse ...

KT: ... is that the bets are extreme. Instead of creating a conversation, you're scared. Yes, you're right to be scared. Let's start with that. You don't want refugees; I understand. But I'll show you something, OK? There's a Tareq, there's a Kim Thúy, there's that doctor who's treating you … and that reassures you that, oh, it's true, they can be something. For sure, if you look at them walking in Mexico, in Honduras or whatever, you cannot see what they can become, impossible, because they are just walking, they are half-dead. But those challenges will make them so much stronger, with a willpower that you will never see in a person who has always grown up in a peaceful country.

MS: I like your description of the people in the refugee camp as "like butter": that's the best part of the milk that's been churned and turned into something wonderful. You use culinary metaphors a lot …

KT: [laughs]

MS: … and your cookbook *Le Secret des Vietnamiennes* is also sort of a combination of, that combination of writing and cooking, and I wondered if you wanted to talk a little bit more about how cooking informs your writing, and how your writing informs your cooking.

KT: I never thought that cooking was a thing, you know, for me but …

MS: But you owned a restaurant. You know cooking is your thing!

KT: But I think that it's because that's the common denominator. When I talk about food, everybody understands. When you have many cultures, you never run out of options. Why? Because, if you have an eggplant in the fridge, let's say you don't know what to do. OK, you only have olive oil: if you're only Italian, what are you going to do, there's no tomatoes, that's it, but, if you have eaten Lebanese food, or Syrian food, or whatever, you know with some olive oil, I can make it a baba ghanoush, no problem! But if you don't have olive oil, you don't have tomatoes, but you have fish sauce, and if you have already eaten Vietnamese food, you go, ah! I'll grill it and make it with green onions and fish sauce. So, you never run out of options when you have many cultures.

And that's always the best door opener, it's the key to anything. I was invited to La Maison des Femmes of Molenbeek in Brussels. I was there for the Book Fair, and in the program, I was sent to this thing in Molenbeek. The only thing we know about Molenbeek in the news is that it's the incubator for the terrorists of Bataclan, right?[12] So I said, oh my God, why are they sending me to this place? Even though

I know the news is just the news, that you should never trust it and believe that what you see is the whole reality, but still, even if you know that, your brain can play tricks on you and make you feel fear. And I felt fear when I saw the word Molenbeek. But I talked to myself, and I said, "I have somebody who will accompany me to go inside this place. I have the Book Fair people. It's gonna be OK."

So, I went there and I asked, how far is it from my hotel? And they said about fifteen minutes' walk to the place, or in a taxi, five minutes. I said, I want to walk because I want to feel, slowly, the pulse. So I walk for a while, and then ask, "Are we there yet? Where is Molenbeek?" My host said, "You've been walking in Molenbeek for the last five minutes." I said, "That's it? That's Molenbeek?" Because I didn't feel any difference with the rest of the city. Of course not, right? It's not like in the news at all. And then we got lost a little bit so we asked people where to go, directions, and people were super nice and so … You know, I expected something and I was all geared up inside, like I'm gonna go into a war zone basically, right? And then I went into this Maison des Femmes, and to tell you the truth, I have Muslim friends, but they are not veiled or anything, so that is like a new frontier for me and I had a lot of apprehension. I didn't know how to react. I walked in there with all my apprehension and before you knew it, it took maybe half a second, for all of them to come, and hug me, kiss me … and then we started talking and I said to the Book Fair [representative], maybe we can cook together. They had already invited one author before, but just for a talk, and I said, I'm not sure, because these are women who are learning how to write, how to read, so I don't know, maybe cooking is a better way to approach things. Literature is too far away, it's not a common tool. So I said, let's cook, and I chose the eggplant, because I know they use eggplants. I'll go in with eggplants cooked my way, but they'll recognize it, so, it was easy! We started talking. It was the first time that they ate fish sauce. It was the first time they spoke to a Vietnamese woman from Canada, of all places. We had so much fun. It was supposed to be for one hour; it lasted for four hours and a half. We became friends.

So, food is that door opener, or that key to anything. We started talking about food, and then slowly they started talking about the difficulty they have as women arriving in a new place, many of them illiterate, and they have children now who grow up and to whom they cannot speak. You understand their situation so much better, after this kind of meeting, and you understand why they wear that veil. I'm not talking about everybody in Molenbeek; I'm just talking about this group of women who didn't have a chance to learn how to read, how to write, early on. You need that link and that bridge to start a conversation, right? And because of that, we had a great conversation and one asked me how I speak to my teenager, and we shared experiences, the political situations, the discrimination or no discrimination …

MS: The loss of a culture … And how you decide what you're going to keep, how can you keep certain things that are important to you.

KT: Right. And so, I think food carries so much of the history of each culture, but at the same time, it's the common denominator. It's all about happiness, you know, when you eat. It's a meal, and even when we just share a piece of fruit; you cannot be mad at an orange [as she eats one].

MS: Happiness on a plate.

KT: So I think it's because we have that in common, we all eat … We all love food.

MS: So that's a part of the question I wanted to ask you about history. In *Vi*, in speaking about the large communities of expatriate Vietnamese, you write, "The history of Vietnam and the Vietnamese endures, evolves, and grows in complexity without being written down or told."[13] I think your writings do address that complexity or that "complexification" that goes with globalization of your people, but your novels also feel to me like it's an effort … to tell this evolving history of your people across the world.

KT: Because I find it so beautiful, just to see the Vietnamese in the US, so much bigger and larger [in stature] than the Vietnamese in France or in Canada. It's already a fascination. How come? So context, environment does affect the way we look. If you go to California, there are so many Vietnamese who came there in the seventies like us, but they have kept the culture, so they look exactly like the 1970s fashion trends in Viet Nam. Whereas if you're in Montreal, you blend in, right? As you know, expats are the ones who keep the culture static. They are more Vietnamese than the Vietnamese. And for the Estonians, it's the same; when I talked to [my Estonian friend] Eva, she said she met some Estonians here in Canada, and she said they have kept traditions. No Estonians today would do it. And their language is kept like back in the fifties, in the forties even. They have not moved on, because they are so scared of losing it. And it's the same thing with French in Quebec.

MS: Absolutely. It's the preserved accent of the time of the colonization.

KT: Yes, and also because we are so scared of losing it, we are stricter on rules and traditions and so on, whereas if you enter the country, *le pays mère*, you just evolve with life. That's why I talked about this French guy, an *anthropologue* [anthropologist], where, in order to study some Chinese traditions, he was not to go back to China, because there, they are already gone. You have to go to places where the Chinese have established, you know, their …

MS: Outposts.

KT: Outposts, yeah.

MS: You have some of that in your family, you have Chinese heritage.

KT: Yeah. But we lost it all, we were not so much into [it] because of my grandfather who was not, he chose to be Vietnamese because the mother was Vietnamese, right? And because he was not in business, he was in politics. The scientists were with the French, so you kind of choose because of your interests, almost, whereas if you do business, then you stay with the community. And that's why the family split into two. So I find it fascinating how and why we have evolved so differently, from one country to the next, even though we came exactly from the same roots at the same time, it's just that we're all spread out. So the Vietnamese are no longer just Vietnamese. Today being Vietnamese has so many variations. With very different ways of looking at things or treating things, because it's being reinterpreted according to the culture where we have established, you know, our new homes, and we don't realize it.

MS: Do you read other Vietnamese writers? Of your generation or of earlier generations?

KT: I haven't much. There's one called Ocean Vương.[14] ... I cried the whole night. I read the whole of his poetry book. His first poetry book. How do you say that?

MS: Collection.

KT: Collection. First one, at twenty-five years old. He's writing or finishing his first novel right now, and his novel is already bought by Gallimard, for fifty thousand euros. And it was a *vente aux enchères*.

MS: So it was a bidding war.

KT: It was a bidding war for this first novel. And I love him to death. I love his work to death, because there's so much beauty, and he talks about the most horrible things. I still remember this image where the character pulled his father out of the sea, and he [the father] had a hole in his shoulder, and the son could see all the seawater in it ... you see the image, right? This hole filled with the seawater, and he kind of said something like, "it was my father who was no longer my father," like he didn't recognize this father, but then he said something like all the following crises in his life were about trying to find his father again, but it's so well said.[15] So well written, oh my God.

MS: Can you talk about any projects that you're currently working on?

KT: I always think it's my last book. The last book is always the last book, right? And then things happen and ... But I have more stories to share, what am I going to do? What I'm currently writing about is a story that happened a month before the end of the war in Viet Nam. There was an operation called Operation Babylift, where they took children, orphans, and most of them were mixed [race]; that was President Ford's plan, to take these children out of Viet Nam. The message being sent was that the children who were half American and half Vietnamese were going to be punching bags when the Communists arrived in South Viet Nam. And the majority of those children were the orphan children of American soldiers. So the plane was sent and because it was a cargo plane, there were very few seats. I believe there were seventy-seven seats, and the rest was cargo space; so the children were put in, in cardboard boxes. They were small babies, with a belt to hold them in place, at the back of the plane. The older ones were attached to the sides. When the plane took off, there was a mechanical problem with the door, which flew open. There was a violent decompression because of the air pressure and the cargo door opening. The pilot succeeded in bringing the plane down and in landing it on its belly in the rice fields near the airport. Half [of those aboard] managed to survive, and they [the children] are now [living] all over. On the operation altogether they took out more than three thousand children, who were adopted.

What struck me was that there was an American soldier who was sent to the site of the accident to recover the survivors. He described a scene in which the dead and the living all looked the same, because all those who survived were unconscious. So all he saw were bodies lying in the rice fields. He said he picked up a baby in his hands, certain beforehand that that baby was living because he hadn't a scratch, no wound. But when he picked up the baby, he said, "It was like a bag of marbles," because all the bones inside were broken. And forty years later he still remembers "the feeling of picking that baby up," a baby who resembled "a bag of marbles." That was the sensation.

There were other planes that were sent to get [the] three thousand children who left. They all arrived at the same time in California, at [an air force base]. Hugh Hefner, the owner of *Playboy* whom you know of and who knew some of the parents who wanted to help, sent the Playboy plane, a private jet, to the base to pick up the children and take them who knows where, but to transport them. And he also sent along Bunnies to lend a hand to the nurses. Can you imagine? So there are photos of the parents holding the babies and behind them is the plane with its door open, and the stairs, and on the door there's the big Playboy logo, the image of a Bunny. Extreme circumstances create extreme situations, thus this situation at once tragic and comical. You have to imagine Bunnies going to help the orphan children in Hugh Hefner's private plane. And so, my main character is one of the little girls who survived the [initial] crash.

One of the [surviving] children is now a journalist in Australia. She tried to look back at the event and see what happened. She met with the guy who was behind the program, who designed the program for President Ford. And he laughed, because he said this idea, it was an image operation. These children were children of dust. In Vietnamese we call them children of dust. So he took the word from the Vietnamese; so they were basically nothing. He said no Communist would use them as scapegoats. Nobody cares about them. It was an operation for their [the US's] image before the withdrawal. That's it. It shocked me to know it, because I totally believed the first message, for forty years. And when you think about it, it's logical. No Communist would care about the orphans. They cannot even care for themselves. They cannot even care for the population. Why would they care about these orphans?

MS: Yeah, that is a logical thought, but that it was an image operation, that's just so shocking ... but it wasn't about humanity.

KT: No, it has nothing to do with humanity, but, of course, at the same time three thousand children were saved. Many of them would say that if they had stayed back, maybe they wouldn't have a good life. But still, these children were not all orphans. There were many mothers who were convinced that if you keep your children, you go to prison, and they might be killed, and so on and so forth. So [they chose to] leave them, [to] let them go; so, some mothers were still waiting for the children, hoping to see them again, and many of them did go back and meet with them again.

And so I said, "We have to tell this Operation Babylift [story]. We have to lift up the curtain, that veil." There was a *reportage* [story] about this but not so many people have heard about it. We, each of us, have to talk about this story so that the story could [be] kept alive ... because it could happen to any country; it's not just about Viet Nam, no, no ... and maybe people are going, oh no, she's talking about Viet Nam again, but it's beyond Viet Nam, right?

MS: Absolutely. I think it's going to be very important to tell that story even if it's through the vehicle of fiction, because I think you're right, I think that people don't understand, they don't remember if they saw the report, it didn't stick with them and until you make it that human story, it doesn't stay.

KT: Because Operation Babylift, right, three thousand babies, OK – but if you tell the story of one or two of those babies ... We are all victims. That war was decided by maybe less than five people. Altogether? I think it was, tops, five people, maximum ten, but I think it's less than five who made the decision to have a war or not, and we are just *les exécutants* [the implementers] and victims of the war. You've seen [*The*] *Vietnam* [*War*] by Ken [Burns and Lynn Novick], that long documentary of nine hours? When Nixon called the general and said "bomb the hell out of it"? And the general said, "We can't, it's a cloudy day," whatever, so they could not see the targets, and [Nixon] said he needed a first page in the newspaper, a diversion from Watergate. And you hear Nixon saying, "I don't care, just bomb." And they bombed. So you always know that [in] a war, you are just those pieces on the chessboard, right? That people play with that, because they don't see anybody as humans anymore. It's just, "I need a diversion." Kill some people because we need a diversion.

MS: Yeah, "throw some immigrant children in a cage. I need a diversion."

KT: You know, but that's the problem with power, right? And the problem of being taken away from beauty. These people don't live in beauty anymore. That's it. And that kills them. So, our role is to let people get closer to beauty, be touched by beauty constantly, as often as possible, and that's what arts and culture are for, it's our only way to resist ... I don't see any other way.

NOTES

1 Translated into English, this title means *The Sound of the Stranger*.

2 Thúy, "En remontant les rus de l'enfance," 154.

3 Kim Thúy speaks of this in her 2019 interview "I Don't Understand Countries That Don't Want Immigrants" and in "Q&A with Kim Thúy."

4 Kim Thúy had just gotten back from a European book tour, including a stop in Ukraine, prior to the June 2019 portion of this interview.

5 Chan explains that the seventeenth-century Jesuit missionary Alexandre de Rhodes romanized the writing of Vietnamese "using diacritical marks to indicate the tones of Vietnamese words" (*Vietnamese American 1.5 Generation*, 9), and this writing system is in use today.

6 Pears makes a similar point and contextualizes it, in *Remnants of Empire in Algeria and Vietnam*: "the reformed script of the Vietnamese alphabet, Quoc-Ngu, instituted by the French, effectively separated ensuing generations of Vietnamese students from their own national literature, because they could no longer read it ... The ultimate result of Vietnamese written with a Roman alphabet was ignorance of Vietnamese literature" (18).

7 k.d. lang is an award-winning singer-songwriter from Alberta.
8 This Pulitzer Prize–winning photograph was taken by Nick Ut in 1972, and the girl in the photo is identified as Phan Thị Kim Phúc.
9 This 2015 photo of deceased child Alan Kurdi by Nilüfer Demir is credited with changing some Europeans' attitudes to the Syrian refugee crisis.
10 This portion of the interview comes from a conversation after the 2020 COVID-19 pandemic led to government orders to stay at home, on both sides of the Canada-US border.
11 See Dickson, "Sweet Story." The story of this refugee family's success was made into a film by Jonathan Keijser, *Peace by Chocolate* (2021).
12 This is a reference to the 2015 attacks in Paris by Syrian-backed Islamic terrorists based in Molenbeek, Belgium.
13 Kim Thúy, *Vi*, trans. Sheila Fischman (Toronto: Vintage Canada, 2019), 91.
14 Vietnamese American writer Vuong's first poetry collection, *Night Sky with Exit Wounds*, won the T.S. Eliot Prize, the Whiting Award, the Thom Gunn Award, and the Forward Prize for best first collection. See "About," Ocean Vuong's website, accessed 24 October 2022, https://www.oceanvuong.com/about. He was awarded a 2019 MacArthur "genius" grant the same year he published his first novel, titled *On Earth We're Briefly Gorgeous*.
15 Vuong, "Telemachus," in *Night Sky with Exit Wounds*, 7–8.

Afterword

A Few Thoughts about Em

Jack A. Yeager with Miléna Santoro

Like Kim Thúy's earlier work, *Em* (2020) is firmly grounded in the history and culture of Viet Nam, from the colonial period to the two wars and after. The first line of the novel is clear enough: "La guerre, encore" [War, again].[1] Specific historical references anchor the text and set the stage for the fictional stories that develop and evolve against this background. In typical fashion, Kim Thúy engages her readers immediately with numerous characters quickly sketched, instantly humanizing of the effects of war, violence, and death, and with the accumulation of examples, demonstrating the extent to which everyone was touched in some way by the conflicts. This narrative strategy recurs in an expanded section focusing on the My Lai massacre, a historically documented war crime that figures prominently as it directly affects the life of one of the key characters in the novel (*Em*, 40–51), where Thúy offers quite graphic descriptions of the violence, destruction, and murders of the civilians who lived in that village.

The exploitation of the Vietnamese during the colonial period through the example of the rubber plantations further sets the stage for the novel. In the Libre Expression first printing of *Em*, "L'or blanc" is linked by a gold thread to the first interior chapter, "Caoutchouc," and the history of its cultivation for economic reasons (*Em*, 13) recalls Marguerite Duras's famous description at the opening of Part II of *Un barrage contre le Pacifique*.[2] Echoing Duras, Kim Thúy writes, "Les coolies savaient que les hévéas valaient plus que leur vie" (*Em*, 15) [The coolies knew that the rubber trees were worth more than their lives (7)], and "chaque goutte de latex obtenue valait la goutte de sang ou de sueur versé" (*Em*, 18) [Every drop of latex obtained was worth the drop of blood or sweat it had cost (9)]. In this specific context, armed conflict and the presence of foreign soldiers, rubber logically evokes its use in condoms and by extension sex workers during the colonial period and the wars. What may seem to be a merely factual accounting of how the French language influenced Vietnamese through loan words such as *xích lô* (*cyclo*) and *cà phê* (*café*) in the chapter titled "France," the listing concludes with the narrator telling her readers that some Vietnamese words were and are also used in French. The French colonials, however, "les ont étoffés en leur donnant un second sens" [[were] expanding them, giving them a second meaning (30)], and the narrator then cites the pejorative use of *con gái* in French (*Em*, 36–7),[3] a prime example that is crucial to the novel. The word in Vietnamese means daughter or young girl; in French, however, it signifies mistress or prostitute in Kim Thúy's telling.[4] Furthermore, the *métis/se* children born of the relationships between Vietnamese women and Western men, be they French or American, emerge as a major thread in *Em*.

The first of these characters is Tâm, the child of the rubber plantation owner Alexandre and his worker Mai, who bears a daughter. Both are killed in a revolutionary attack, but their Vietnamese nanny rescues the young child, taking her back to her own village, My Lai. Several years later, and according to the wishes of the girl's parents, the nanny arranges for Tâm to take the entrance examination for the *lycée* Gia Long in Saigon. Accepted, she moves to the southern capital with the nanny, but they then return together to My Lai on the occasion of a school break, during which the American attack occurs. As apparently the sole survivor of the massacre, by pretending to be dead among bodies thrown into a ravine, Tâm is thus doubly orphaned. Spotted by an American helicopter pilot who sees not only the adolescent girl moving but, in her, an image of his own daughter, she is rescued once again and entrusted to Catholic sisters working as nurses. Sent to Saigon with a baby who is slated for adoption, Tâm becomes stranded there by cancelled flights, weather, and military manoeuvres. While in Saigon she meets the helicopter pilot, the narrator tells us from her ironic distance, but they do not recognize each other. Three years have passed since the massacre. Still, their first glance leaves them thunderstruck. Three nights of love and promises eventually reveal Tâm's identity to the unnamed pilot; her earlobe is missing, and he remembers it falling into his hand during the rescue. The possibility of redemption lingers as he returns to his base with a promise to return to her. Days pass and he does not reappear, himself another fatality of war. Desperate, Tâm – Alexandre and Mai's daughter, a *con gái* – does all she can do; she takes a job in one of Saigon's many bars and becomes a prostitute, the other meaning of *con gái*.

If this story of a single character relies on coincidence and chance, it also harks back to the cover illustration of *Em*, a box with the top flaps barely open and from which emerge gold and red threads. These are the colours of Tết, the lunar new year, the most important holiday of the Vietnamese calendar, and the same hues of banners in Vietnamese and Chinese, gold on red, to wish the best of luck during the coming year. The threads on the cover are tangled, yet the colours remain separate, as two threads, one red, one gold, reappear on the back cover and extend to the back flyleaf over the photograph of Kim Thúy herself. The gold thread then reappears in selected chapters in the book with chapter titles of the same colour. The threads reflect the weaving of a text, of course, but also the unexpected connections among the characters in *Em* as exemplified by the story of Tâm, among others.

However, the threads also remind us of the brief sketches in the very first, "framing" chapter of the novel, one in which Kim-as-narrator, invented by the writer, promises to tell the truth as she knows it, saying, "Je vais vous raconter la vérité, ou du moins des histoires vraies, mais seulement partiellement, incomplètement, à peu de chose près" (*Em*, 9) [I'm going to tell you the truth, some true stories at least, but only partially, incompletely, more or less true (1)]; and also "j'ai cherché à imaginer" (*Em*, 10) [I tried to imagine (2)]. She exhorts the reader, an explicit "vous," to imagine her own truth in reading this imperfect version, as "Kim" admits: "Dans ce livre, la vérité est morcelée, incomplète, inachevée dans le temps et dans l'espace. Alors, est-elle encore la vérité? Je vous laisse répondre d'une manière qui fera écho à votre propre histoire, à votre vérité. Entre-temps, je vous promets dans les mots qui suivent un certain ordre dans les émotions et un désordre inévitable dans les sentiments" (*Em*, 11) [In this book, truth is fragmented, incomplete, unfinished, in both time and space. Then is it still the truth? I'll let you reply in a way that relates to your own story, your own truth. Meanwhile, I promise you in the words that follow a certain ordering of the emotions, along with feelings whose disarray cannot be denied (3)]. In emphasizing the verbs *imaginer*, *s'imaginer*, and *envisager*, Kim-as-narrator encourages the reader to be open to this text and its story, to understand it on an emotional level, where truth resides, which for Kim-the-writer eventually leads back to love; "L'amour, encore" are the first words we see on the front inside flyleaf. Chapters at the end of the book also function to complete the frame for the stories told inside. The threads, too, thus symbolize how all are affected by the violence and death of war; what may appear as coincidence or chance is nothing of the kind, for narrative threads are connected visually by the meandering threads on the book's pages and, figuratively, by the vicissitudes of life.

The chapter on rubber mentioned above leads to that titled "Coolie" and to "France" and to "Points de vue," in which the narrator explains that what is known in the US as the "Viet Nam War" is referred to by Vietnamese as the American War (*Em*, 47). These chapters are then connected to one called "R & R" (*Em*, 60). The threads of two colours also figure *métissage* and the biracial children born to Vietnamese mothers and Western fathers. Tâm – like Kim Lefèvre, as we know from her remarkable autobiography *Métisse blanche* (1989), also the child of a French father and a Vietnamese mother – is visibly different, a difference treated consciously by Kim Thúy in *Em*. The narrator mentions "ses cheveux clairs et ses yeux caramel" (27) [her fair hair and her caramel eyes (19)] and adds that "son teint lumineux éblouissait les yeux les plus saturés" (*Em*, 39) [her luminous complexion dazzled the most jaded eyes (32)]. The nanny "la protégeait des regards curieux" (*Em*, 33) [protected her from curious gazes (26)] and "les mauvais mots des mauvaises langues" (*Em*, 34) [the ugly words of gossips (27)]. Tâm's physical difference serves as a constant reminder of the betrayal and moral downfall of her mother, Mai.

"R & R" makes the diversity of these biracial children explicit in mentioning that the military may have treated the STDs that soldiers contracted but did nothing for the "graines ... semées à l'intérieur de certaines de[s] femmes [des bars]. Voilà pourquoi des populations asiatiques autrement homogènes, comme celle du Vietnam du Sud, se sont diversifiées avec des enfants aux cheveux pâles ou crépus, aux yeux ronds et aux cils longs, à la peau foncée ou avec des taches de rousseur, presque toujours sans père et souvent sans mère" (*Em*, 60) [seeds they'd sown inside the bodies of some of the women. That is why Asian populations that were once homogeneous, such as that of South Vietnam, became diversified, with children who had hair pale or curly, eyes round and long-lashed, skin dark or freckled, almost always fatherless and also, often, without a mother (57)]. Unsurprisingly, Tâm, too, will give birth.

In *Em* the existence of the *métis/se* children in Viet Nam logically raises the question narratively of Operation Babylift in April 1975. With the impending arrival of the North Vietnamese in Saigon, the US government devised a plan to evacuate children from orphanages and especially those resulting from the involvements of Vietnamese women with American military personnel. Kim Thúy focuses particularly on the first plane out of Tạn Son Nhut airport in Saigon early in the month. She recasts this tragic event for dramatic effect, writing that the plane exploded and crashed on takeoff. The plane did indeed crash, as the pilot tried to land the damaged aircraft at the airport, killing nearly half the passengers and crew.[5] The chapter "Operation Babylift" is one of those linked by golden thread (*Em*, 79–81) to others. Stories of survivors adopted and raised in the United States are interwoven in the remaining pages of *Em*, extending the wars' effects that persist to this day.

There are threads that link *Em* to Thúy's previous works as well, and not only because of the historical and geographical rootedness of the narrative. The notion of care, of mothering that occurs both within and beyond bloodlines, of the role food plays in identity formation, of the secrets that come to light and those that do not, of roles both familial and social that are shaped by migration, of the influence of languages and words on our (self-)perceptions – "tous ces fils de vie sur le fil du temps" (*Em*, 145) [All these threads of life as time goes by (144)] that *Em*'s narrator notes in her "Conversation lunaire" [Lunar Conversation (144)] with the artist who painted the cover image of the box, Louis Boudreault – these form a web of associations and connections that our contributors have deftly explored in writing about Thúy's earlier publications for the chapters of this volume. There are some threads, of course, that are dropped, critical avenues that remain unexplored, or that may not seem relevant now but may someday be more so. We can never, in fact, cover every topic in a single book, just as in a narrative, the writer may not tie up all the loose ends. As Thúy herself writes, playing on the double meaning of *fils* ("thread" and "son" or "sons") in French: "J'ai cherché à tisser les fils, mais ils se sont échappés pour rester sans ancrage, impermanents et libres. Ils se réarrangent par eux-mêmes selon la vitesse du vent, selon les nouvelles qui défilent, selon les inquiétudes et les sourires de mes fils" (*Em*, 128) [I tried to interweave the threads, but they escaped, and remain unanchored, impermanent and free. They rearranged themselves on their own, given the speed of the wind, the news streaming by, the worries and smiles of my sons (129)]. We have pursued a similar goal in this project, and in the process have also found ourselves buffeted by the pandemic, by personal challenges, as well as by political upheavals here and elsewhere. We have encountered delays and obstacles but were sustained throughout by the inspiration that Kim Thúy's work has offered and the bonds that have been strengthened through our collaboration. We were particularly delighted to have Kim Thúy offer her own original contribution to this volume, the previously unpublished passage that follows, titled "Les mots au milieu des mots" (Words within words). In reading it, and Jack A. Yeager's translation, we hope you too will feel the joy and the challenge of working with the words of an author whose search for beauty is far from over.

NOTES

1 Kim Thúy, *Em* (Montreal: Libre Expression, 2020), 9; Thúy, *Em*, trans. Sheila Fischman (New York: Seven Stories Press, 2021), 1. Subsequent references to this novel refer to these editions. The English translation will appear in square brackets after the original French, with the page number in parentheses.

2 Duras, *Un barrage contre le Pacifique*, 167–9.

3 The narrator explains that after the birth of his daughter, he never again used this common Vietnamese term in French, even though Tâm was his female child.

4 See also the discussion of the term in chapter 1 of this volume, "*Récits* and *Recettes*: Preserving and Recreating Culture and Identity through Writing and Cooking."

5 Due to a faulty latch repair, the rear cargo door of the Lockheed C05A blew off at altitude over the South China Sea out of view of Saigon, causing a rapid decompression that damaged the control cables in the tail of the plane. The pilot was able to return the heavily damaged aircraft to the airport and make a crash landing, short of the runway. Seventy-eight children and 46 military and medical personnel died in the crash; 176 survived (*Em*, 79–81). See Martin, "Remembering the Doomed First Flight of Operation Babylift"; and Wikipedia, s.v. "1975 Tân Sơn Nhứt C-5 Accident," last modified 12 August 2022, 01:39, https://en.wikipedia.org/wiki/1975_Tân_Sơn_Nhứt_C-5_accident. See also "Chasing Beauty," pp. 172–3 in this volume.

Les mots au milieu des mots

Kim Thúy

J'aime les mots. J'aime jouer avec les mots. J'aime chercher les mots au milieu des mots. Et parfois, des maux.

Les mots s'offrent à moi avec candeur et souvent sans prévenir. Ils s'échappent de la même manière, c'est-à-dire soudainement comme un éclair de génie, un pincement passager ou une simple impression. Pourtant, ils me font vivre les émotions les plus riches, les plus vives, les plus diverses.

Il y a des mots qui sont aussi doux que les nuages et d'autres plus lourds qu'une boule d'acier.

Il y a des mots si brûlants qu'on peut à peine les tenir dans nos mains et d'autres qui glissent entre nos doigts comme le silence.

Il y a des mots aussi timides que les premiers rayons de soleil qui, après une nuit blanche, s'immiscent à travers les persiennes et d'autres, aussi bruyants qu'un fou rire pendant une prière.

Il y a des mots qui nous soulagent des malentendus, des glissements de sens, des mauvaises langues.

Il y a des mots dits et oubliés, promis et écartés, fidèles et rebelles tout en étant charmants et paresseux, embêtants et élégants, profonds et perdus.

Il y a des mots qui se veulent mystérieux, insondables, énigmatiques pour dissimuler leurs besoins de tendresse, de sympathie, d'intimité.

Il y a des mots éblouissants, étourdissants, étonnants qui font danser les papillons dans le ventre et les étoiles dans les yeux.

Il y a des mots qui nous guident vers la lumière des lanternes d'automne et d'autres qui nous bercent avec grâce et patience comme si les heures avaient perdu leurs minutes et les mois, leurs jours.

Il y a des mots imperméables aux intempéries, aux épreuves, aux obstacles mais qui se renversent au premier baiser.

Il y a des mots qui caressent les cheveux, d'autres les joues, quelques-uns le creux du cou.

Il y a évidemment des mots cruels qui forcent la vérité, la lucidité, l'obéissance alors que d'autres tentent de convaincre par la délicatesse, la finesse, la souplesse.

Il y a des mots si subtils qu'on les croit inutiles et sans personnalité.

Et pourtant, ils offrent subrepticement la légèreté, l'adresse, le raffinement.

Il y a des mots qui s'effacent, s'oublient, s'annulent pour célébrer l'abnégation, le sacrifice, la compassion, le don de soi.

Il y a des mots solidaires, complices, partenaires pour nous encourager à poser des gestes braves, courageux et radicaux.

Il y a tous ces mots qui tourbillonnent, qui se font valoir, qui tentent d'être audacieux, grandiloquents et sophistiqués mais aucun n'arrive à la cheville de ce mot qui rafle tout sur son passage. Lorsqu'on choisit ce mot, lorsqu'on l'anime, personne, ni rien ne peut y résister.

Il est intangible, inodore, indépendant, insaisissable, indescriptible mais tout en étant omniprésent, essentiel, pur, vital, naturel, attachant, fondamental, grandiose.

Il est notre dénominateur commun, notre raison d'être, notre humanité.

Grâce à lui, nous sommes capables de soulever les montagnes, traverser les océans, faire face aux tempêtes sans cligner des yeux.

Quel est ce mot, vous le devinez, n'est-ce pas? Si vous avez encore des doutes, je vous offre un autre indice: il est composé de 5 lettres en français. En chinois, selon une leçon que j'ai reçue d'un amoureux, il est un idéogramme qui contient trois caractères, soit une main, un cœur et des pieds parce que le mot "aimer" demande à ce que nous prenions notre coeur dans notre main et par la suite, marcher jusqu'à la personne qu'on aime pour le lui offrir.

Merci à vous d'avoir marché jusqu'à moi pour m'offrir tout votre temps avec tant de cœur.

Words within Words

Kim Thúy, translated by Jack A. Yeager

I love words. I love playing with words. I love finding words within words. And sometimes their wounds.

Words offer themselves to me with candor and often without warning. They escape in the same way, that is, suddenly like a stroke of genius, a passing twinge, or a simple impression. However, they bring alive the richest, the most intense, and the most varied emotions within me.

There are words that are as soft as clouds and others heavier than a steel ball.

There are words that are so fiery that we can barely hold them in our hands and others that pass between our fingers like silence.

There are words as timid as the first rays of the sun which, after a sleepless night, penetrate the shutters, and others as noisy as giggling during a prayer.

There are words that comfort us from misunderstandings, shifts in meaning, spiteful tongues.

There are words said and forgotten, promised and set aside, faithful and rebellious, all the while being charming and lazy, annoying and elegant, profound and lost.

There are words that want to be mysterious, unfathomable, enigmatic in order to hide their need for tenderness, sympathy, intimacy.

There are dazzling, intoxicating, surprising words that make butterflies dance in our stomachs and the stars twirl in our eyes.

There are words that guide us toward the lanterns of autumn and others that cradle us with grace and patience as if the hours had lost their minutes and the months their days.

There are words that are impervious to bad weather, to hardships, to obstacles but that swoon at the first kiss.

There are words that caress the hair, others, the cheeks, some, the hollow of the neck.

There are, of course, cruel words that compel the truth, lucidity, obedience while others attempt to convince with delicacy, finesse, suppleness.

There are words so subtle that one believes them useless and without personality. And yet they surreptitiously offer lightness, skill, refinement.

There are words that are erased, forgotten, nullified in order to celebrate abnegation, sacrifice, compassion, the gift of oneself.

There are words that show solidarity, complicity, partnership in order to encourage us to take brave, courageous, radical actions.

There are all those words that swirl around, that try to get noticed, that attempt to be audacious, grandiloquent, and sophisticated, but not one measures up to the ankle of the word that sweeps away everything in its path. When you choose this word, when you give it life, no one, nothing can resist it.

It is intangible, odorless, independent, imperceptible, indescribable while being omnipresent, essential, pure, vital, natural, captivating, fundamental, grandiose.

It is our common denominator, our reason for being, our humanity.

Thanks to it, we are capable of lifting up mountains, crossing the oceans, facing storms without blinking an eye.

What is this word? You can guess, can't you? If you still have doubts, I offer you another clue: it is composed of five letters in French. In Chinese, according to a lesson I learned from a lover, it is an ideogram that contains three characters: a hand, a heart, and feet because the word "aimer," to love, asks that we take our heart in hand and then walk up to the ones we love to offer it to them.

Thank you for walking up to me to give me all your time with so much heart.

Bibliography

Note: Vietnamese authors with the family name first – that is, in traditional order – are listed in this bibliography without punctuation.

Al Masri, Maram. *Le Rapt*. Paris: Éd. Bruno Doucy, 2015.

Ammour-Mayeur, Olivier. "Écrire l'amour: Enjeux des poétiques asiatiques chez Duras." In *Marguerite Duras: la tentation du poétique*, edited by Bernard Alazet, Christiane Blot-Labarrère, and Robert Harvey, 137–53. Paris: Presses Sorbonne Nouvelle, 2002.

Anderson, Benedict. *Imagined Communities: Reflections on the Origin and Spread of Nationalism*. London: Verso, 1983.

Atsufumi, Kato. *Weaving Women's Spheres in Vietnam: The Agency of Women in Family, Religion, and Community*. Leiden: Brill, 2016.

Austin, John L. *How to Do Things with Words*. Oxford Paperbacks. Oxford: Oxford University Press, 2009.

Bach Mai. *Le Bouddha couché*. Paris: L'Harmattan, 2017.

– *D'ivoire et d'opium*. Sherbrooke: Éditions Naaman, 1985.

– *Hier encore Saigon*. Paris: L'Harmattan, 2009.

– *Rivages du Mékong*. Paris: L'Harmattan, 2012.

Bacholle-Bošković, Michèle. *Linda Lê, l'écriture du manque*. Lewiston, ME: Edward Mellen Press, 2006.

Baloup, Clément. *Mémoires de Viet Kieu: Quitter Saigon*. Paris: Boîte à Bulles, 2006.

Barnes, Leslie. *Vietnam and the Colonial Condition of French Literature*. Lincoln: University of Nebraska Press, 2014.

Berrouët-Oriol, Robert. "L'effet d'exil du champ littéraire québécois." *Vice Versa* 17 (1986–87): 20–1.

Berrouët-Oriol, Robert, and Robert Fournier. "L'émergence des écritures migrantes et métisses au Québec." *Québec Studies* 14 (1992): 7–22.

Bethune, Brian. "Kim Thúy on How 'Refugee Literature' Differs from Immigrant Literature." *Macleans*, 11 April 2018. https://www.macleans.ca/culture/books/kim-thuy-on-how-refugee-literature-differs-from-immigrant-literature.

Bhabha, Homi K. *The Location of Culture*. London: Routledge, 1994.

Boué, Rachel. *L'Éloquence du silence: Celan, Sarraute, Duras et Quignard*. Paris: L'Harmattan, 2009.

Bourdeau, Loïc, ed. *Horrible Mothers: Representations across Francophone North America*. Lincoln: University of Nebraska Press, 2019.

Bouvier-Laffitte, Béatrice, and Anne Prouteau. "Le texte épistolaire comme mise en scène de l'exil au féminin," *Intercâmbio*, 2nd ser., no. 4 (2011): 59–71.

Britto, Karl Ashoka. *Disorientation: France, Vietnam, and the Ambivalence of Interculturality*. Hong Kong: Hong Kong University Press, 2004.

– "Kim Thúy: A Way with Words." *Public Books*, 15 October 2014. https://www.publicbooks.org/kim-thuy-a-way-with-words.

Burns, Amy Jo. "Author Amy Jo Burns on Her Debut Novel 'Shiner.'" Interview by Scott Simon, *Weekend Edition Saturday*, NPR. 9 May 2020. https://www.npr.org/2020/05/09/853216996/author-amy-jo-burns-on-her-debut-novel-shiner.

Burns, Ken, and Lynn Novick, directors. *The Vietnam War*. Florentine Films and WETA, Washington, DC. Eighteen-hour WETA series, first aired in 2017. http://www.pbs.org/kenburns/the-vietnam-war/home.

Cancian, Sonia. *Families, Lovers, and Their Letters: Italian Postwar Migration to Canada*. Winnipeg: University of Manitoba Press, 2010.

Carrière, Marie. "Mémoires du *care*, féminisme en mémoire." *Women in French Studies* 6, Conference Issue on Memory (2015): 205–17.

Carrière, Marie, and Catherine Khordoc. "For Better or for Worse: Revisiting *écriture migrante* in Québec." In *The Oxford Companion to Canadian Literature*, edited by Cynthia Sugars, 621–38. Oxford: Oxford University Press, 2015.

– eds. *Migrance comparée: Les Littératures du Canada et du Québec*. New York: Peter Lang, 2008.

Castillo Durante, Daniel. *Les dépouilles de l'altérité*. Montreal: Éditions XYZ, 2004.

Chan, Kwok Bun, and Louis Jacques Dorais. "Family, Identity, and the Vietnamese Diaspora: The Quebec Experience." *Sojourn: Journal of Social Issues in Southeast Asia* 13, no. 2 (1998): 285–308.

Chan, Sucheng, ed. *The Vietnamese American 1.5 Generation: Stories of War, Revolution, Flight, and New Beginnings*. Philadelphia: Temple University Press, 2006.

Chartier, Daniel. *Dictionnaire des écrivains émigrés au Québec, 1800–1999*. Montreal: Éditions Nota Bene, 2003.

Chaudey, Marie. "Kim Thúy raconte sa renaissance." *La Vie*, 26 January 2010. https://www.lavie.fr/papier/2010/3361/kim-thuy-raconte-sa-renaissance-49528.php.

Chen, Ying. *Les lettres chinoises*. Montreal: Leméac, 1993.

Cheng, François. *Vide et plein: le langage pictural chinois*. Paris: Éditions du Seuil, 2006.

Chihiro, Miyazawa. "Rethinking Vietnamese Women's Property Rights and the Role of Ancestor Worship in Premodern Society: Beyond the Dichotomies." In *Weaving Women's Spheres in Vietnam: The Agency of Women in Family, Religion, and Community*, edited by Kato Atsufumi, 57–80. Leiden: Brill, 2016.

Chin, Mee-Jung. "Family Attitudes and Gender Role Divisions of Married Women in Contemporary Vietnam and Korea." *International Journal of Human Ecology* 12, no. 2 (2011): 65–75. https://doi.org/10.6115/ljhe.2011.12.2.65.

Ching, Julia. *Chinese Religions*. London: Macmillan, 1993.

Chiu, Lily. "Alter/Native: Imagining and Performing the Native Woman in Francophone and Vietnamese Literature." PhD diss., University of Michigan, 2004.

Collins, Holly. "The *Littérature-monde* vs. the Parisian Publishing Empire." *Romance Notes* 55, no. 3 (2015): 495–508.

Connell, Raewyn. *Masculinities*. Cambridge: Polity Press, 1995.

Courville, Rosemary Harrington. "Melancholic Epistolarity: Letters and Traumatic Exile in the Novels of Three Francophone Women." PhD diss., Louisiana State University, 2013. https://digitalcommons.lsu.edu/gradschool_dissertations/964.

Cung Giu Nguyen. *Le domaine maudit*. Paris: A. Fayard, 1961.

Demetriou, Demetrakis Z. "Connell's Concept of Hegemonic Masculinity: A Critique." *Theory & Society* 30, no. 3 (2001): 337–61.

Den Toonder, Jeannette. "Migrant Writing in Quebec: Female Mobility in Kim Thúy's *Ru*." In *Exiles, Travellers and Vagabonds: Rethinking Mobility in Francophone Women's Writing*, edited by Kate Averis and Isabelle Hollis-Touré, 33–53. Cardiff: University of Wales Press, 2016.

Denis, Claire, director. *White Material*. Why Not Productions, 2009.

Desloges, Josianne. "Publishing in Québec 2018: Across the Invisible Frontier: Heather O'Neill and Kim Thúy." Translated by Katherine Hastings. *Publishers Weekly* 265, no. 39 (21 September 2018). https://www.publishersweekly.com/pw/by-topic/international/international-book-news/article/78130-publishing-in-qu-bec-2018-across-the-invisible-frontier-heather-o-neill-and-kim-th-y.html.

Desroches, Vincent. "Présentation: En quoi la littérature québécoise est-elle postcoloniale?" *Québec Studies* 35 (Spring/Summer 2003): 3–12.

Dickson, Janice. "Sweet Story: 'Joyful' Syrian Refugee Gains Canadian Citizenship." *Globe and Mail*, 3 January 2020. https://www.theglobeandmail.com/politics/article-sweet-story-joyful-syrian-refugee-gains-canadian-citizenship.

Doan, Kim. *Retour*. Paris: Plon, 2005.

Donaldson, Michael. "What Is Hegemonic Masculinity?" *Theory & Society* 22, no. 5 (1993): 643–57.

Dumontet, Danielle, and Frank Zipfel, eds. *Ecriture migrante/Migrant Writing*. Hildesheim, Germany: Georg Olms Verlag, 2008.

Duras, Marguerite. *Un barrage contre le Pacifique*. Paris: Gallimard, 1950.

– *The Lover*. Translated by Barbara Bray. New York: Pantheon, 1985.

Dusaillant-Fernandes, Valérie. "Du Vietnam au Québec: Fragmentation textuelle et travail de mémoire chez Kim Thúy." *Women in French Studies* 20 (2012): 75–89.

Eisen, Arlene. *Women and Revolution in Viet Nam*. London: Zed Books, 1984.

Elliott, Bruce S., David A. Gerber, and Suzanne M. Sinke, eds. "Introduction." In *Letters across Borders: The Epistolary Practices of International Migrants*, edited by Bruce S. Elliott, David A. Gerber, and Suzanne M. Sinke, 1–25. New York: Palgrave, 2006.

El Nossery, Névine, and Amy L. Hubbell, eds. *The Unspeakable: Representations of Trauma in Francophone Literature and Art*. Newcastle upon Tyne: Cambridge Scholars Press, 2013.

Erhart, Walter. "Das zweite Geschlecht: 'Mannlichkeit,' interdisziplinar. Ein Forschungsbericht." *Internationales Archiv fur Sozialgeschichte der deutschen Literatur* 30, no. 2 (2006): 156–232.

Esme, Jean d'. *Thi Ba, fille d'Annam*. Paris: La Renaissance du Livre, 1920; Paris: Kailash, 2001.

Espiritu, Yen Le. "Thirty Years AfterWARd: The Endings That Are Not Quite Over." *Amerasia Journal* 31, no. 2 (2005): xiii–xxiii.

Firpo, Christina Elizabeth. *The Uprooted: Race, Children, and Imperialism in French Indochina, 1890–1980*. Honolulu: University of Hawai'i Press, 2016.

Fitzpatrick, Anna. "Kim Thúy's *Mãn* Is a Story of Realism Told like a Fable." *Globe and Mail*, 26 September 2014. https://www.theglobeandmail.com/arts/books-and-media/book-reviews/kim-thuys-man-is-a-story-of-realism-told-like-a-fable/article20804546.

Fluck, Winfried. "Reading for Recognition." *New Literary History* 44, no. 1 (2013): 45–67.

Ford, Michele, and Lenore Lyons, eds. "Introduction." In *Men and Masculinities in Southeast Asia*, edited by Ford and Lyons, 1–19. Oxford: Routledge, 2012. https://doi.org/10.4324/9780203197394.

Frenette, Yves. "Introduction." In *Envoyer et recevoir: Lettres et correspondances dans les diasporas francophones*, edited by Yves Frenette, Marcel Martel, and John Willis, 1–16. Quebec City: Presses de l'Université Laval, 2006.

Girard, Jean-Yves. "Les joies de Kim Thúy." *Châtelaine*. 8 December 2011. https://fr.chatelaine.com/societe/entrevues/les-joies-de-kim-thuy.

Government of Canada. "Canada: A History of Refuge." Last modified 16 January 2020. https://www.canada.ca/en/immigration-refugees-citizenship/services/refugees/canada-role/timeline.html.

Green, Mary Jean. "Transcultural Identities: Many Ways of Being Québécois." *Textualizing the Immigrant Experience in Contemporary Québec*, edited by Susan Ireland and Patrice J. Proulx, 11–22. Westport, CT: Praeger, 2004.

Groulx, Lionel [Alonié de Lestres, pseud.]. *L'appel de la race*. 1922. Reprint, Ottawa: Fides, 1956.

– *The Iron Wedge*. Translated and introduced by Michel Gaulin. Ottawa: Carleton University Press; Montreal and Kingston: McGill-Queen's University Press, 1986.

Guy, Chantal. "Kim Thúy et Pascal Janovjak: D'écrits et d'amitiés." *La Presse*, 7 September 2011. https://www.lapresse.ca/arts/litterature/201109/07/01-4432148-kim-thuy-et-pascal-janovjak-decrits-et-damitie.php.

Harel, Simon. *Les passages obligés de l'écriture migrante*. Montreal: Éditions XYZ, 2005.

– *Le voleur de parcours: Identité et cosmopolitisme dans la littérature québécoise contemporaine*. Longueuil, QC: Le Préambule, 1989.

Hargreaves, Alec, Charles Forsdick, and David Murphy, eds. *Transnational French Studies: Postcolonialism and Littérature-Monde*. Liverpool: Liverpool University Press, 2010.

Harrisson, Brigitte, and Lise St-Charles, with Kim Thúy. *L'Autisme expliqué aux non-autistes*. Montreal: Les Éditions du Trécarré, 2017.

– *L'Estime de soi et l'autiste*. Montreal: Les Éditions du Trécarré, 2019.

Hernández, Ángeles Sánchez. "L'oeuvre de Kim Thúy: Une écriture née de la fêlure biographique." *Anales de Filologia Francesa* 27 (2019): 311–30.

Hirsch, Marianne. *The Mother/Daughter Plot: Narrative, Psychoanalysis, Feminism*. Bloomington: Indiana University Press, 1989.

Hirschman, Charles, and Vu Manh Loi. "Family and Household Structure in Vietnam: Some Glimpses from a Recent Survey." *Pacific Affairs* 69, no. 2 (1996): 229–49. https://www.jstor.org/stable/2760726.

Hoang Xuan Nhi. *Heou-Tâm*. Paris: Mercure de France, 1942.

Hong, Terry. "Kim Thúy's *Ru*: An Apple for the Reader." *Bloom*, 16 September 2013. https://bloom-site.com/2013/09/16/kim-thuys-ru-an-apple-for-the-reader.

Horlacher, Stefan. "'In Reality Every Reader Is, While He Is Reading, the Reader of His Own Self': Reconsidering the Importance of Narrative and Savoir Littéraire for Masculinity Studies." *Men and Masculinities* 22, no. 1 (2019): 75–84.

Howell, Jennifer. "À chaque recette, son histoire: Viet Kieu Food Writing and the Emergence of a Transnational Poetics." *Contemporary French and Francophone Studies* 21, no 1 (2017): 72–80. https://doi.org/10.1080/17409292.2017.1299348.

Ionescu, Mariana. "L'écriture de Kim Thúy et Liliana Lazar: Résilience ou résistance?" *www.revue-analyses.org* 9, no. 3 (Autumn 2014): 95–111.

Ireland, Susan, and Patrice J. Proulx. "Negotiating New Identities in Québec's Écriture Migrante." *Contemporary French and Francophone Studies* 13, no. 1 (January 2009): 35–43.

– eds. *Textualizing the Immigrant Experience in Contemporary Quebec*. Westport, CT: Praeger, 2004.

James, Jenny M. "Frayed Ends: Refugee Memory and Bricolage Practices of Repair in Dionne Brand's *What We All Long For* and Kim Thúy's *Ru*." MELUS*: Multi-Ethnic Literature of the United States* 41, no. 3 (Fall 2016): 42–67.

Jamieson, Neil L. *Understanding Vietnam*. Berkeley: University of California Press, 1993.

Jordan, Miriam. "On Migrant Journeys with WhatsApp and Google Translate." *New York Times* (international edition), 3 June 2019. https://www.nytimes.com/2019/05/29/technology/personaltech/migrants-whatsapp-google-translate.html.

Jullien, François. *La Valeur allusive: Des catégories originales de l'interprétation poétique dans la tradition chinoise: Contribution à une réflexion sur l'altérité interculturelle*. Paris: Presses universitaires de France, 2003.

Kerstetter, Jim. "WhatsApp Is Embraced by World's Immigrants." *New York Times*, business section, 16 December 2016. https://www.nytimes.com/2016/12/22/technology/daily-report-whatsapp-is-embraced-by-worlds-immigrants.html.

Khordoc, Catherine. "From Migrant to Transnational: Contemporary Québécois Writing (1999–2010)." *Québec Studies* 63 (2017): 79–98. https://doi.org/10.3828/qs.2017.6.

Kistnareddy, Ashwiny O. "'Against the Flow': Exile and 'Willful Subjects' in Malika Mokeddem's *Mes Hommes* and Kim Thúy's *Vi*." *Contemporary Women's Writing* (forthcoming).

– *Migrant Masculinities in Women's Writing: (In)Hospitality, Community, Vulnerability*. Cham: Springer International and Palgrave Macmillan, 2021.

– "Transnational Vietnamese Refugee Families: Childhood and Filiation in Kim Thúy's *Ru*." In *Transnational Families, Transnational Novels*, edited by Annette Brueler Dietrich and Amelie Daigle. London: Palgrave Macmillan, forthcoming.

Kurmann, Alexandra. "*Aller-retour-détour*: Transdiasporic Nomadism and the Navigation of Literary Prescription in the Work of Kim Thúy and Thanh-Van Tran-Nhut." *Australian Journal of French Studies* 55, no. 1 (2018): 65–78.

Kurmann, Alexandra, and Tess Do. "Children on the Boat: The Recuperative Work of Postmemory in Short Fiction of the Vietnamese Diaspora." *Comparative Literature* 70, no. 2 (June 2018): 218–34. https://doi.org/10.1215/00104124-6817419.

Labelle, Maude. "Les Lieux de l'écriture migrante: Territoire, mémoire et langue dans *Les lettres chinoises* de Ying Chen." *Globe, Revue internationale d'études québécoises* 10, no. 1 (2007): 37–51.

Lambert-Perrault, Marie-Christine. "Des affects plein l'assiette: Migration, nourriture et agentivité chez Kim Thúy." *Atlantis* 38, no. 2 (2017): 79–91.

Laozi. *Tao Te Ching*. Translated by D.C. Lau. Harmondsworth: Penguin, 1963.

Larochelle, Samuel. "'Les secrets des Vietnamiennes': Kim Thúy concocte un livre culinaire … touchant." *HuffPost Québec*, 11 June 2017. https://quebec.huffingtonpost.ca/2017/11/06/les-secrets-des-vietnamiennes-kim-thuy-concocte-un-livre-culinaire-touchant_a_23268174.

Larue, Monique. *L'arpenteur et le navigateur*. Montreal: Fides/CETUQ, 1996.

Laval, Martine. "*Ru* de Kim Thúy." *Télérama* 3130 (4 January 2010). Updated 18 September 2013. http://www.telerama.fr/livres/kim-thuy-ru,51130.php.

Lê, Linda. *Calomnies*. Paris: Christian Bourgois, 1993.

– *Lettre morte*. Paris: Christian Bourgois, 1999.

– *Un si tendre vampire*. Paris: La Table Ronde, 1987.

– *Slander*. Translated by Esther Allen. Lincoln: University of Nebraska Press, 1996.

– *Les trois parques*. Paris: Christian Bourgeois, 1997.

Le Bris, Michel, et al. "Manifeste pour 'une littérature-monde' en français." *Le Monde*, 15 March 2007. https://www.lemonde.fr/livres/article/2007/03/15/des-ecrivains-plaident-pour-un-roman-en-francais-ouvert-sur-le-monde_883572_3260.html.

Le Bris, Michel, and Jean Rouard, eds. *Pour une littérature-monde*. Paris: Gallimard, 2007.

Leclair, Bertrand. "Mort de Linda Lê, grande figure contemporaine de la littérature de l'exil." *Le Monde*, 10 May 2022. https://www.lemonde.fr/disparitions/article/2022/05/10/mort-de-linda-le-grande-figure-contemporaine-de-la-litterature-de-l-exil_6125511_3382.html.

Lefèvre, Kim. *Métisse blanche*. Paris: Éditions Bernard Barrault, 1989.

– *Retour à la saison des pluies*. Paris: Éditions Bernard Barrault, 1990.

– *White Métisse*. Translated by Jack A. Yeager. Honolulu: University of Hawai'i Press, 2018.

Le Van Phat. *Contes et légendes du pays d'Annam*. 1913. Saigon: Nguyen Van Cua, 1925.

Lim-Hing, Sharon. "Vietnamese Novels in French: Rewriting Self, Gender and Nation." PhD diss., Harvard University, 1993.

Lohka, Eileen. "Senteurs de l'ailleurs: Mémoire culinaire chez Kim Thúy." *Nouvelles Etudes Francophones* 32, no. 2 (2017): 184–94.

Lu, Alexander, and Joel Wong. "Stressful Experiences of Masculinity among U.S. Born and Immigrant Asian Americans." *Gender and Society* 27, no. 3 (2013): 345–71.

Luong, Hy Van. "Vietnamese Kinship: Structural Principles and the Socialist Transformation in Northern Vietnam." *Journal of Asian Studies* 48, no. 4 (1989): 741–56. https://doi.org/10.2307/2058112.

Ly Thu Ho. *Au milieu du carrefour*. Paris: Peyronnet, 1969.

– *Le mirage de la paix*. Paris: Promédart/Les Muses de Parnasse, 1986.

– *Printemps inachevé*. Paris: Peyronnet, 1962.

Maclure, Jocelyn. *Récits identitaires: Le Québec à l'épreuve du pluralisme*. Montreal: Québec Amérique, 2000.

Malarny, Shaun Kingsley. *Culture, Ritual and Revolution in Vietnam.* Chippenham, England: RoutledgeCurzon, 2002.

Martin, Rachel. "Remembering the Doomed First Flight of Operation Babylift." *Weekend Edition Sunday*, NPR, 26 April 2015. https://www.npr.org/2015/04/26/402208267/remembering-the-doomed-first-flight-of-operation-babylift.

Micone, Marco. "Speak What." *Jeu: revue de théâtre* 50 (March 1989): 83–5.

Moï, Anna. *L'Écho des rizières: Nouvelles.* La Tour d'Aigues: Éditions de l'Aube, 2001.

– *Nostalgie de la rizière.* La Tour d'Aigues: Éditions de l'Aube, 2012.

– *Parfum de pagode: Nouvelles.* La Tour d'Aigues: Éditions de l'Aube, 2004.

– *Le pays sans nom: Déambulations avec Marguerite Duras.* La Tour d'Aigues: Éditions de l'Aube, 2017.

Moisan, Clément. *Écritures migrantes et identités culturelles.* Montreal: Éditions Nota Bene, 2008.

Moisan, Clément, and Renate Moisan-Hildebrand. *Ces étrangers du dedans: Une histoire de l'écriture migrante au Québec, 1937–1997.* Montreal: Éditions Nota Bene, 2001.

Moss, Laura, ed. *Is Canada Postcolonial? Unsettling Canadian Literature.* Waterloo, ON: Wilfred Laurier University Press, 2003.

Moura, Jean-Marc. *Littératures francophones et théorie postcoloniale.* Paris: PUF, 1999.

Nepveu, Pierre. "Écritures migrantes." In *L'écologie du réel: Mort et naissance de la littérature québécoise contemporaine*, 197–210. Montreal: Boréal, 1988.

Nguyen, Hoai Huong. *Déserts.* Paris: L'Harmattan, 2009.

– *Parfums.* Paris: L'Harmattan, 2005.

Nguyen, Linh. *Lemongrass, Ginger and Mint: Vietnamese Cookbook.* Berkeley, CA: Rockridge Press, 2017.

Nguyen, Nathalie Huynh Chau. *La Mémoire est un autre pays: Femmes de la diaspora vietnamienne.* Translated by Patricia Fogarty and Alain Guillemin. Paris: Riveneuve Éditions, 2013.

– ed. *New Perceptions of the Vietnam War: Essays on the War, the South Vietnamese Experience, the Diaspora and the Continuing Impact.* Jefferson, NC: McFarland, 2014.

– Vietnamese Voices: Gender and Cultural Identity in the *Vietnamese Francophone Novel.* Dekalb: Northern Illinois University Press, Southeast Asia Publications, 2003.

Nguyen, Viet Thanh. "The Ideas That Won't Survive the Coronavirus." *New York Times*, 10 April 2020. https://www.nytimes.com/2020/04/10/opinion/sunday/coronavirus-america.html.

– *Race and Resistance: Literature and Politics in Asian America*. Oxford: Oxford University Press, 2002.

– *The Refugees*. New York: Grove, 2017.

Nguyen, Vinh. "Refugee Gratitude: Narrating Success and Intersubjectivity in Kim Thúy's *Ru*." *Canadian Literature* 219 (2013): 17–36.

Nguyễn Du. *The Tale of Kiều, a Bilingual Edition of Truyện Kiều*. Translated and annotated by Huỳnh Sanh Thông with a historical essay by Alexander B. Woodside. New Haven: Yale University Press, 1983.

Nguyen Duc Giang. *Vingt ans*. Vinh: Éditions de la "Nouvelle Revue Indochinoise," 1940; rev. 2nd ed., 1942.

Nguyễn Giáng Hương. *La Littérature vietnamienne francophone (1913–1986)*. Paris: Éditions Garnier, 2018.

– ed. *Pham Van Ky et son oeuvre: Un taoïsme littéraire*. Paris: Démopolis, 2019.

Nguyen Phan Long. *Le Roman de Mademoiselle Lys*. Hanoi: Imprimerie Tonkinoise, 1921.

Nguyen Thi Van. "Confucianism 'Three Obediences and Four Virtues' Theory and Its Impacts on Vietnamese Women Nowadays." PhD thesis, Ho Chi Minh National Academy of Politics, 2014. https://hcma.vn/Uploads/2014/6/4/nguyen_thi_van_en.pdf.

Nguyen Tien Lang. *Les Vietnamiens I: Les chemins de la révolte*. Paris: Amiot-Dumont, 1953.

Nguyên Van Ky. "Rethinking the Status of Vietnamese Women in Folklore and Oral History." In *Viêt-Nam Exposé: French Scholarship on Twentieth-Century Vietnamese Society*, edited by Gisèle L. Bousquet and Pierre Brocheux, 87–107. Ann Arbor: University of Michigan Press, 2002.

Nguyen Van Nho. *Souvenirs d'un étudiant*. Hanoi: Publications Revue Indochinoise, 1920.

Nguyen Van Xiem. *Mes heures perdues*. Saigon: Imprimerie de l'Union, 1913.

O'Brien, Tim. *The Things They Carried*. Boston: Houghton Mifflin, 1990.

O'Riley, Michael. "Discerning the Empire's Other: Literary Interventions in the Culture of French Modernity." PhD diss., University of Oregon, 1998.

Palumbo-Liu, David. *Asian/American: Historical Crossings of a Racial Frontier*. Stanford, CA: Stanford University Press, 1999.

Pâquet, Martin, and Stéphane Savard. *Brève histoire de la Révolution tranquille*. Montreal: Boréal, 2021.

Paquin, Stéphane, and X. Hubert Rioux. *La Révolution tranquille 60 ans après*. Montreal: Presses de l'Université de Montréal, 2022.

Paterson, Janet M. "Identité et altérité: Littératures migrantes ou transnationales?" *Interfaces Brasil/Canada*, Rio Grande 9 (2008): 87–101.

Pears, Pamela. *Remnants of Empire in Algeria and Vietnam: Women, Words, and War.* Lanham, MD: Lexington Books, 2004.

Pham, Andrew X. *Catfish and Mandala.* London: Flamingo, 2001.

Pham, Mai. *The Best of Vietnamese and Thai Cooking: Favorite Recipes from Lemon Grass Restaurant and Cafes*. Rocklin, CA: Prima, 1996.

Pham Duy Khiem. *Légendes des terres sereines*. Hanoi: Imprimerie Taupin, 1942; Paris: Mercure de France, 1951. Reissued 1989.

– *Nam et Sylvie*. Paris: Plon, 1957.

Phạm Quỳnh Phương, and Chris Eipper. "Mothering and Fathering the Vietnamese: Religion, Gender, and National Identity." *Journal of Vietnamese Studies* 4, no. 1 (Winter 2009): 49–83. https://www.jstor.org/stable/10.1525/vs.2009.4.1.49.

Pham Van Ky. *Blood Brothers*. Translated by Margaret Mauldin with an introduction and notes by Lucy Nguyen Hong Nhiem. New Haven: Yale Southeast Asia Studies, 1987.

– *Des Femmes assises çà et là*. Paris: Gallimard, 1964.

– *Frères de sang*. Paris: Éditions du Seuil, 1947.

– *L'homme de nulle part*. Paris: Fasquelle, 1946.

Pictet, Christine, ed. *Femmes du Vietnam: Visages d'hier et de demain.* Mane, France: Éditions de l'Envol, 1996.

Plamondon, Jean-François. "Les manifestes québécois, acteurs et témoins d'un champ en évolution." *Francofonia*, no. 59 (2010): 59–74. www.jstor.org/stable/43016552.

Poe, Edgar Allen. "The Purloined Letter." 1845. Accessed 5 December 2022. https://poestories.com/read/purloined.

Proulx, Patrice. "Writing Home: Explorations of Exile and Cultural Hybridity in the Correspondence of Nancy Huston and Leïla Sebbar." *L'Esprit Créateur* 40, no. 4 (Winter 2000): 80–8.

Robin, Régine. *Nous autres, les autres*. Montreal: Boréal, 2011.

– *La Québécoite*. Montreal: Québec Amérique, 1983.

Roy, Marie-Josée R. "ICI ARTV: La table d'amitié de Kim Thúy." *Le Journal de Montréal*, 18 December 2019. https://www.journaldemontreal.com/2019/12/18/ici-artv--la-table-damitie-de-kim-thuy.

Rye, Gill. *Narratives of Mothering: Women's Writing in Contemporary France*. Newark: University of Delaware Press, 2009.

Said, Edward. *Orientalism*. London: Routledge & Kegan Paul, 1978; Vintage Books, 1979.

– *Reflections on Exile and Other Essays*. Cambridge, MA: Harvard University Press, 2000.

Saint-Martin, Lori. *Le Nom de la mère: Mères, filles et écriture dans la littérature québécoise au féminin*. Montreal: Éditions Nota Bene, 1999.

Santoro, Miléna. *Mothers of Invention: Feminist Authors and Experimental Fiction in France and Quebec*. Montreal and Kingston: McGill-Queen's University Press, 2002.

Schnyder, Peter, and Frédérique Toudoire-Surlapierre, eds. *Ne pas dire: Pour une étude du non-dit dans la littérature et la culture européennes*. Paris: Classiques Garnier, 2013.

Selao, Ching. *Le Roman vietnamien francophone: Orientalisme, occidentalisme et hybridité*. Montreal: Les Presses de l'Université de Montréal, 2011.

Shakespeare, William. *Shakespeare's Sonnets: An Original-Spelling Text*. Oxford: Oxford University Press, 2016.

Sing, Pamela V. "Kim Thúy: A Gentle Power." In *Ten Canadian Writers in Context*, edited by Marie Carrière, Curtis Gillespie, and Jason Purcell, 179–93. Edmonton: University of Alberta Press, 2016.

– "Migrance, sensorium et translocalité chez Ying Chen et Kim Thúy." *International Journal of Francophone Studies* 16, no. 3 (2013): 281–301.

Soucy, Alexander. "Vietnamese Warriors, Vietnamese Mothers: State Imperatives in the Portrayal of Women." *Canadian Woman Studies/Les Cahiers de la femme* 19, no. 4 (2000): 121–6.

Statistics Canada. "150 Years of Immigration to Canada." Canadian Megatrends. Released 29 June 2016, last modified 17 May 2018. https://www150.statcan.gc.ca/n1/pub/11-630-x/11-630-x2016006-eng.htm.

Stur, Heather Marie. *Beyond Combat: Women and Gender in the Vietnam War Era*. New York: Cambridge University Press, 2011.

Taylor, K.W. *A History of the Vietnamese*. Cambridge: Cambridge University Press, 2013.

Taylor, Philip. "The Goddess, the Ethnologist, the Folklorist and the Cadre: Situating Exegesis of Vietnam's Folk Religion in Time and Place." *Australian Journal of Anthropology* 14, no. 3 (2003): 383–401.

Thai, Hung Cam. "Low-Wage Vietnamese Immigrants, Social Class and Masculinity in the Homeland." In *Men and Masculinities in Southeast Asia*, edited by Michele Ford and Lenore Lyons, 56–67. Oxford: Routledge, 2012.

Thomas, Suzanne, Stephen C. Willis, and Hélène Plouffe. "Mon Pays." In *Canadian Encyclopedia*. Historica Canada. Article published 20 November 2011; last modified 4 March 2015. https://www.thecanadianencyclopedia.ca/en/article/mon-pays.

Thúy, Kim. *Em*. Montreal: Libre Expression, 2020.

– *Em*. Translated by Sheila Fischman. New York: Seven Stories Press, 2021.

– "En remontant les rus de l'enfance: Interview avec Kim Thúy." Interview by Jean-François Plamondon. *Francofonia* 60 (2011): 149–60. http://www.jstor.org/stable/43016979.

– "Habiller le vécu de mots et d'images: Le projet de Kim Thúy." Interview by Valérie Dusaillant-Fernandes. *Voix Plurielles* 9, no. 2 (2012): 164–177.

– "I Don't Understand Countries That Don't Want Immigrants: They're Super Men and Super Women." CE *Noticias Financieras* (English edition), 24 November 2019. ProQuest.

– "Interview with Kim Thúy: *Secrets from My Vietnamese Kitchen: Simple Recipes from My Many Mothers*." Interview by Anelyse M. Weiler. *Gastronomica* 20, no. 1 (Spring 2020): 80–2.

– "Kim Thúy: Fan finie de la francophonie – Les visages de la francophonie." Facebook, 10 July 2020. https://www.facebook.com/watch/?v=518330808939206.

– *Mãn*. Montreal: Éditions Libre expression, 2013; Paris: Liana Levi, 2013.

– *Mãn*. Translated by Sheila Fischman. Toronto: Random House Canada, 2014; Toronto: Vintage Canada, 2015.

– "Q&A with Kim Thúy." Interview by Terry Hong. *Bloom*, 18 September 2013. https://bloom-site.com/2013/09/18/qa-with-kim-thuy.

– *Ru*. Montreal: Éditions Libre expression, 2009; Paris: Liana Levi, 2010; Montreal: Pocket ed., Éditions Alain Stanké, collection 10/10, 2014.

– *Ru*. Translated by Sheila Fischman. Toronto: Random House Canada, 2012.

– *Le Secret des Vietnamiennes*. Montreal: Les Éditions du Trécarré, 2017; Vanves: Hachette Livre Marabout, 2018.

– *Secrets from My Vietnamese Kitchen: Simple Recipes from My Many Mothers*. Translated by Sheila Fischman. Recipes translated by Marie Asselin. Vancouver and Toronto: Appetite by Random House, 2019.
– *La Table de Kim*. Six one-hour episodes. First aired January-February 2020. IciARTV. https://ici.artv.ca/emissions/la-table-de-kim.
– *Vi*. Montreal: Éditions Libre expression, 2016; Paris: Liana Levi, 2016.
– *Vi*. Translated by Sheila Fischman. Toronto: Vintage Canada, 2019.
Thúy, Kim, and Pascal Jankovjak. *À toi*. Montreal: Editions Libre Expression, 2011; Paris: Liana Levi, 2011; Montreal: Éditions Alain Stanké, collection 10/10, 2015.
Thúy, Kim, and Rogé, illustrator. *Le Poisson et l'oiseau*. Montreal: Les Editions de la Bagnole, 2019.
Tran Van Tung. *Bach-Yên ou la fille au coeur fidèle*. Paris: J. Susse, 1946.
Trinh Thuc Oanh, and Marguerite Triaire. *En s'écartant de ancêtres*. Hanoi: Imprimerie d'Extrême-Orient, 1939.
Truong Dinh Tri, and Albert de Teneuille. *Bà-Đầm*. Paris: Fasquelle, 1930.
Une Mangeuse Avertie [pseud.]. "La touchante sensibilité de la cuisine vietnamienne." *Le Guide du Mangeur Averti* (blog), 24 August 2013. http://guidedumangeur.blogspot.com/2013/08/ailleurs-la-touchante-sensibilite-de-la.html.
Vigneault, Gilles. "Mon Pays." In *Avec les vieux mots*. Quebec City: Editions de l'Arc, 1964.
Vuong, Ocean. *Night Sky with Exit Wounds*. Port Townsend, WA: Copper Canyon Press, 2016.
– *On Earth We're Briefly Gorgeous*. New York: Penguin, 2019.
Winston, Jane Bradley, and Leakthina Chau-Pech Ollier, eds. *Of Vietnam: Identities in Dialogue*. New York: Palgrave, 2001.
World Trade Press. *Vietnam Women in Culture, Business & Travel: A Profile of Vietnamese Women in the Fabric of Society*. Petaluma, CA: World Trade Press, 2010. ProQuest Ebook Central.
World Trade Press. *Vietnam: Society and Culture*. Petaluma, CA: World Trade Press, 2010. ProQuest Ebook Central.
Xavier, Subha. *The Migrant Text: Making and Marketing a Global French Literature*. Montreal and Kingston: McGill-Queen's University Press, 2016.
Yeager, Jack A. "Authorial Identities in the Work of Linda Lê." *South East Asia Research* 25, no. 1 (March 2017): 80–97.
– "Bach Mai's Francophone Eurasian Voice: Remapping Margin and Center." *Québec Studies* 14 (Spring/Summer 1992): 49–64.

– "Blurring the Lines in Vietnamese Literature in French: Kim Lefèvre's *Métisse blanche*." In *Postcolonial Subjects: Francophone Women Writers*, edited by Mary Jean Green, Karen Gould, Micheline Rice-Maximin, Keith L. Walker, and Jack A. Yeager, 210–26. Minneapolis: University of Minnesota Press, 1996.
– "Culture, Citizenship, Nation: The Narrative Texts of Linda Lê." In *Post-colonial Cultures in France*, edited by Alec G. Hargreaves and Mark KcKinney, 255–67. London: Routledge, 1997.
– "Invention, appropriation et adoption d'identités dans les romans francophones de Kim Doan, Kim Thúy et Minh Tran Huy." *La Francophonie en Asie-Pacifique*, no. 1 (September 2017): 65–74.
– "La Politique 'intimiste': La production romanesque des écrivaines vietnamiennes d'expression française." *Présence francophone* 43 (1993): 131–47.
– *Vietnamese Literature in French*. New Orleans: CELFAN Edition Monographs (Tulane University), 1999.
– *The Vietnamese Novel in French: A Literary Response to Colonialism*. Hanover: University Press of New England, 1987.

Contributors

ASHWINY O. KISTNAREDDY is Leverhulme Early Career Fellow at the Refugee Studies Centre, University of Oxford. She has published a monograph on Ananda Devi's works, *Locating Hybridity* (2015) and a monograph titled *Masculinities in Women's Writing* (2021) and is currently working on a monograph on Vietnamese refugee writing, *Refugee Afterlives*. She is also working on a project on refugee children. She has published a number of articles on Ananda Devi, Kim Thúy, Fatou Diome, Maryse Condé, Léonora Miano, Malika Mokeddem, Nathacha Appanah, and Ying Chen and has a long-standing interest in francophone women's writing, race, gender, and migration.

DR. NGUYỄN GIÁNG HƯƠNG is the head of the Southeast Asian (Vietnam, Laos, Cambodia) Languages and Civilization Division at the François-Mitterrand site of the National Library of France and fellow researcher at the Institute of Modern Texts and Manuscripts (ITEM), under the French National Centre for Scientific Research (CNRS). She completed a PhD in French literature in 2015 at Université Paris Nanterre. Her research focuses on Vietnamese francophone and diaspora literature, and she works more broadly on intercultural and exile issues in Vietnamese-French writing. Her first monograph, *La littérature vietnamienne francophone (1913–1986)*, was published in 2018. Her latest publications include *Pham Van Ky: un taoïsme littéraire* (2019), an anthology of critical articles and unpublished texts by the writer, and *Le Portail France-Vietnam* (2021), which considers Viet Nam as a transnational space of cultural transference.

AMY B. REID is professor of French and gender studies and director of the Gender Studies Program at New College of Florida, where her teaching focuses on the representation of women and women's voices in French and francophone literature. She is an award-winning translator whose work has been recognized by the Modern Language Association, the French Voices Award Program, and the National Endowment for the Arts. Her most recent translations include Patrice Nganang's *A Trail of Crab Tracks* (2022) and Mutt-Lon's *The Blunder* (2022). Translations of works by Canadian-based authors Blaise Ndala (*From the Belly of the Congo*) and Marie-Célie Agnant (*An Alligator Named Rosa*) are forthcoming.

JULIETTE M. ROGERS is professor of French and francophone studies at Macalester College in Saint Paul, Minnesota. Her main areas of specialization are nineteenth-century French women writers, especially those of the *belle époque*, and Quebec women writers from the twentieth and twenty-first centuries. She has published numerous articles on both these topics in journals such as *The French Review*, *Québec Studies*, *L'Esprit Créateur*, and *Société et Représentations*, and her book, *Career Stories: Belle Epoque Novels of Professional Development, 1900–1914*, was published in 2007. In 2019, she was awarded a Fulbright Research Fellowship to study women writers "of the north" in northern France and southern Belgium. She has served as president of the American Council of Quebec Studies and the Women in French organization, and as editor in chief of the journal *Women in French Studies*; she is currently serving as associate editor for book reviews for *Québec Studies*.

MILÉNA SANTORO is a 2019 recipient of the Ordre des Francophones d'Amérique, and winner of the 2018 Prix du Québec and the 2017 Grand Prix de la Francophonie. She has built her career on exploring the transnational and cross-cultural connections between Quebec's rich literary and filmic practices and its North American and global francophone counterparts and influences. Her research on Quebec's feminist literary tradition, Quebec's transatlantic cultural exchanges, and its Indigenous cinema appears in her book *Mothers of Invention: Feminist Authors and Experimental Fiction in France and Quebec* (2002) and in two co-edited volumes: *Transatlantic Passages: Literary and Cultural Relations between Quebec and*

Francophone Europe (2010) and *Hemispheric Indigeneities: Native Identity and Agency in Mesoamerica, the Andes, and Canada* (2018). Her work on Indigenous filmmakers also features in a 2013 special issue, titled "Québec Cinema in the 21st Century," that she co-edited for the *American Review of Canadian Studies*, the flagship journal in the field. In 2017, Professor Santoro received one of fifty "Médailles hommage 50e" created by the Québec Ministère des relations internationales et de la Francophonie to commemorate fifty years of public diplomacy and conferred upon partners and exponents of Quebec from around the world. In 2018, she was additionally honoured with one of three Certificates of Merit in Canadian Studies bestowed annually by the International Council for Canadian Studies. Santoro has been a professor at Georgetown University for over two decades, where she teaches Quebec Studies and Film and Media Studies, and is one of the founding members of the Americas Forum, an interdisciplinary hemispheric research and discussion group.

JACK A. YEAGER, a Fulbright scholar at Vietnam National University in Hanoi in 2016, is professor emeritus of French studies and women's and gender studies at Louisiana State University in Baton Rouge. He studied Vietnamese at the Defense Language Institute in 1969–70, and in Hanoi in 2009, and earned his PhD at the University of Wisconsin-Madison where he began delineating the parameters of narrative literature in French from Viet Nam, the primary focus of his research. His publications include *The Vietnamese Novel in French: A Literary Response to Colonialism* (1987; winner of the New Hampshire Book Prize), *Vietnamese Literature in French* (1999), and the co-edited *Postcolonial Subjects: Francophone Women Writers* (1996), as well as the translation of Kim Lefèvre's *Métisse blanche* as *White Métisse* (2018). His articles have appeared in such journals as *La Francophonie en Asie-Pacifique*, *South East Asia Research*, *Intersections*, *Michigan Quarterly Review*, *Présence Francophone*, *Notebooks in Cultural Analysis*, *The Vietnam Forum*, *L'Esprit Créateur*, and *Québec Studies*. In addition, he has published book chapters in *Pham Van Ky et son oeuvre: un taoïsme littéraire* (ed. Nguyễn Giáng Hương, 2018), *France and Indochina: Cultural Representations* (ed. Kathryn Robson and Jennifer Yee, 2005), *Le Viêt-Nam au féminin* (ed. Gisèle Bousquet and Nora Taylor, 2005), *Textualizing the Immigrant Experience in Contemporary Quebec* (ed. Susan Ireland and Patrice Proulx, 2004), *Of Vietnam: Identities in Dialogue* (ed. Jane Bradley Winston and Leakthina Chau-Pech Ollier, 2001), and *Post-colonial Cultures in France* (ed. Alec Hargreaves and Mark McKinney, 1997). These publications include work on novels by Bach Mai, Ying Chen, and Kim Thúy.

Index